A Place to Talk

by

John N. DeFoore

A PLACE TO TALK

First edition. August 16, 2024.

Copyright © 2024 John N DeFoore Sr..

ISBN: 979-8227711106

Written by John N DeFoore Sr..

Table of Contents

from the editor

In the mid to late 1970s, John N. DeFoore had a popular television program called, "A Place to Talk," broadcast out of Abilene, Texas. He was a popular speaker at retreats and conferences during that time as well. This book is a collection of talks given by John DeFoore on "A Place to Talk" in 1975 and at Laity Lodge retreats in 1973 and 1978.

The recordings of the sessions were transcribed and collected into this book. Much liberty has been taken in sentence structure to keep the conversational manner of John's talks. He tends to connect his series and thoughts with "and" and parenthetical comments (usually enclosed in emdashes here). Sometime that tends to create a long run-on sentence, but those conventions have been left in to allow the reader to follow his uninterrupted train of thought and read the talks in John's manner of speaking them.

It should be noted that these were telecasts and in-person sessions, so John does sometimes comment about putting "something on the board." For the most part these references to diagrams can be interpreted or "imagined" by the reader. They remain, because often within the reference hide nuggets of wisdom or insight.

These recordings were of conversations and talks from over forty years ago—a different era when gender roles were more defined. With that in mind, the reader will need to look beyond any stereotype situations and read words of wisdom which are just as relevant and timeless today as they were when the sessions were recorded.

Ernestine M. Haas, Editor

about the author

John DeFoore was born in 1919 in the small town of Sidon, Mississippi. He grew up surrounded by cotton fields and dense forests. He left home at age 17 and went to work with a highway construction group. He finished high school, started college, and entered the Army before WWII began. He served seven years, enlisting as a private first class and being discharged as a major. He was in the infantry and saw service in New Guinea, the Netherlands East Indies, and the Philippines. He was awarded the Bronze Star during an amphibious landing on Morotai Island.

After the war, John was ordained as a Baptist minister and graduated from Mississippi College with a Bachelor of Science degree and Southern Baptist Theological Seminary with a Master of Theology degree. He further studied at New College in Edinburgh, Scotland, Princeton, Harvard, and the Jungian Institute in Zurich, Switzerland.

He served as a missionary in Alaska for five years and then pastored in Mississippi, Alabama, and Texas for over 30 years. At 65, he began his second career as a counselor and international business consultant and retired from this practice at 98. He and his wife, Marion Sue, live in Boerne, Texas. He is the father of four sons.

At 105 years old, John still spends his days writing and reading. Since retiring, he has written more than a dozen books.

Cover art is "John DeFoore" by Janice Yow Hindes, a renowned artist residing in San Antonio, Texas, where she owns Hindes Fine Art Gallery and Atelier.

January 1975

OUR 24-HOUR DAY

The thing about this 24-hour period that we call a day is that you will determine how you will employ this length of time. Every one of us has the same amount of time. A very wise man told me one time that you were supposed to use eight hours for play, eight hours for work, and eight hours for rest.

When you say this to a lot of people, it sounds ridiculous. To say 16 hours of work and 8 hours of rest doesn't sound so strange, but to say that we should play 8 hours really hooks some people and makes them worry about the waste of time.

I have been talking a lot since you and I have had this place to talk about a life that affords us the maximum amount of health and happiness and enjoyment and sense of fulfillment. To be able to move continually towards this is the most successful experience a man can have. We are moving in this direction.

You are moving in this direction if you can look back at the place you were a year ago and see that you have made progress in the last 365 days. If you can do this, then you are doing great. This might be a really good test if you don't take it too seriously. Now if you see that you haven't made much progress or that you are regressing, then it might be the time to say that this year is going to be different.

What I want to .continue to work on now is the way you employ your 24 hours and whether or not you are ready to make the decision to live one day at a time. Most of us employ 8 hours of our day at work, preferably at some kind of gainful employment that brings some kind of financial gain. It may not be financial, but each one of us needs some kind of return from the employment of our physical energy.

Incidentally, next week I am going to talk about the meaning of work, and the next week about the meaning of play. In this time, we will discuss what work can mean other than money, and what play can mean other than whatever it means to you.

Now, this day is all you have in your own lifetime. Yesterday is gone, and tomorrow is not here. All you have is today. The way you employ today is probably the way you have employed most of your life.

A friend gave me a little computer the other day and I figured up the number of days that I had lived. It was shocking. We know a week is 7 days, but we don't think of days in terms of thousands and ten thousands. Each day is a packet in itself .Today is all of your life that you will have. Yesterday is gone, and it is gone forever. Tomorrow has not come, and you cannot do a thing now to control tomorrow. You can make plans and set up appointments, but the future, fortunately, is out of our hands.

Incidentally, I like the idea of God's forgetfulness— that God forgives and God forgets. I like to know that God doesn't spend time over our past mistakes— that he sees us how we are part of what we are today. I think that is very beautiful.

Now look at today: This is the only part of time that you and I have. When you are living one day at a time, it. brings all your energies and all of your strength and focuses on now, here with me. Some of you may even want to focus on what I am saying, and not remember the mistakes you made yesterday, and the anxiety and fears you have about tomorrow. Let them go, and then you are free to bring all your strength and energy to today.

Sometimes, you may have talked to someone who is preoccupied at the time, and engaged in. something completely away from you. Every once in a while, he might look at you and say, "Uh-huh, yes, yes," but he is really somewhere else. And while he is talking to you he is looking over your shoulder and speaking to other people. These people are not living in the present, and generally we are insulted, or at least concerned, when they will not focus on what we are saying.

Living one day at a time means that you can focus all your strength on present relationships, and it makes you a stronger person. Actually, it increases your potency when you are all here. A lot of you are not all here some of the time, but when you are all here, you have a lot more strength than when you are thinking about something in the past or future. Now the first thing I want you to consider is having a few shallow term goals—just for today—not for tomorrow. Decide what you are going to do.

I used to know a man who got out of bed during the night and wrote on a pad what he was going to do the next day. A person may be able to keep this up for a while if he has a good supply of tranquilizers or antacids, or if he can keep his mind partially paralyzed by alcohol or work, but a man can't live continually under these pressures, because the mind needs rest just like the body does.

One thing to consider today, and not tomorrow or next week, is to have a few short- term goals for yourself. The first thing I want to know is if you will do a few things for yourself. This is just taking care of you. Bathe yourself, dress yourself, shave yourself, and decide that today you are going to take your time and enjoy it.

The most important thing today is that you aren't going to have expectations. If you will say today that I am going to have a few short-term goals for myself, and I am not going to have any expectations for anybody. For when I have expectations of you—unless I very clearly verbalize these expectations and let you know exactly what I am expecting and unless you agree on what I expect from you—I am going to be disappointed. How would you feel about going through the day not expecting anything from anyone? Without requiring anything or demanding anything?

When you lay your money down on the counter, you can reasonably expect the clerk to deliver the goods, and when you pay for gasoline at the service station, you can expect to get it. These things are not what I am talking about.

Keep this in the mainstream of your life. If you expect your children to appreciate you, or if you expect your wife to cater to you, or if you expect your husband to remember to do certain things, or to come in and volunteer to help you do the dishes, this is one of the ways you set yourself up to be disappointed, and if you will watch yourself and free yourself from expectations of others, there will be a lot less disappointment in your life, and your relationships with others will improve. Consider, instead of having expectations for others, setting a few goals for yourself. Put yourself first, and take care of your own physical health and needs.

I was in California a few days ago with friends and we visited an old sailing ship. It was beautiful. It was a four-master, and the sails were still tied to the deal that goes out, and the mast and the rigging were still there. We walked around the ship, and there was just enough swell in the water to rock the boat a little bit. It creaked as we walked, just like it does in the movies. It was really a beautiful experience. I had never been on one, and I felt,. especially as we walked below deck, that I was in another world, There was a little painted plaque there with the instructions given to the new deck hands the first time they went to the full mast, to lower the top sails. It was a very dangerous assignment. It was the same for all the men on those old ships. They would say to the new man, "One hand for yourself, one hand for your work, keep you mind on your job, and don't look down." I looked at that and thought what a beautiful recipe for life. Take care of yourself, take care of your work, keep your mind on what you are doing,. and don't look back.

When I stood there on the deck of that ship and looked at the mast, I pictured myself climbing up, and my first impression was that for some of the jobs we do today, one hand is not enough. One of the things that makes counseling and guidance so important and makes your doctor a very close friend, or makes your psychiatrist, psychologist, or your pastor so necessary in your life, is that some people spend all their time with two hands on the job and the self begins to roam and slip away.

That's the most important thing I want to say this morning.. You are important. Take care of yourself, make a few short-term goals for each day, and then make sure your family is taken care of emotionally as well as physically and financially.

If you have a daughter or son at home, take some time and make some plans. Have a goal for today. Today, I'm going to let that little girl know that I love her. Today I'm going to let that little boy know I love him. Today, I'm going to walk around the block with my son. Today, we are going to spend 10 minutes on the floor. Ten minutes isn't long in 24 hours. Today I'm going to touch my son's face. Today, I'm going to tell my wife I love her. Today I'm going to spend some time with my parents. Today I am going to spend some time with a close friend.

This is where you keep your life in close context.

YOU live in your body. Take care of it. The body lives in the setting of your friends and your family. Take care of them. You see, what we are talking about is making the world a safer place for you. You can do this as long as you live today. You won't spend a lot of time with yourself or your family if you're busy rehashing yesterday. Yesterday is gone. You can't change the things that happened. Only God could change yesterday, but I don't think I 've ever read of an instance in which he did it. God can change the past, but God doesn't. Maybe this is evidence that the past is not important enough for God to bother with it. If God doesn't bother with it, why do we?

I don't really know if this is the problem, but after you take care of yourself and your friends and your family, take care of your job. Do this so you will be happy and pleased with the job you do, and you can consider yourself a craftsman in any trade or profession. You can look back over your 8 hours of work with pride and say, "I did that. I like my work I enjoy my work, and I'm proud of the work I do."

The mistakes you made yesterday are not important. Concentrate on today's work, today's job, and today's play.

After this, I want you to consider some short-term goals concerning rest. You can take a 30-second vacation. You can sit down on your coffee break, or when you go to the restroom, or when you have any time and rehash last Sunday's football game. You can, in 30 seconds, relive the thrill of it. If you had a vacation with your family last summer, you could remember that. You can remember some good friend, some New Year's celebration, or you can remind yourself of any good time you've had. This is one of the ways you renew yourself'.

Another way to get rest is to come out of the work you are doing. Leave the work on the bench or in your automobile., and then when you take your coffee break, concentrate on the present. Stay in the present. Be where you are, and enjoy the moment. It's not a bad idea to thank God that you can walk, that you have two arms and two hands, and that you have the normal mental, emotional, physical facilities that a human being needs. You can spend 30 seconds being thankful for these things.

I guess you can do it better if you've ever had to do without these. I want to recommend these as short-term goals. and in this way, the strength and force and vitality of your life is focused on right now, and you will become a different person. As long as you are expecting things from another person and they do not know what you are expecting, the only way your expectations are filled is if these people read your mind.

So today, I want you to consider living up to your expectations of others. Also, you might want to give up your expectations of yourself; the expectation that you will be perfect, or that you will be a millionaire, or that you will be a pro football star. Accept the fact that you are who you are, and where you are, and that as you are, you are Okay. One of the most beautiful things to me about this man named Jesus is that He, of all people, knew the dimensions of the planets and the measurements and limits of the universe. He knew what it was to be God, with unlimited power, with unlimited might. But He spent the first 30 years of His life being a carpenter. He spent His life as a tradesman, and if you lived in Nazareth, you could have hired Him to repair your door.

He lived approximately thirty -three and a half years. The first thirty years were spent doing a job. The first thirty years of His life He spent being a person. The last three and a half years, He moved in another direction. so that you and I could learn the facts of the hallowing of God's name, and the coming of Christ's Kingdom. Not in eternity but in the present.

January 1975

WORK'S PLACE IN YOUR LIFE

We have been meeting at this place to talk for about sixteen weeks, and that, for me, seems to be an awfully long time. Sixteen weeks constitutes eight hours of talking. When I put that in terms of talking to someone, eight hours is a lot of talking.

I wanted to pick up on something I said last week. I was reading a book, *What Do You Say After You Say Hello?* The author said something that was very helpful to me. It has to do with staying in the present and living one day at a time. This is right now. The thing that Eric Berne said in this book that I thought was beautiful was that we reached back and used time. He called this "reach-back." He said that we use time before an event takes place worrying and being anxious; not planning intelligently, but being overly anxious.

For instance, if I plan to go hunting tomorrow, and I spend my time in anxious planning about what I am going to take, or what I am going to forget, or how I am going to get hurt, or what I am going to tell my family— this is "reach-back." It means from this point in time, you actually reach back and spoil your time.

Some adult planning is necessary, but when this pollutes and contaminates the work responsibilities and the play responsibilities or the interpersonal relationships— when it reaches back into our prior period—then this is just a way to defeat ourselves.

If you want to see how much you reach back, check this: if you are going to church on Sunday, see if all day Saturday you ruin everyone's day by making sure that their clothes are ready, and trying to get your own clothes ready, and trying to make sure that everyone is perfectly groomed and perfectly happy. If this is true, then you are reaching back and spoiling your time.

I had a friend who said that by the time he got to church on Sunday morning, God didn't have a chance. He had such a hassle getting there that the whole purpose of worship had been destroyed.

We do that sometimes on vacations. I have heard kids say that they remember the miseries of a vacation where the whole family was together and one of the parents was determined that they were all going to be happy and have a good time—This is a way of reaching back.

Another thing that Berne says is that he has something he calls "after-burn." It is just what the name implies. It is after an experience is over when you keep referring to it in your mind. The way I do this is, after I have had a conversation with someone, I think, "Why didn't I say this or that? I rehash the conversation in my mind. I think "When he said that, I wish I had said this." Sometimes I am so wrapped up in the after-burn that I forget the present. I am really moving backwards in my thinking when I do this.

One of the advantages of living one day at a time is that there is enough beauty and enough joy and enough excitement in any one moment that all our emotional, mental, and physical faculties can be involved in enjoying the moment if we only allow ourselves to be aware. So, in talking about living one day at a time, the purpose is to say, be aware and enjoy.

We talked about the meaning of work. When I was a child, in the town where I grew up, work was sacred. It was one of the ways a person could learn his worth and value. I'm not in favor of that at all. Play was sort of an afterthought. I think that sometimes work can be a little too sacred.

One of the things that always makes me pause is when I think of a man who has worked for 25 years and is getting ready to retire, and they have a banquet and present him a gold watch with his name on the back. The he retires on a certain day, and the next day they move in a new desk with new name plate on it, and the man—for all practical purposes– is forgotten.

This has to be, in order for some businesses to survive—I'm not criticizing this business. I would just like to use this as a point in the meaning of work.

When God made the earth, He worked six days, and in His dealings with man today, He says, "I want you to follow the example I have set. You work six days and rest one." We talked earlier about the days being divided into 24-hour periods: 8 hours for work; 8 hours for play, and 8 hours for rest. It is good when a man can enjoy 8 hours in work, play, and rest without excessive overlay. It is hard to work and rest at the same time.

There are exceptions to everything I say. If you can maintain a clear and decisive line between these areas of your life, you have already moved a long way toward maturity in mental, spiritual, and emotional areas, and you will probably have a very rewarding life. There is, of necessity, some overlay.

We don't do anything in the area of human life perfectly. We don't do anything entirely and completely with everybody in every circumstance. So, if work can be a certain, distinct period of employment and we can give ourselves to be creative and productive during this period of time when you employ all your senses, you are maturing, I think.

I am probably talking more about man's work here. Woman's work has puzzled me. I think it is very commendable that a woman can clean house and wash dishes and cook and care for children and then see it torn down every day, and get up the next morning and do the same thing all over again. That requires a dedication and devotion that I'm glad I don't have to muster up. I have always admired my wife for her willingness to cook a meal and clean up the dishes.

You give yourself to your work, and you can see the work as an extension of yourself. The work is not you, but rather an extension of you. It represents the employment of energy, the extension of one's own self-image, and creativity. It represents the creativity and dynamic in a person's life.

When you go to the doctor's office and he give you a prescription or performs surgery, or whatever he does, it is an extension of the doctor's training, knowledge, and wisdom. When you are an attorney or a carpenter or a plumber, —or when you work with the city sanitation department and you pick up garbage, and your work results in the cleanliness or the improvement of an area—this represents the employment of your life, and it means your life has been employed and improved. Work makes a difference.

It may be that you look at your work and see if it is worthwhile. Some people look at their job and say, "This job is not really worth anything." So, they find a job that they decide is worth more of themselves.

Now, when you work, the financial return from your work makes possible play time and rest time. It may be that you don't like your job that much, but it pays well, and it allows you to play and to rest. Work sometimes makes these two areas possible, but unless these two areas exist, there will be no energy for you to work.

One thing about God's work is that He performed His task, and He looked at it and said, "That's good." —Everything He created. It seems as though He kind of backed off, surveyed this whole scene, and said, "That's good. I did a good job."

He also said, "That's good" when he made man. When God made you, you were the result of God's working— the employment of the creative force of the life of God. This is where you came to be. You didn't make yourself. You are not an accident. You are upon this earth as a result of the creative work of God. You have worth, and you have value, and God worked, and so you live. I'm glad that God allowed us to be a part of His infinite plan and purpose–that God allowed us and gave us the responsibility to be creative people.

I visited a factory in Detroit one time. I was with a group of ministers and we interviewed this man on the assembly line. He had a job slipping a pin in a chain, and hitting it with a sort of stamping machine, and then shoving the chain back on the assembly line. That's all he did all day, every day. During a break, we talked to him and he was thoroughly bored with the job. That kind of job I don't have an answer for. If I had his job, I'd probably get another one.

If you are an automobile mechanic, I really appreciate you and I couldn't function unless you fix my car. I appreciate plumbers–especially when the plumbing in my house or office is not working. The same thing goes for those in the heating and cooling business. I appreciate people who take care of the electrical work or the roofing. You see, all the trades and professions are necessary in order for us to function. If you look at the end result of your work, then it will take on a new meaning.

I like the work I do now. I like to see people change. I have seen people grow and have a new capacity for loving, caring, and laughing, and the freedom to have healthy relationship with their family and friends.

Now, the work is entitled to a certain proportion of my life and time. Work is entitled to a proportion of my energy, to a proportion of my intelligence. There is one thing that has been very important to me—I dare not sell my soul to my job. I have been, for a large part of my life, a compulsive worker. I have used it as one of the means of finding my worth and value. I am not at that place today. When a man goes to his job having already decided that he has worth and value and meaning as a person, it will be a different type of day—instead of going with the feeling of having to earn his worth.

I am saying this: don't sell your soul to the agency or the individual for whom you work. Tennessee Ernie Ford used to sing a song with a line in it, "I owe my soul to the Company Store." Some men tell their families, "I have to work. This is the only way I provide a living for you and the family. That's now I can give you and the kids a nice place to live."

If your work comes before your wife and family, then it may be that your work is your god. However kind your employer may be, he can't do for you what God can. So, give to your work it's just dues in energy, strength, vitality, and time, but don't sell your soul to your store, to your business, or to your office, or employer. Your office or employer can't carry the burden of your soul.

It is necessary for me to remember at times that when I am gone, they will find someone else to fill my place. I have been a pastor of churches and have moved from one to another, then have come back in five years, and my name wasn't written on it anywhere. The church that was so important to me while I was there and to whom I had been so important, had found someone else.

I just want to say that businesses, institutions, agencies, and employers have ways of finding replacements; so, it is necessary to keep these different areas of life in balance. You can give yourself the freedom to work and to retain the right to play and retain the right to rest. Watch to see that there is no excessive overlay in any of these three areas.

I often wonder what God did when He rested. Maybe He did nothing more than sit on a big rock and enjoy the work of His hands. This may be one of the ways your work can give you freedom to rest.

January 1975

PLAY'S PLACE IN YOUR LIFE

We have been talking about a lot of things on this program, and when it comes time to talk about play, I ask myself why I put this off until the last of the series. When these programs first started, I listed about 20 things I wanted to talk about, and the last thing I listed was play.

This is because play has been one of the things that I have spent more time working on than anything else. I have decided something: play is an essential part of a person's life. I have never talked to anyone who was in serious emotional stress who knew how to play.

Now we will probably have to define the word, but I want to suggest to you that it is as important as your work, and that the quality of work you do over the long haul will possibly depend on the play in your life.

In the concept of life in which we work, I want to tell you that life is a very delicate and fragile thing. Life–in order to exist and to continue–just must have balance. The human body depends for its permanence and its survival, on balance. When we upset or destroy the balance in the human body, we get into trouble. When we get upset and destroy the balance or thinking processes, our mind has its own way of reacting. The same think is true in schedule. A person can overwork and he gets in trouble, and a person can overeat and get in trouble, and a person can overplay and get in trouble. The balance is very, very important.

I have watched people very carefully for the last couple of years and have found that those who are getting the most out of life–who seem to have reached a new plateau–are those who are free to work, free to play, and free to rest.

Probably the most important thing you and I will every do in this earth is to establish healthy, changing, growing relationships with the persons nearest us. Now that will probably take some looking at.

Last time we talked about the fact that on this planet, God saw fit to give us 24-hour days, and since a day has 24 hours, and man's body is constructed as it is, the day can be divided into work, rest, and play.

I mentioned on an early program that a friend of mine wrote a book called *Confessions of a Workaholic.* I wonder if there will ever be a book written called *Confessions of a Playaholic.* I want to see how that sounds to you, because in our society, it is all right for a man to work excessively. He gets a sort of disguised admiration. But a man who plays excessively sometime is viewed with scorn or contempt.

If a man spends excessive time sleeping and resting, we say that he is sick. If he goes overboard in play, we say that he is no good, and if he goes overboard in work, we say that he is dedicated. Here he dies with a heart attack, but we say he was very dedicated. Here we say he is sick and needs to be hospitalized, or here we say he is a playboy and is no good. If you stay in bed 12-14 hours a day, you do need to talk to someone. That's a hard-core fact. If you refuse to work or have any sort of gainful employment for yourself, you need to talk to someone. If you spend excessive time working–and if working has become your life–you also need to talk to someone about yourself, and eventually you will. Either your doctor or the undertaker will relate to you silently.

I want you to look at something about these 8 hours in work, 8 hours in rest, and 8 hours in play. The line between them must be reasonably clear and definite so that you can leave work completely and enter into a play period.

You are not playing when you spend time rehearsing what you are going to do during the day. If you are an attorney and your playtime is spent rehearsing what you are going to do in the courtroom, you may want to see if you can find a more gainful means of play. If you are a surgeon and you spend your time rehearsing your surgical procedure, and if you are a plumber and you spend your time rehashing the problem you found in Mrs. Jones's sink, that would be boring. I really don't see how this would be playing at all. If you are a housewife and you go over to a friend's for playtime, and you think of all the things you have to do at home, it may be that this period may not be productive in your life.

Watch the ways you tend to move your work time into your play time because of the anxiety and lack of comfort you feel in play. Some people have to have permission to play. It's easy for me to play after a good day's work.

I take a vacation and the first few days I always have to slow myself down to establish a new schedule. I think a growing person might possibly be able to shift gears and slow himself down daily, and move into an area of living that is characterized by certain things.

Play is characterized by a person's being free. I don't mean you have to be a potter working at a potter's wheel, or an artist, or a composer, or an author. I am talking about your freedom to participate in activities that are a full expression of yourself, without regard to being judged by other people, and without any need on your part to be competitive.

It is this part of your life that is planned by God to make you a free, spontaneous, creative person where you will allow your inner self to flow without stopping. It is a time for inner personal growth; a time when the inner self is reconstructed, and a time when the inner self is reorganized.

The particular form that play take is subordinate to the inner attitudes that you assume towards this portion of your life. It may be that you have a desk job, or your work is confining, and you will enjoy some kind of physical play. It may be that you will want to participate in athletics or sports. The important thing is that you have moved out of the work area of life into play. Here, without the rules or the schedule of work, is a time when you can unshackle you can unharness your body and mind, and play. Here you can allow yourself to be a creative, spontaneous, happy, uninhibited person.

I am convinced that this is an essential and vital part of the life of God. I am convinced that Jesus of Nazareth did it, and I am convinced that every great man has times of quiet, times of reflection, times of escape, and time where he gets away from the pressing, consistent demands that his intellect has imposed on him.

I heard one of the happiest things about a man in my hometown. This man had carried a very heavy load of responsibility. I asked a friend of his one day how he managed to carry such a tremendous load, and the friend said to me, "I know how he does it."

I stopped. Are you aware of times when people are talking to you that the level in which they are talking to you moves? This is what happened at that moment. When I stopped, this man told me that the man we were discussing came home every day at five o'clock and watched the kiddie cartoons on TV.

I about fell out of my chair. I couldn't imagine this man, with all his responsibilities, sitting there watching those cartoons. But, you know what? Sometimes when I have come home for lunch or in the middle of the afternoon, I have watched a couple of them. I was afraid at first that someone would come in and find me watching them, and I kept watching the door. And I made up my mind that if anyone came in I would say, "Well the TV was on when I came in and I was just killing time."

Then I decided that I had the right to watch them. I'm not advertising cartoons, but I am saying that this man, by watching cartoons, found himself at the other end of the world from the responsibility of the relationships in his office.

At this time, his mind lay down and relaxed. He is what we would call elderly. He is in his 80s, but he is still peppy, and he has a beautiful smile. He is a productive and friendly person. I think that the balance he has found in life has given him the health that he enjoys. He has an unshakable faith in God, which impressed me. He believes, and he worships, and he works, and he plays. Maybe this man knows that the times of play are as important as those of rest and work. I don't mean watching cartons is all he does for play. I watched cartoons 30 minutes one day, and the first 15 minutes were okay, but the last 15 minutes I was just about climbing the walls. This was just an example.

In your office, you can play by taking your coffee break time and going for a walk, or to the post office, or across the street. Or you can walk to the window and spend 30 minutes standing before it. This will do you as much good as a hot cup of coffee. Thirty minutes in which you see the sky, the landscape in which you see people moving up and down the street, the wide- open fields. Whatever the beauty is, you take yourself out of its work setting, and for 30 minutes, you can play.

Another way to play is to stand and look at the sky and realize that light, traveling 186,000 miles a second, 60 seconds a minute, 60 minutes and hour, 24 hours a day, 365 days a year, sometimes take three billion light years to reach you and me.

This is a big world, and a big universe, and God made it, and it might be all right for you to rest and play. God worked, but Gold also rested, and although I can't quote your scripture, chapter, and verse, I am convinced that there was also a balance in the life of God. I think God plays and participants in some type of change in the life of mankind, and I am also convinced that this balance can come into my life.

You may feel guilty and that you are wasting time playing. Guilt over play is no more realistic that guilt over work or over rest. You are entitled to it.

So, since this is a fairly new year, you might want to say that during this new year of 1975, "I promise for myself a new experience of play, so that I can keep balance in my life. You need to play for the sake of playing. Play will get you in touch with your inner self. You will find yourself more free and more creative, as you continue to allow yourself to find the balance in life that comes when a person balances work and play and rest. You'll experience a new kind of happiness and a joyous abandonment that characterizes the life of a person. You'll find yourself dealing less and less with inhibitions, fear, guilt, anxiety, and doubt. You might even find out that while you are playing, you will look around and you'll see God smiling.

May 1975

TIME

In this discussion that we have been having about using our time, a lot of you have responded to me and said the use of time is so often beyond one's control, and that's true to some extent, depending on the commitments we've made. You've a certain commitment to your family, and you have a commitment to where you make your living, some of you have commitments to an educational process and this commitment is a constant and a continuing thing, and we give a certain amount of our time to these commitments. The thing that's important to me is that I stay in control of my time. And I reserve the right to continue the commitment or to discontinue the commitment as I see fit. This is necessary, it seems to me, in order to give a person a feeling of identity and integrity. Once you lose control of your time there's a real possibility that you've lost control of your life.

Compulsive working or compulsive playing or excessive sleeping are bad signs. These are signs when properly used that can enable us to improve the quality of the particular lifestyle that we've chosen. The division that we have discussed here, eight hours work, eight hours play, and eight hours rest is a good beginning place.

It needs to be discussed further, however, the things we include under each one of these, someone asked, "Where do we worship God in this?" I think maybe worship would include a little bit of time in all three of these sections. It seems to me it would be a real happy experience for a person to know some play in his worship, and for a person to know some rest in his worship. I don't know if work should be a part of worship or not, I guess so. I guess there are times when the mental and emotional processes should be geared to working in order to call the whole being forth, I don't know if that would be work. I'd certainly include play and rest in worship and I think probably include a dimension of the work time.

If the experience of worship takes a substantial part of your life and includes the totality of your whole being, it will make your life richer and fuller and happier. And I wondered, too–after talking with some of you who listen and give me some feed back–I wonder, too, if one's work should include a dimension of play and a dimension of rest. Now, this might require a lot of readjusting, on the part of some of us, but it seems to me that instead of the day,—and this I want you to think about—instead of the day being divided into these neat little compartments, it seems that if there's a dimension of work, play, and rest in everything you do, that it would give life a freedom, give you a freedom and give you a sense of belonging, producing, being creative that a person does not normally experience. I believe, with all of my heart, that's it's possible for a person to have a life and to live at something better than just a plain existence. And the reason I believe it is because I experience it sometime and I keep working toward it, I keep struggling for it.

Okay, this is the way we talked about dividing the day. Now I think that maybe in the work there must be some worship and a dimension of worship in play and a dimension of worship in rest. Now, if you can include these three dimensions in your vocation, in the way you make your living, man, you're living at a higher level than the average person. And I think your capacity to laugh—to laugh with people, to laugh at yourself—will have a lot to do with this.

If your vocation extends so that it includes all these three areas, one of the things then you might ask yourself is, how much fun is your job. And how much enjoyment do you experience with getting up and going to the office, or going to the shop or going to the farm, or whatever you do each day, how much fun is there included in that and if there's no fun in it, it may be that the time has come for you to change jobs. And it may be that you'll be much happier in doing some other kind of work.

Now, some people get awfully panicky when they talk about changing jobs. If you've had ten jobs in two years you could stop and look at what you're doing with yourself. But if you've been unhappy and miserable on the same job for twenty-five years it's also time for you to stop and look. We have a great deal of respect here in America for the way a person stays with a job. And some people say I've been on the same job for twenty, twenty-five, thirty years . And that's good if the job has contributed to your life and if you, through the job, have made a contribution to society and to the world in which you live. But there's no virtue in being miserable and unhappy and disgruntled and grouchy and remaining on the job.

One thing that came out of war and experiences that a lot of us had is that we said every soldier gripes, and if the soldier is not griping he's not happy. I doubt that. The happiest soldiers I found during the war were not gripey.

They had found something better to do with their time than to gripe. I don't particularly like the experience of being around a man who's always complaining and who's always criticizing and cutting other people down. I think the reason for this, rather than lying in the character or the nature of the individual, the reason for this may be in the way this man has chosen to structure his time. Unhappiness does not have to be due to an emotional disorder. Unhappiness may be caused by the poorly structured time frame in which this person lives.

So, I just want to say, you can take charge of your time and choose the way you will employ yourself, you will employ your hours during the day. The commitment to your family will probably have to be constant, the commitment you have to your employer or your employees will have to be constant. I submit to you that this rarely takes more than twelve hours a day. Now some of you housewives will challenge that, but that's alright, I've lived with a housewife for quite a while, and I think it's possible for a woman to do her work in twelve hours, some do it in less, a lot less. And there is some time here where a woman can get out of the house, get away from the family, and find some time and situations in which she can experience some affirmations of her own identity. That sounds pretty stiff. There are times in every family's life where a woman can get out and away from the family and just enjoy being herself, and enjoy being a person and be with other human beings who will affirm her as a person and who will accept her as a person, so that when she goes back home she goes back a total and complete and a happy person, and she gives the family a gift which they can get from no other source. This is compared to the woman who stays at home and who works hard all day and is a frenzied, frantic mother, then when the family comes in in the evening, she's ready for a fight.

Your decision may possibly mean that you've chosen to preserve your marriage. You know one of the reasons that I have found that marriages don't make it—some marriage—some marriages don't make it because the husband doesn't make it as a person or the wife doesn't make it as a person, and when the man in a marriage just gives himself completely to the tasks of being a mechanic or a barber, doctor, counselor, or teacher and a husband, this many will eventually be unhappy. When the woman in the marriage gives her life over totally to being just a wife and just a mother, this woman is eventually going to be unhappy, and here's where a lot of marriages lose their way. The business of preserving the marriage and not just surviving in the marriage, but really growing and enjoying the marriage, can I think, be summed up in the way an individual uses his time. And you know, if you'll take a sheet of paper and divide the sheet of paper into three columns, in work, play, and rest columns —and be honest with yourself for a week, for a seven- day week, you can understand more about yourself in this little simple exercise than sitting down with a counselor and talking half a dozen times.

I mentioned before that there are some people who need to counsel with a professional person. Most people do not, I'd say nine out of ten do not. That's just a figure out of the air. But this is one of the ways you find out things about yourself, first your capacity to be honest with yourself about how you use your time, and secondly, your persistence in doing this for a week—if you don't want to do it for a week, do it for three days. You will really find out some things about the way your employment of time controls your life. The freedom to make a decision is something, hey, you know something, I've come back to the freedom to make the decision. This is one of the fascinating things to me it's one of the fascinating things about this Jesus Christ that we talk about and worship. He had about three and a half years to do on earth what no human being ever would do again in all of eternity, and we never have one recorded instance or one indication. The Bible describes them as teaming multitudes. He looked at the crowd, and He looked at the disciples and said, "Let's get out of here." (That's a free translation.) And they went out into the mountains to rest. Now most of us would have called a meeting and set up a lot of preaching and teaching and made arrangements to feed them and house them. But Jesus chose to employ His own time in such a way that as His own needs were met that He could continue to live through and enjoy each day, and I'm convinced that this man enjoyed life at a level no other person has ever since or before experienced the sheer joy of living. I'm sure that's right. The freedom to make the choice on the way you use your time.

Now here's where you can check yourself out again. If you kind of keep a chart or a graph in the way you use your time, then you may decide you want to make some changes and your freedom to make the changes is again an indication of how much you're in control of your life. If you're out of control, then you need some help. If you're still in control, man, Hurray! That's the name of the game.

Now, it may be that you'll need to sit down and say to your wife, I have chosen to take Thursday afternoons off, or Thursday evenings I won't come home for supper, I'm going to mee some of the boys and we're going out to dinner, and — well, I don't know what you and your men friends do on your night out, that's your business. But whatever you do you might want to say to your wife, I've made this decision, and I've made this choice, and I just want to let you know. If you happen to be that wife, and you can say, "Good, that's a great idea and I'm glad that you're going to do it." If you can say that that means that you are secure and you're in control of your life and, girl, you're rich when you can do that.

Now, on the other side of the picture, for the woman. When you can say to yourself, "When you all get home tonight, I won't be at home. I've made a date with a friend, preferably female, specifically female. I've made a date with a friend and we're going out the movies."—or whatever you like to do on your nights out—"Cheese will be in the refrigerator, the bread will be where it usually stays, so tonight for the evening meal you are going to have cheese sandwiches, and if you really want to splurge, you can toast them. But I won't be at home tonight." Now I think it is necessary for the husband and wife to do this together sometimes, it's necessary for the wife to do it apar, and the husband to do it away from the wife. It's necessary for the parents to be away from the children at times; it's necessary for the children to be away from the parents. And your freedom to make this choice is also your freedom to experience at a qualitative higher level than most people ever know. This we call time structure.

I'm saying the decision is yours, it was not taken away from you at birth; have both the right and the responsibility to make the choice. And when you find yourself shackled to your job, or shackled to your family, or shackled to your home, you need to look at those shackles and see whose hand make those chains that are binding you to that monotonous, unhappy existence.

Another thing about this time structure, the restructuring of your way of life might mean that you will be uncomfortable initially doing new things, and if it does, that's all right. You see, there's no learning without change; there's no growth without change. Sometimes the experience of change produces some anxiety. It's because we are unfamiliar with the new schedules, the new routine, and we're unfamiliar with the new experiences we create for ourselves in making the changes, so don't expect to be totally comfortable It may be really hard for you to be away from home and allowing your family to fix their evening meal. It will probably be easier for you to know that you were missed and the family appreciates more than ever the work that you do. It may be hard for you not to go home when you leave the job, if you're the man, and to spend the evening with friends. It also may be easier; however, it may be easier for you to know that you're appreciated. And you're appreciated for the fact that you do come home with regularity and promptness and contribute to the life and enjoyment of your family.

Separation is as much a healthy part of relationship as closeness, physical closeness, and physical intimacy. Now, structuring your time so that you have both closeness and separation is a healthy part of growth and adjustment. It's necessary for you to structure your time so that you are separated from the familiar surroundings of your home. Vacations are for that, too. And sometimes when we don't make the choice, it's made for us because sometimes when we don't make the choice or decision to rest, it's made for us and we get our vacation in the bed in the hospital. That can happen, so the decision you make to control your time can possibly be the measure of the extent to which you are in control of your life. Time is probably one of the most valuable commodities that you have on this earth. I wanted to say this morning, that nobody, but nobody, is ultimately responsible for the way your time is used but you. You can use it or abuse it. You can waste it or you can make it count, but the decision ins yours. That's the way God made you; that's the way God made time.

August 1975

REASON FOR BEING

Did you hear the story about the man who died and went to Heaven, and got to the gates and St. Peter, or whoever the custodian is, stopped him and the man introduced himself and said, "I'm so and so, and I live in Texas, and I've come to spend the rest of eternity in Heaven."

St. Peter said, "Well, I need first to know how many points you have."

The man said, "They never told me anything about points down on earth, I never heard such a thing."

And the story goes... St. Peter said, "Well, we had a staff meeting here last night, and we decided a man had to have 3,000 points to get in." And the man stood there and scratched his head. St. Peter said, "Tell me, what did you do on earth."

The man said, "Well, I was a devout church goer, and I attended church regularly, and I paid my tithes, and sometimes gave over on special occasions. And I visited for the church, and I was an officer in the church, and I was there every time the door was open and attended every service.

St. Peter said, "That's one point." The man stood and scratched his head. St. Peter said, "What else did you do."

The man said, "Well, I belong to very prominent civic club, and I fulfill my duties very well, and I left a good insurance program, I provided well for my family on my departure, I was a model father, and I was a faithful and devoted husband, I kept the lawn trimmed, and I took care of my aged and widowed mother, and I gave every year to the United Fund, even donated a little blood, when the blood bank made an appeal for blood."

St. Peter said, "That's two points." And the man stood there and scratched his head and shuffled his feet, and he looked and he said, "St. Peter, nothing but the grace of God is going to get me in here." And St. Peter said, "Good, that's the other 2,998 points, come on in."

This story and stories like this help us to keep in perspective the value of work as opposed to the value of being and believing and trusting in terms of our relationship with God. And that's a valid story. It really is. The thing that's important to me is, that we keep in balance and proper perspective the necessity for a man finding a goal or an objective, or I like to think of it as a focal point for his life. Not long ago there was a movie, a play, later a movie that made popular a song titled, "To Dream the Impossible Dream;" I don't know if that was the title, but that's the meaning of it. I think this very beautifully portrayed the need that we all have to feel deeply challenged and deeply moved and feel ourselves attested and drawn out, and our whole life brought to focus and brought to bear on some particular purpose. I know a lot of women find this in their families, a lot of men find this in their jobs, some people find it in sports and in avocation, as well as in vocation, and that's fine. The important thing it seems to me is that you find it. I mentioned once on a previous program here, that the French have a term called, *"raison d'etre."*

Now, what that means in English, is simply this. It means "reason for being." And this is what I want you to look at for just a minute and if you won't reach a conclusion ahead of me, I'll appreciate it. This is one of the ways that a man identifies himself in this world, and this is one of the ways a man focus his life or brings it to bear in a certain direction for a certain purpose. In this "reason for being" we're talking about the totality of a man's life, not just what he does. It's a fullness of being, and it's not a reason for doing sort of life, it's a reason for being. And the emphasis that I have chosen for myself is emphasis on the being. I've been a doer most of my life, about the only thing I ever got was tired. It's fine to be a doer, as long as doing is kept in perspective.

This is where I think we miss the point. We don't find the balance between who we are and what we do; we don't find the balance between the works of our hands, the strength of what we're able to accomplish ourselves, and the necessity of trusting in God. It seems to me, and I've talked to you once about this before; it seems to me that balance in life is an absolute necessity and it is something that has to be achieved and attained every day, I get the feeling that my scales change several times a day and sometimes more, but they particular change at night and when I get up every morning, I have sort of a mental picture–not every day but occasionally–a mental picture of one who sets the scales, where the pivot is in the center, you know, has a little fan on either side like you seen in old movies wherever they go. And I have to balance that thing out early in the morning and I particularly have to do this later in the day. It has to be balanced for me with work and play. It has to be balanced for me with laughter and seriousness, it has to be balanced for me with joy and sorrow, spontaneity, and commitment. That sort of balance gives me a larger overall feeling. I don't mean that this is a conscious thing, I think it would be very boring if it were conscious all of the time. I do mean this: I must exercise my files of choice in order to focus the energies of my life on the things that need to be done at the moment.

At the moment the thing that might need doing is play. I played a lot of tennis about 10 years ago. I said every year, I really enjoyed that, and I'm going to get back to it. Buy me a racket, get some new shoes, and I'm going down to the tennis court. Last year, when I was out of town on a retreat, I played with one person,... no two years ago. Then I said, I really enjoyed this. I'm going to get me a racket, get some shoes and get back on the court. Two weeks ago, I did it again, I played tennis four times, thoroughly enjoyed it, loved it and I said, "I'm going to get me a racket," and then I caught myself and said, "I may not."

Now, to me that's freedom, to me that's being. It's the freedom to make a choice and make a decision and make a commitment, it eliminates the have to, it eliminates the ought to and eliminates the should. And leaves me free to choose to do this if and when I make up my mind and enjoy it when I do but not feel guilty because I didn't.

> One of the reasons for being is a healthy balance between play and work. The parent, grandparent generation, most of the people that I know, have a healthy respect for the work effort. Now for some of our children and grandchildren, I have observed that there's not the same respect for work that we have, that's okay ... if they can live. Now, we don't have to tell people that work is a necessity—most people we don't have to tell. Some of the young friends that I have don't have the same respect for work, and I respect their opinions. Most of the time we do our work the problem is, we are not at the point of commitment with play that—let me say that over— we don't have the same respect for play that we have for work. The balance here is where you save your life and keep yourself in .a healthy, functional frame of mind.

And I wanted to say the purpose in life will of necessity include play, as well as work. It will also include good judgement, good sound sensible judgement. It will also include a dimension of forgiveness. The reason for being that you choose to pursue will include a dimension of good judgement and objective evaluation. It will also include a healthy dimension of forgiveness. No forgiveness in one's life means that everything becomes sterile and sad. Every man that I know has a sense of right and wrong, who doesn't always agree with mine any more than mine always agrees with his. But where one has exceeded his own sense of rightness or wrongness, there's a feeling of guilt that comes, and the only remedy that I know anything about is forgiveness. Forgiveness in terms of my relationship to the creator, forgiveness in terms of my relationship to myself. It's necessary for me in my being to accept the forgiveness of God; it's necessary for me in my being to accept the forgiveness of myself.

Sometimes I need the help of a friend, we've talked about this, I won't go back into it. To go to a friend and get help and assistance and forgiveness where I can come to terms with myself. And really, you know I was thinking the other day, we live such a restrained, inhibited, harnessed, shackled life. I do not believe God intended any of this. Most of the shackles that I have worn as an adult were chains that I had forged with my own hands. They were not put on me by another person. One of the freedoms and privileges of an adult is to enter into the kind of understanding that will remove the ball and chain that you put there yourself. Now this is not true of everybody. I have some friends when I meet them and look at the weight of their burden, and at the tremendous obstacles which they have to overcome, I am appalled at their ability to stay alive—and some of you who watch this telecast, too. God bless you, Sir, I tip my hat to you. I cannot understand, and I certainly will not try to explain, why things in your life have happened as they have. I mean things that are completely, totally beyond your choice and that you received without your hope or your approval. Maybe it takes people like you to teach the rest of us what bravery really is. Maybe it takes people like you to teach me faith. But for the rest of us we have a choice, of giving up the chains, of moving out of nature's cave and coming into the sunlight, and allowing our eyes to become adjusted and accustomed to the sunlight. And choose learning to live in the sunlight and experience the green fields of God, rather than live in the dank, damp, dark, hollow, empty cave of fear and despair and depression and gloom and hopelessness. You have a choice.

Then, I've decided to tell you, there's also the choice of purpose toward which you can direct your commitment. I believe more in people now, than I ever have.

> I am constantly amazed when I find people who are more than willing to help others, who are more than willing to be open and understanding toward others. The people that I meet who are harsh, judgmental, and critical are in the very small minority. They sometimes just make more noise than the others. And we begin to think that everybody is that way. Is this the way people treat me? No, it's not. This is a very small minority; they just have big mouths. It's good when you can ignore them, and count noses and see this is not really the majority. of people.

> In this reason for living, this reason for existence, as you learn to experience the balance of work and play and rest and sleep, creativity, and solitude, all of those moments; then people take on a different complexion with you. I mentioned in the introduction that every man has his price. I do not know if this is true.

> I have met some people and I never found their price. I think some men who are addicted to certain forms of

living have a very low price. Their price is the addiction and they are for sale. There are some other men whose price runs considerably higher, but in some ways, some men succumb easier to flattery than they ever would to bribery with money or position. Whatever your price is, I think it would really have to do with your reason for being, with your reason for existing on this earth. If *you* want a neat little experiment, you could sit down and ask yourself, "What is *my* price'; and what do *I* sell for? What would it take for my family to buy my time?" And some men's price is priceless. The price of some men is tragic. When he hits his so-called bottom, that's his price. That means I'm willing to be stopped, arrested— not by the officers of the law—but arrested mentally and emotionally and turned around because I've hit bottom. I talked to a very beautiful person the other day, and I ask this person, "When did your life change? And the person knew instantly and said, "It was today – when this happened."

Now, that's when the person makes a decision, it is in a manner of speaking, the person's price. And when you're aware of your price, you can also more clearly define the reason that you're here on this earth and the purpose that you have for being.

My own reason for being is–call it, "this need to relate to people nearest to me." You know, a lot of times we have the idea that we could do something for the people who have been hurt by earthquake or flood, or the victims of famine in different parts of the world, and I'm glad there are people who minister and take care of people in situations like this.

I think that's great. People like this I've known who do this kind of work, I've been surprised to find that their relationship with people closest to them at home *is* very poor. Now, I don't want this to be a generalization because I'm *really* not talking about them. I'm talking about you, and I'm talking about me and saying, "How much kindness do you show your wife? How much kindness do *you* show your son or daughter? How much kindness do you show your mother and father, your husband, or your grandparents?" Now, this is where the water hits the wheel; this is bedrock. Reason for being on this earth, if it excludes the persons closest to you, and if it eliminates the relationships which are greatest importance because of the primacy which they have in your life, then maybe you need to reexamine your reason for being in the world. I've known this particularly among some pastors—great servants among the family of God, and total strangers to their families.

I think this is wrong, I don't think there's any way you can justify this, and I think the scriptures substantiate this. I've known, also, some great humanitarians, some doctors, who cared tenderly and patiently for other people, but had no *time* to listen to their wife or their son or their daughter. I have known men who were very prominent in civic and community life, and one day I talked to a son of such a man, and I said without thinking, "You must be very proud of your dad." and he answered immediately, "I don't even, know him." And I realized then that the man must have paid a very high price for the publicity he had enjoyed— apparently, he had paid the price of alienating his son.

If it's true that every man has his price, it might be good to stop and look to see what yours is. And along with the price it might be wise to examine the reason that you 're here on this earth. I believe that if I understand this man from Nazareth, He achieved a beautifully balance in being. Hey, I don't believe He had a price. I was just trying to think. I know of one occasion, when offered three different bribes, He didn't take any of them. His price wasn't his life, because He was given an opportunity to save it and did not. His price wasn't safety because He was offered an opportunity for flight and didn't take it. His price wasn't his own personal security and personal safety. It seems to me that I remember a group of people saying one time, "Save thyself," and He never did.

I had thought that this morning I would sum up for you His reason for being. Now we do this a lot of times in our worship with little cliches and aphorisms and memorized phrases. I think when we do this, we do this Man an injustice. It may have been that his reason for being, first, was to be **who** you are. For of all men who ever lived, none was ever more nobly himself. Maybe that constitutes his reason for being." Of all the men who ever lived none ever more nobly gave to me and to you, both the freedom and the capacity—and the permission for us to be ourselves.

March 1975

HAPPINESS

Since you have to live life you can choose to live it happily or you can choose to be miserable. You can choose to enjoy it, or you can choose to live it depressed. Either way —you've got to live it. Now the choice is what we're going to talk about here this morning on this program which we call "A Place to Talk."

To me, it means to meet a person who enjoys life and who is experiencing it every minute, who's in contact with himself and his feelings, a person who likes people and enjoys them. I don't mean someone who likes everybody. I think a person who likes everybody doesn't really have any convictions. But the kind of person who enjoys life, who experiences it, who's aware, and who's sensitive and perceptive is really exciting, and I enjoy being around him. Admittedly there are not a lot of them running around loose, but if you ever know one, or if you ever have the opportunity to be around one, you're aware of it. You're usually aware of it when you're with him. I would say you're

I was with a person like this recently. I wanted to tell you I went back to Mississippi for a speaking engagement last Sunday night and Monday morning. And I mentioned on a previous program the experience of going back to bury my Mother. This time I didn't go back to my hometown; I just went back to a larger city nearby where I spoke and I found myself being picked up by some emotions that had very subtly and casually entered into my thinking and feeling and which I'd allowed to come in. I was with a man and his wife and we were looking at a piece of property they had bought recently. We were walking out on the grounds, and the grounds were beautiful. When we were walking out the woman picked a huge handful of azaleas.

Some of them were deep red and some were kind of pink, and when we went into the house she laid them on the table. Something in this action struck a familiar chord in me and I was for a minute sort of overwhelmed with nostalgia and memory. It was almost as if a wave had swept over me and I found myself in that moment very sad and wanting to cry. I didn't, but I did say to myself, "This is grief and it's all right to be sad and it's all right to grieve." And I did for just a moment there. I didn't know this couple too well. I thought about it later, you know I could have just told them that, but I decided not to. I make this decision a lot. They would have understood. I think probably the thing that was significant there was, I was not ready to be understood or willing at that moment. But I was talking about this incident later with another friend, and we discussed the awareness·that comes when you talk about these experiences and this awareness sometimes doesn't come unless you're willing to talk about these experiences with other people. This friend is the kind of person I was just discussing a minute ago. He's not particularly an outstanding individual in the world, but he has a qualitative experience of life, he has a capacity to enjoy life that, Man, it's just beautiful. And when I leave this guy, I like me and I like the world, I like people a whole lot better. It is just really a good experience to be around him.

And one of the things that came out of my meeting with this guy, and incidentally this came out of some of the mail and telephone calls. In the next several weeks or a month, we're going to have a program that will deal with single parents and their responsibilities in rearing children. There are a lot of people in this boat. Fully a third or more of the married population of the United States is in this condition. So, we're going to talk about that and I have some friends who are doing this and who are doing a good job. We'll be sharing that with you. Another thing that I thought we'd do is we'll have friends come who know something about relating to children—how to talk with them and how to establish a healthy growing relationship with a child. Another thing we're going to do is we're going to be talking about your health and your heart. The way that the emotions tie in with a person's physical health. Another thing I thought we'd talk about is your anger and your digestion, because this is a factor.

I read more and more articles in popular magazines about anger. And I get a lot of questions regarding anger in the mail, too. I think we've had a lot of bad teaching about anger, hostility, and resentment—and give it any name you want to. This is a very powerful emotion, and I'm convinced that when properly used, it can be very creative in a person's life. So, I think this will be a big help, it will to me to work on it. I hope it will be to you when you're hearing it.

The experience of living out the rest of your life, which is where we started, is one of the choices that you will make. Incidentally, your capacity to choose is one of the greatest capacities that you have. You've chosen to watch this television program for this span of time and you have chosen to take yourself and employ yourself this way either intently watching or casually watching while you're getting ready for church or Sunday school or whatever you're doing with your time. The thing I want to say is this: it's not a matter of whether or not we have choices—because you choose, you make choices all the time. You choose to go to work or stay at home or play with the kids or be alone. You choose either to be depressed or to be happy. The choice is yours; nobody makes it for you, and the thing I'd like you to consider is that you can choose exactly what you're going to do with your life.

I was on a trip one time and on the way home I was kind of wrestling with some problems; so, I decided to stop and call a friend. He was a home, and his office was near his home; so, I went over and visited with him. I Planned to stay two hours— stayed two days—a good two days. He first introduced me to what I said to you this morning. He's a very wise man, he's not an old man either. He said,

"John, you can choose how you are going to live your life, and you can choose what you're going to do with it. You can either be happy, or you can be sad, and all you have to decide about is right now while you're sitting in this chair. I was sitting in his office, he sells real estate and business was not too good at that time, incidentally. And he said, "All you have to do is decide right now how you're going to feel." and he said, "Now relax and enjoy with happiness."

So, I did. And I said, "Yes, but what about when I go back home?"

He said, "You're not back home now, you're just sitting in that chair, stay with your happiness right there where you are."

Now this is the decision. You can be happy, you can enjoy the experience of living right now, right where you are, you can be excited, you can be stimulated you can be thrilled, you can be comfortable and secure right now watching this television. program or washing the dishes, or getting ready for wherever you're going. When you make the decision that this is where you're going live and what you're going to experience today, now all you have to do to stay happy is to make the decision to be happy in the present. I'm more than ever convinced, and a year or two years ago I would have argued with you about this 'til the world turned blue, all you have to do to be a happy, contented, peaceful person is to make the decision that you're going to enjoy life in the present tense right here, right now, right there where you are. This is where the action is. And once you start doing that , the continuation of the present decision is a guarantee of future happiness on out into the rest of your life.

Do you remember the things you were miserable about a year ago on February whatever today is? Do you remember the things you were miserable about a year ago this Sunday? I don't. Do you remember the things you were unhappy about two years ago at this time or five years or ten years? Being unhappy is a dirty habit that we acquire, some people acquire this in childhood, but you do not have to stay with it.

You can choose right now to be free from it as you make the decision to be happy in the present and stay with it. A part of this decision to be happy is your acceptance of the forgiveness of God. And what more liberating experience can a man have ·than the experience that he is completely acceptable to God. That God has nothing against you. That you're totally, completely, freely forgiven by God through Jesus Christ.

Hey, Man that's good news, no wonder they call it that! Then you live in the present tense without guilt and anxiety. Forgiveness, accepting forgiveness, will give you freedom from anxiety and fear, and guilt. It will also do something else: It will relieve you of the dubious privilege of worrying about the past.

Man, when I think of the mistakes I made yesterday and the day before and the day before that, I can literally climb the walls, as long as I keep my mind focused on the past. If you decide not to focus on the past but rather to live in the present, then you don't spend all the energy which you can employ in present happiness by focusing on past mistakes. Like I said last Sunday, you can spend your time and energy being a winner, rather than spending your time and energy wishing that yesterday you had not done this or you had done that, wishing you had said it another way, wishing you had waited or wishing you had started.

None of these past experiences can be changed, but, Sir, you can change the present. You can change your mental attitude; you can change your personal relationship with other people; you can change the way you feel about yourself; you can change the attitude of the emotional state that you're in right now. Nobody on earth can change it but you, but you can change it.

This is the part of it I like, There's something else. You can change the relationship with the people who are closer to you. I think this is so important, and you know I've been changing some relationships with people, thank God! —People that I work with and some friends—and the change has usually come about in–well not the same way with everybody– but in different ways. I have to say to people, "Hey, I'm not satisfied or I'm not happy with our relationship an I'd like to talk with you." In every case, I've found the person ready to talk, not quite understanding maybe a direct approach. But the people in your family, Sir, the other members of your family, really do want a better relationship with you. Or Mother, the other members of your family really do want to understand you, and they would like to be closer. Let me say if you are a son or a daughter, I can almost guaranty you, without question, that your mother and your father would really like to know what goes on in your mind.

Now there are exceptions to this. The truth of the matter is some parents don't care. the truth of the matter is some children don't care. I think if you are in a position where your parents obviously do not care–or maybe they have told you that–you can find substitute parents, there are a lot of them. Your doctor, your minister, or a friend can help you find substitute parents. If you're in a position where your child does not care about you, then–I hadn't thought of this,–but I guess you could find a substitute child. There are a lot of agencies that provide substitute children. There's one very good one called Foster Parent Agency. I don't know the address, and I'm not pushing that organization, but there are a lot of ways that you can find people who need your love and need your friendship and are interested in sharing. The decision to enjoy life in the present tense, which means you've got a guaranteed happiness for as long as you live—the decision to do this brings you into better relationship with people around you. Nothing is more important than this. If you're in a bad relationship with your family, you know you've got to spend the rest of your day down at the office,–and that's gets old– or on the job, or wherever you work. But improved relationships in one's family makes a big difference in the way you come home, or the way you leave home, or when you think about it.

A little clarification in the relationships is the beginning step in building better relationships with family. I think probably, I'm an advocate of straight talk. When I say straight talk, I don't mean criticism. I do not enjoy talking with people who are critical or who come home with "Well, I want to tell you something for your own good." When I hear that, I begin thinking, "How can I get away from this person as quickly as possible." When I say straight talk, I mean straight talk like "I'd like for us to have a better relationship... I've got something that I want to say to you; this is what I feel and what going on between us and our family, ...or I need your help and I need you to do this for me. Would you do it?...or I want to offer my help," or whatever the opening statement should be in establishing better relationships in families.

Living this happy, full life begins with the decisions you make about what you're going to do and act or say and feel right now. I want to make this clear, when I say you can live life in a rich, full, and happy way, I am not talking about living in a world of fantasy on a superficial level while you're running around giggling and giddy. That is not what I'm talking about. I have neither desire nor intention of living that way. What I am saying is you can know a measure of contentment, you can know a measure of peace, and you can know a measure of self-assurance, you can know a measure of friendship, warmth, and—I'm convinced—joy in every day to some degree in different ways, now that's what I mean. I am not talking about living on an emotional high. Now there are a lot of people today, who, well...there are some religious groups that are advocating living on a sort of—what I consider to be—living on an unrealistic plane of excitement, joy, and stimulation. I think this is what some people hope to get out of alcohol and some other people hope to get out of drugs, but it never lasts. If you are in some situations, you know, joy and excitement and happiness would be totally out of place. So, what I want to get across is that I'm talking about propriety. I am talking about being proper. The emotions corresponding to the situations and the individual retaining his own identity, his own selfhood, and his own personhood. I'm saying it's possible for you to live your life and to retain your own sense of identity regardless of what goes on in the world around you.

Hey, I'd like you to hear this: I'm not selling anything; I'm not trying to get you to join anything. Man, this is for free; it's for you. It's not something you ought to have it's something you have already. It's not something you ought to be doing, or should be doing, it's something that one decision will give you. And the extent of the gift, the measure of this gift is only determined by your willingness to receive. God is rich, did you know that. Man, He's rich, and everything God has, He's made available to His kids. He's a good parent and God is a good God. All that God has is available to you as much as you need to live by and more. Man, He's a generous giver., and the only way you can live on poverty road or on misery street,–only way you can do that–is to choose not to accept the gift that God has for you. I mentioned this before, and I keep on saying it because of the beauty that I've seen in the life of this one person.

I have a friend who has been living in an iron lung for twenty-three years. Did you hear me? She's been living in an iron lung for TWENTY-THREE YEARS! I defy you to show me any one person who gets more out of life than she does. It's not where you are or what you're doing that's important, it's the decision that you make about the present; it's the gifts of God already available for you. Th decisions you make about accepting these gifts and about utilizing them. It's also the decision you make about the people closest to you and how much you're willing to be close to these people. The decisions you make as to whether or not you will give yourself permission to enjoy today, to enjoy this moment, enjoy the experience of being alive. You're just one decision away from a rich, full, happy life. That's what God intended for you when He created you and gave you this day.

August 1975

GUILT

l have been getting some mail and decided to come back and touch base with you at one of the places where we started, one of the first things, in fact the first time I talked to you here at this Place to Talk, I talked about guilt.

About ninety percent of the mail I received asks that I repeat or emphasize or cover other areas of guilt. I think that this is one of the biggest problems that we face as individuals today, and there's also corporate guilt. There's sort of a cultural guilt that we, as Americans, have.

I was interested not long ago, In talking with someone from another country who had been on an extended visit here. This was this person's first visit to the United States, and he asked me a question, "Why are the people of the United States so guilty, why do they feel so guilty?" And I didn't have an answer. I can't explain, but I can comment on it, and I am sure that it's true. I have gotten some letters; I asked two people and one of them did it—I asked two people to list eight or ten things that they would like for me to discuss here on this program. I got a nice letter from a good friend within two or three days after I'd requested this. I'd like to say if you are available and if you are interested, if you'd like to have a part of this conversation so that it's two-way and not one-way, I wish you'd sit down and list some things you'd like for me to talk about, ask some questions, or make some statements, and I'll be glad to do it.

I'm going to work today on this business of guilt. first, to say I can't take your guilt away; second, you can give it up. Thirdly—before you would let anybody take it away if they could, or before you would give it up—it would be necessary for you to decide that you're willing to live without it and that's the hard part. When you're willing to make the decision to live without guilt, then you're on the threshold of giving it up. Now all the time I'm talking I want you to be aware of the fact, that you've got something invested in guilt, particularly if you are twenty, thirty, forty, fifty years of age or older; and you've had this feeling of guilt for a long time . When you carry a feeling for a long time and you continue the same feeling you have a lot invested in it. By having something invested in it, I mean you like it, I mean you get some good results and you're going to stay with it. So, it would be useless for you to think about guilt or talk about it until you ask yourself, "Do I really want to give it up; and if I gave it up and I had no guilt at all—but just didn't feel guilty at all—what would life be like? and what would I do with my time? and what primary feeling would I have? That's the starting place. Now, here's what I'm going to say in the next twenty-three minutes.

I'm going to say there are two kinds of guilt. There's a real guilt that leads to behavior changes or leads to confession and forgiveness—That's real guilt. Real guilt has a focal point and a solution; that's **healthy** guilt. Corrects your behavior. Every person whose reasonable normal will have this. Because we all make mistakes and so this is one of the ways to correct it. Another type of guilt is not really valuable—it's **unhealthy** guilt. This unhealthy guilt is a kind of guilt that has no focal point that you can't do anything about it, where you can't confess it, or make absolution, or I mean make amends, and get absolution, that kind of guilt is a sick guilt. It's a kind that continues over a long period and you just learn to live with it and you develop a habit of feeling—"feeling guilty."

Here's a picture, I'll even draw you a picture of the two kinds. Okay you want to 'see me draw. This is a picture of real guilt. I did something here; I did something wrong here. And I feel guilty. And so, I take this thing I did wrong, and I hurt my wife and I go to my wife and say, "I did this, and this is wrong will you forgive me?" And

I'm dealing with it, and this is with a friend, and this is with a relative, and this is with a stranger—I can deal with those four things. And I know why I'm feeling guilty or if you want to substitute another word, It'll be fine. Call it remorse; call it regret; call it shame—call it whatever you want to, if the feelings are of discomfort, then it's time to do something about it. Now that's healthy guilt. You can identify the cause; you can do something about it.

Now there's another kind of guilt, that's unhealthy, this is a picture of unhealthy guilt. It's like this: it just goes on and on and on; it doesn't have any focal point in it. It's just sort of a vague blob; it just keeps running on point, any dimension. Goes on and on; you say , "I just feel guilty, don't know why I feel guilty. When I do this, I feel guilty; when I don't do it I feel guilty, when I sleep late, I feel guilty, when I don't sleep late I feel guilty. When I go to church I feel guilty; when I don't go to church I feel guilty."

Now this kind of guilt I'm going to talk to you about in a minute. First, I want to talk to you about healthy guilt. In this kind of relationship, the purpose of this is to correct and to change your behavior. This is healthy. When I say "healthy," I don't mean comfortable. You can identify the cause, you can generally– and when you identify the cause of the guilt,–or that might be an incident: it might be that you hurt someone, you infringe on someone else's body-space—and you can generally identify the person involved or more than one person. When you can identify the cause and then you can identify the person, then you'll know what to do to correct it. You'll also find a remedy. It might be an apology; it might be a confession; it might be you have to make amends to this person and repay him in some way; then, after this is the forgiveness or the new feeling of whatever you want to call it. Forgiveness is the big thing. It takes a lot of room. So, when you have a feeling of regret, remorse, or guilt, you'll find out what causes it. You'll find out what person you injured, you'll do what's necessary to correct it; you will accept forgiveness whether the other person feels forgiving or not—that's true. When you've done your part, then you'll accept the forgiveness of God and grant yourself forgiveness—even if it doesn't come from another person.

Then I want to say, you're through with the guilt. If you carry it beyond this point, you are into a racket and you're into a bad form of behavior and you're kidding yourself. You're beating yourself unnecessarily you're wearing a hair shirt, and there's no value in this at all–for anyone– most of all there's no value in it for you.

Now there's another kind of guilt that's unhealthy, and you can almost take the opposite of these things and transfer them over here. I've heard it illustrated like this: When a person has this unhealthy sense of guilt, probably it's an experience that you had as a child. It may have been your mother or your father were not forgiving persons; they may not even have known this. But a child can grow up with a sense of guilt, and I've talked to some adults who said, "All my life I've had the feeling that I was guilty. "Now that's this kind of feeling. When guilt becomes a way of feeling and it's just the way you live, and it's just the persistent– what we call a "favorite feeling." "Favorite" means it's with you most of the time. This kind of feeling can identify the specific cause, you can't take it to a particular person, there's no remedy and there's no forgiveness. Now in this kind of situation, you move totally out of the world out of realty and into the world of fantasy. The person probably uses skill as a means of keeping distance between him and other people. Here's what I mean: I mean if I decide I don't want to be close to somebody, or if I decide that I don't feel comfortable being intimate up close to someone, I'll say to myself, "I'm guilty," or sometimes we'll add to it, "I'm inferior or I'm worthless or I'm ugly or I'm useless, then I won't have to get close." You may even find that you will do things like this. You will do things so you will feel guilty and add it to your backlog of guilt. I know of people who have not been comfortable feeling forgiven and have worked really hard to find something for which they could feel guilty; then bring it back into their mind.

I want to tell you about this healthy guilt. It's very important when you have the feeling of guilt to take it somewhere and deal with it. It's very important that you take the guilt and that you deal with it at a particular time and a particular place; then, you make a decision. I've confessed this; I accept the forgiveness of God even whether or not the other person is willing to forgive me. I accept the forgiveness of God; Now listen—I am forgiven. It is at this point that a person forgives himself in the light of the fact that God has forgiven you. How do you hear this? When you accept the fact that God has forgiven you, and in the light of God's forgiveness, you forgive yourself. Then the complexion of your world is going to change. If you have a healthy guilt, then for you that ploy is over, and you will not be guilty anymore. Now, that's real healthy guilt. It's the kind of guilt that corrects and changes human behavior. It will terminate when you have dealt with it responsibly and appropriately; it will change your behavior; it will make you a better person. As a result of this, you'll grow.

Now, an unhealthy guilt is probably nothing more than a dirty little childhood habit. It is probably a hangover from a bad experience in childhood. I've known people who have all their adult lives felt guilty for something they did in childhood, and they've carried it all the way through their adult years. One of the things about guilt is that guilt is malignant. It's malignant and contagious, and if you start with a little growth of guilt as a child, it will enlarge and expand, and attract emotional rubbish and debris, and other things will flock to it. Then, after you've done this for a while you won't just have a feeling of guilt, you will have decided you are a guilty person. I've been there. There was a time in my life when I was guilty of eating or sleeping or breathing or bathing or dressing or guilty for working or guilty for not working ...and that's gone; I don't carry that burden anymore.

I've found; I believe—and I'll leave this open for question—I believe that a lot of people feel that being guilty is synonymous with being Christian. But for a person to be a good Christian and to be humble, you have to be guilty. It would be nice if a person like that heard the good news and didn't have to carry the burden of guilt. For the person who has the unhealthy sense of guilt, he decided that he was guilty, that he would never really be forgiven, that God wouldn't forgive him.

Some people even say, "Yes, I know that God has forgiven me, but I won't forgive myself." In this way, that person puts himself in a position superior to God. When you accept the forgiveness of God, and refuse to forgive yourself, what you're saying is "I'm greater than God, and my authority is greater than God, because God has pronounced me forgiven. But I assume a position higher than God. God may have forgiven you but I won't." It's ridiculous, isn't it? This is what we call a racket. One of the ways we keep ourselves inferior. One of the ways we tell ourselves that we're failures. It's one of the ways of telling ourselves that we don't have the right to succeed, that we don't have the right to win, we don't have the right to friendship or love or any of these things. and that's not true. It is an unhealthy habit; it is an unrealistic fantasy and nothing more. I want to say to you that some of you as adults have been whipping yourselves for things that you did in childhood. That if you spoke it out loud to someone else, they would laugh in your face. Most of the time we sentence ourselves to suffering and pain for ridiculous things.

Some people have carried the guilt for a whole lifetime, a guilt that is completely out of proportion to the crime of the mistake they made. Some people who've done things wrong, you know, sentenced themselves to a lifetime of emotional imprisonment, for which there is no pardon, no release, unless this individual, by the grace of God, really encounters the grace of God. The nice and promising and hopeful thing about this is, you see, Jesus Christ made this unnecessary. When Jesus Christ died on the cross, he died to take away your guilt. Now, if you're not a Christian, and you work this out some other way, that's fine, suites me fine.

I'll speak now just to Christians. Jesus Christ died; he died to take away your guilt. And he lived a perfect life. He completely obeyed all of God's laws and applied himself as one single solitary human being to the task of living on this earth. He lived a full, rich, happy, abundant life. He did not waste himself and he did not waste the people around him. Then this same man comes to you, and He comes to me and He comes to me, and He takes all of my guilt on himself and He takes all of your guilt on himself. In the place of the guilt which he took away from us, He gives us credit for the perfect life that he lived. I want you to get this picture. Here stands Jesus before God and you. The two of you standing before God. He is guilty—as guilty as all of your sins have made him—and you're righteous—as righteous as his perfect life has made you. That to me is the incredible thing about the story of Jesus Christ. That He could love us enough to become guilty for our misdoings and our wrong deeds and to give us in place of his guilt, full credit for the perfect life that He lived. So, when God looks at you, He sees you as righteous as Jesus Christ.

Did you hear me? He sees you as righteous as Jesus Christ; when he looks at Jesus Christ, he sees Him guilty for all of your sins. So, Jesus Christ goes with all of your sins and with all of mine, and all of our guilt, He goes to the cross and there is put to death in your place and in mine—in full, complete, and total payment for every wrong thing you have ever done or ever will do. All the wrong things you have ever done or ever will do and then you're free to be the total, complete, justified person before God. I'm saying before God, you're clean; Jesus Christ is guilty. Before God, you're free; Jesus Christ is in prison. He has done this for you so that you don't have to live guilty in this world. A continuing feeling of guilt is the choice that you make to reject the work that Jesus Christ did for you in this world on the cross and our time. You're wasting your time, you're not doing anybody good, and I want to tell you as directly and as positively as I can, God is not impressed by your suffering. Your suffering doesn't impress God a bit. You wouldn't look good hanging on the cross, not even in your Best Sunday suit or dress. What God wants from you, is for you to accept His Grace, to accept His Love, to accept His Forgiveness and go on and live an abundant life.

The best, clearest way that I can picture this for myself is—I want you to just imagine something with me now—just imagine that you had a son or daughter, let's say about ten years old. And you're sitting there reading the paper at the end of the day, or watching TV or making exciting, intimate conversation with your wife, whatever you do when you come home. And your son comes in and says, "Daddy I did something and it was wrong." And he tells you what he did, and he says, "I'm sorry, I apologize, forgive me."

Would you forgive him? Yes, most of us would. Or you might even say, "You're grounded for a week." But then a week later, he comes back, and he confesses the same sin and says, "Daddy, I did this and I'm sorry, and it was wrong. Forgive me." And you'd say, "Well, I've already forgiven you once, but if you're feeling bad about it, I forgive you." If he came back the next day and the next and the next, and over and over and over, every time you saw your son, all he had to say was, "I want to confess, I'm sorry, forgive me." What would you say?

Now, be honest. What would you really say? You know what I'd say, "Hey, we've dealt with that—forget it. Leave me alone, quit bugging me. Let's find something else to talk about." I wonder how many people on this Sunday morning have treated God just that same way. Every time you go to Him, all you've got is your dirty, grubby, little ole sins, and that's all you ever want to talk about.

Don't you think God gets bored? I think sometimes God yawns. "So, Hey, what else is new." It may be that in the same way you would be forgiving toward your own child. God would be—not would be— **is**. God is a hundred million times more forgiving than you are. It might just be that God's as good a parent as you are, and He loves His children more, and forgives you quicker than you ever forgive your children. The beautiful part of it is that when God forgives, God forgets. He removes your sins as far from him as the East is from the West. I'm saying you don't need guilt. God has given you the gift of forgiveness.

July 1975

JOY!!

I've just been to the West Coast for a conference; well almost to the West Coast, the conference was on a lake. The closest place we could fly into was Reno. And it was a sort of vacation; so, Telle and I flew into Reno and spent a couple nights there, then went on to the lake where the conference was to be held. It was the first time I'd been to Reno. I'd heard a lot about it, and I thought I was prepared for it.

We visited a lot of things around there and saw some shows and we went into the casinos. I haven't seen a half-acre of slot machines before, particularly slot machines played by intense, determined, stony-faced or sad-faced people. I had anticipated, once before we came through Las Vegas late at night, we'd been living in Alaska and were going to Mississippi, and we stopped there for just a little while, and I'd had a glimpse, but we were in Reno two days, and I looked at this thing again. I had anticipated a place where everybody was having fun—not everybody, you know, but most of the people were having fun—and there was some enjoyment and happy children running around: it wasn't that way.

I don't know what you expect to get out of a nickel slot machine, but whatever it was the people expected to get, they were really determined about getting it. The conference I went to was a conference on fun, on how to have fun as an adult and how to be a winner. But I know a little bit about these two things and I found out that I knew about as much as the people there and determined more than ever now to put it in practice.

I looked at Reno as a play place, which is the way I'd seen it advertised in all of the brochures. It was not a lot of fun and what I saw happening was not really play, the kind that is creative and productive. I did a lot of thinking. The whole sea of grim faces startles me. I was shocked when I walked through these tremendous areas of spaces and people—just thronging those places—and I really was taken aback. The friendliest people were the people who worked in these places. The bright, smiling faces were the faces of those who were making money. I don't mean that the money may make them happy, I think maybe they decided to be happy in order to make the money, in order to do something. But the happiest people were the people who worked in the places. Not the dealers at the card tables or the crap tables, but the little girls they had running around there making change for you. I guess that was the only place I really saw a smile—except I did meet two Texans who looked pretty happy. I think maybe that I saw some smiles there.

Next week I'm going to a conference, where I have spoken in the past. I want to tell you where I am now. In the past, I have spoken on guilt, inferiority, depression, alcohol and drug addiction, and last year I spoke on fear. I was just kind of reviewing this thing and these have been my topics. This year, I'm speaking on Joy, and, you know, I've been looking through reference books that I normally use and some new books that I've just gotten in to find some material that I could quote and let you know I was reading. Do you realize how little writing has been done on Joy outside the area of poetry and outside the Bible? The references to Joy and hope are very, very rare. In writings on mental health and mental growth, and writings on counseling, you'll find volumes written on depression, you'll find volumes written on the classic mental illnesses, you'll find volumes written on divorce and marital adjustment, but the references to Joy and hope are very, very rare. It seems like sometimes this is an emotion or an experience that we assign primarily to the poor or the mystic or the child. I have been amused and perplexed in trying to understand the place we have assigned to Joy and hope.

We almost have to use the two words interchangeably....and I don't know if it were possible for a man to be Joyful unless he had a deep and abiding hope. I believe that hope might be an inseparable compliment to Joy. The efforts that we human beings make at play.

That's not the kind of Joy I'm talking about. I'm not talking about hysterical laughter, or public relations smile, and I'm not talking about a friendly pat on the back. When I say Joy, I mean an inner abiding lasting experience of excitement and anticipation that is continually renewed by Hope. And it's the kind of inner glow that warms the person's whole life and permeates his smile and permeates his relationships with other people. This is what I mean by Joy.

It's the kind of experience a person can enter into and know that will allow him room to grieve, to be sad, to experience nostalgia, and melancholy for a period, the Joy continues. The Joy or Hope would be an abiding and sustaining lifetime position, and it would allow room for the other emotions to take their rightful healthy places within the spectrum of human experience.

Now, I promised you on this program that we would talk mostly about "how-to," not "what" and "where." So, on the "how-to" experience Joy on a continuing basis, the first thing that is necessary is within your grasp and your reach and your choice this morning. I'm not talking about theoretical Joy, I'm talking about something that I strive daily to experience in my own life when previous to this, I 've spent more than half of the years I've been alive depressed.

I did not know it; I was not aware that this was not a normal state. I'm not there anymore—haven't been for twenty years–and thank God for that. I'm not satisfied with the experience of just not being depressed. I've decided that Joy ls available for me, it's available ln the life that I'm living there, that I don't have to go anywhere or do anything or have anything in order to be Joyful, that it's an experience that is available to me in my present world with the things as they are. So, what I'm talking about is something that is available to you and to me—today—it's available to you now while you're watching this television program and the only thing that would prevent you from experiencing Joy right now is the decision that you don't want it.

Now we've talked long enough on this program about trying to change other people... that's out. We've talked about what some people call "the geographical cure," if I lived here, if I lived there, or if I could move to Miami or Seattle things would be better. In Miami or Seattle, the first that will meet you when you move there is yourself. So—no use to move. Now, you can experience this now, you can enjoy this now, and the only thing that keeps it away from you is a decision.

Now the first thing in order to experience Joy is for you to choose to have what we will call the capacity of selective recall. Now, this is doing nothing more than controlling your memories. Okay? Now, this means that when you remember the past, that you select what you dwell on, you don't select what pops into your mind, but you select what you dwell on. I know some persons whose memories of the past are colored by tragic events:

"We had this terrible fire and I've never been the same since."

"My husband died and I've never been the same since."

"My wife left me; or my children left me, or we had this tragedy in the family, and I've never been the same since."

And they measure time from tragic events, I'm saying that doesn't have to be. You can change that and you can choose to recall from the past experiences that were happy, joyful, exciting and where you experienced in these moments, warmth and love and maybe intimacy and closeness or recognition or reward –or whatever you like best–; you select what you remember and what you dwell on out of the past. You remember high school graduation? For some people it wasn't qood—for some it was. It might have been for you. You remember the death of a child. Will you not also remember the birth of others or the birth of that child? Is the birth not as important at the death? You can remember times when spring came, spring comes every year. For every fall and every winter there is a spring and there is a summer and there is autumn and there are sometimes beautiful colors even in west Texas. You can remember times when friends pay you compliments. Hey, let me tell you something. On the way home, my wife and I had an experience; it was real good, it was beautiful, it was warm and it involved some other people. The day after we got home we had a letter in the mail from somebody whose name we did not know, we had never seen the man before, probably will never see him again, but he had taken the time to find our name and address and to write a letter to say thank you. Now, I betcha that guy is happy.

Not all the time, but I betcha, (that's not a real nice way to say it.) I have the feeling that he experiences, in at least a large sector of his life, "Joy." People who are continually saying "thank you" are usually fairly happy people. Did you get that or do you want me to repeat it?—You can replay it in your mind. This is one of the ways to experience a continuing Joy: to decide what your mind will dwell on about the past. You can dwell on tragic events. You can dwell on the sorrowful miserable and unhappy experiences. But, Man, you can also change. Walk around your house and look around your house, you've got some things in that house that you really enjoy. You can experience some Joy from things. You have a reasonable measure of health. You have a reasonable amount of integrity as a person, if you did not have, you wouldn't be sitting at your home or wherever you are in a motel watching television this morning, you've got a little time. You've got some faith in some security, nobody's going to batter down your door. And these are things you can use as a basis however insignificant they may seem to be to you at the time. These are the things that you can use as a basis for building a continuing experience of Joy. The first thing is, decide what you will think about from the past, decide what your mind will dwell on. Say, I'm not going to give my time to remember the scene in the cemetery, or hospital or on the highway or what the doctor said, when the telephone rang, or the police came. That's a waste of time, and it's a bunch of trash.

There is no virtue and there is no beauty in doing this. So, if you select what you remember and you decide to remember the happy, significant, bright events, I promise you your day will be different. Hey, I know one person who writes things down. I'm not joking, he said he had a memory bank like a computer. And he writes things down in order to move from the place, this man's been very sick In the past, he's been so sick that he's been incapacitated Where his mind did not function at all. This man at one time was not able to speak or hear, he had lost all contact with people. Today he lives a relatively happy life. It's not accidental, it's planned. He says that he must take the same care of his mind that he takes of his body, and he says, "I feed my body three times a day, I brush the teeth in my body, I comb the hair on my body, I clip the nails on my body, I shine my shoes, and I make sure that I look nice when I go out every day, I look as well as I can." And he said, "I do the same thing with my thinking processes, As long as I do it with my thinking and with my mind the same way I do with my body I can live in the world of normal people."

Now, you don't have to live like that, but I promise you, Sir, if you will give yourself that kind of care and nurture and attention, life will be different for you. Now if you will use this experience here in relating to the past, then you can move on to plan happy future moments. Now, this is what I want to make clear. This is one of the things I'm doing myself. You can't plan all of your future as a happy experience, but you can plan some moments. Now, whatever it is you like to do and enjoy doing and whatever it is that gives you a kick, you know that really gives you a thrill, and when you think about it, you say, "Boy, I'd love to do that!" give yourself permission to do that and make plans to get it done in the future, are you with me?

Now in the planning of this, watch yourself, pick out something that you enjoy doing the most and then make some preparations so that you'll get to do it and don't let anything interfere—well, I don't mean major crisis. If the house bums down or wife gets sick, you'd better alter your plans, that's not what I'm talking about. But *you* can make plans to have happy future moments. Some people like to fish; you say, "You know, I really love to fish, but I never get the time." You don't like it that much... if you did you'd make the time, I would, too. I don't fish nearly as much as I want to, but I think probably I like work more than I like fishing that's the truth... really came out. But next to work I like fishing and work is compulsive work, working all the time is losing some of its attraction for me, and I'll probably have more time to fish in the future.

Now, it takes planning; it takes some sacrifice because you've got to sacrifice some.of your working/worrying time in order to have fishing time. If you like golf, tennis, swimming, working in the yard–whatever it is, plan time and set aside time in the future however long or however short the time may be. I'm saying give it to yourself. If you do not give it to yourself, nobody on earth can give it to you. But when you can give it to yourself, no one else will have to. That's the good part. That's the part about this that I really like. If you'll take care of yourself nobody else will have to. if you don't take care of yourself, nobody else can. So, by selectively recalling what we remember from the past and what we dwell on, we'll have good memories and by planning happy experiences for the future, tomorrow we will remember the happy things we allowed ourselves to do today. You know, I don't know whether you're living in Lubbock, Odessa, or Midland or Big Springs or Monahans or San Angelo, or Brownwood or wherever it is but the countryside ls particularly beautiful this time of year. I think there's even beauty around Midland and Odessa, further out where it begins to get a little barren; I see a lot of beauty there; it's got some beautiful people. And when you go looking for the beauty you'll find it. When you live with beauty, you'll have a continuing experience of Joy. joy, beauty, hope, love, warmth, closeness, trust, gentleness, kindness, patience.

These things kind of go together. Now, if you take the opposite of these, which I don't care to dwell on, then that puts you in a whole different ball game, mister. But when you look for these things, when you look for the good and you're happy when you find the good, then you're going to have a different relationship with other people.

I know somebody who cannot bear to be with a person until they find the flaws in his character or the cracks in his armor, and when they find them they say, "Ah ha, now, I knew you were that way," and they're comfortable with a person. There are other kinds of people, thank God, I know one or two, one who listens to this telecast every Sunday (thank you), who always looks for the wholeness in a person, who always looks for the pure and the good, the legitimate, the authentic, the beautiful and people like you make this a better world and a better place. I covet for myself the quality of Joy that you experience on a continuing basis. I have a friend that I've told you about who lives in another city who spent nineteen years in an iron lung, nineteen, well twenty now. She knows Joy on a continuing basis. Never moves out of that large tin can she lives in. But I promise you she lives a real quality life. She blesses all of those who have the time... are you listening... who have the time to go to see her. I think that if I know anything about God that it's His will that we should have Joy on a continuing basis.

That's why the Bible says more about Joy and Hope than any other book, I think. And it's not all poetry, it's very realistic formulas for Joy and happiness in the Bible. I think if you'll read carefully about this man Jesus Christ you'll find that He experienced it, too. I want to say that this is available for you, and you can have it today; you can have it this Sunday morning, and you can have it throughout the day by disciplining, using another word, by directing your mind, your thoughts, and your feelings to Joy and Hope.

Of course, I know, as you do, that the basis of this is God, and the love for Him and the fact that He loves and cares for you. That's the whole basis of everything I say. I do not talk to you apart from my faith in God. So; because God loves you and made you, you can have Joy.

October 1978

GRIEF

So many of you have been writing. The programs for the next several weeks will be made up as a result of your requests. I had a lot of requests for some more information on "grief" and so that is what we are going to be discussing. today.

Incidentally, I went fishing last weekend, and caught a barrel of fish, and really enjoyed it. I had a ball, but I am glad to be home.

Today we are going to talk about grief and the process of grieving. I mentioned to you before that we grieve for periods in our lives and we grieve for moments, and we grieve for places. One of the best friends I have had in my lifetime is here with me on the program this morning. We have been friends since we were in college together and have been a lot of places and shared a lot of experiences and people together. This man's name is Everett; and he knows about life, and of experiences. Everett, I'm glad you are here with me on this program and with these people.

As I said, we are going to be talking about grief, and I think before we start, I would like you to take just a minute and tell these people what you would like them to know about you so they can hear you more clearly. Would you do that?

EVERETT: Yes, I would be glad to do that. I am a human being, a man who has experienced a lot of life and a good bit of grief in my day. I have now come to the place in my life where I see grief as being a normal thing. If you care, if you love, sooner or later you are going to get hurt some way as you lose someone or something important to you, and you are going to grieve. My word to you would be simply this: let the grief happen, embrace it, and live through it, and you will see a better, brighter day coming. What I would like you to know about me is that I am just as human as John DeFoore is. He has spoken of our friendship and we cannot say really enough about that because our friendship transcends words, I think maybe even feelings. But I would like you to get to know me. I will want to tell you about some of my own grief and by sharing that with you, help you understand that it is very human to grieve. It is also, I think, very godly to grieve, and we will be talking about that.

JOHN: Do you think God grieves?

EVERETT: Yes, I do think God grieves.

JOHN: Oh, I had not thought about that, Everett. I said to you when we talked about this before— and I think it is necessary to start here— that for some reason God made this body to last about seventy or seventy-five years. I think women live a little longer than men, don't they?

EVERETT: Yes, that bothers me.

JOHN: Well, they don't work as hard. I will not repeat that statement. But this body is bult to wear out. This is something I keep reminding myself. The life that God has given us will go on eternally, but the body that we have, that we are using now, is only designed to last for a brief period of time while we experience life in the time-space environment. Now after this body wears out, there will be a new container. And for this we can be grateful. But during the course of seventy-five-plus-or-minus years, during the course of this life on earth, it is necessary for us to say goodbye to people, places, and things— to release people, places, and things— and your willingness and my willingness and ability to do this is the measure of grief. I would like for you to think this morning about people, places, and things that it has been necessary for you to release. Maybe some of these you are still clinging to after a period of years. If you are interested in growing—and when I say grow, I mean the capacity to experience life in the world of reality with an ever-increasing sense of joy and excitement—you will be a happier, safer, and more secure person if you learn to release whatever it is that is no longer yours, and to place it gently and competently into the hands of God. So, I think, this morning, Everett, the best starting place that I know of is "death."

Let's talk about the grief that comes when we lose a person or any living thing, and I want to include pets here because some people are still grieving over lost pets. I lost a great big Irish Setter dog not long ago. When I was fishing this weekend, I say an Irish Setter running up the coast, and I felt a real hint of sadness because I could never find my dog. I felt some grief then. So, let's talk about the grief that comes first through death. And I want you to start this if you will please, Everett.

EVERETT: Well, when we think about grief, the first thought we have is that it is associated with the loss we have due to the death of someone very dear to us. We read the paper and read about an acquaintance dying or about some whom we have heard about dying, and we are not affected by that very much. Then someone in our family dies and we feel that much more keenly. The closer home it come to us, the more we feel it.

I would like to take a bit personally here about this and tell you that I am acquainted with grief, and the most painful time in my life came when my wife died. She had been ill for a year that we knew about and we anticipated her death. We tried to prepare for it, and in some ways I suppose we did. But when she died that early morning in M.D. Anderson Hospital it really hit me. I was thinking about this just yesterday, as I was talking to someone. About 2:00 A.M. that morning, a mutual friend of ours, who was a nurse in the hospital, came to me. I was sleeping a little, for I was absolutely worn out from having stayed at my wife's bedside around the clock for the last days of her life. And this friend– this nurse–shook me and when she got me awake she said, "Everett, Eulee is dead." Well, I had anticipated this, I knew that she would not live the night through because the doctors had told me that, and I had just spent an extremely painful time in the intensive care unit with my wife shortly before she lost consciousness. At the moment the nurse told me Eulee was dead, a great burden seemed to be lifted from my shoulders. Later on, that morning as I talked with my children, by telephone (They were in Minneapolis.) it really hit me. As the oldest child, a girl of thirteen, and I were talking, I found myself saying to her, "Janice, I have never been more lonely in my whole life. I don't know what I'm going to do."

And she said, Well, Daddy, we're hurt here, too, but we'll carry on."

Sometime after that, I probably was in a state of shock or numbness; Eulee's mother was also in Houston and we arranged for a plane back to New Orleans. There, one of our family was going to meet us and take us on to what we had called home in Biloxi, Mississippi. Hazel, Eulee's mother, and I made that plane trip, and we talked about a lot of things. But there was a heaviness about us. We had a different kind of weight now, and we knew that someone dear to us was no longer available to us. We were met at the plane by Hazel's husband (Not Eulee's father who had died even before Eulee and I were married). Then we waited a little in the New Orleans airport for the three children to come in from Minneapolis. During that period of waiting, I felt heavy; and yet, I experienced some anticipation about seeing my children and was looking forward to seeing the because I had missed them during those days I had been away from them. Seeing them get off the plane kind of allowed me to have a bit of a lift. I didn't feel so very much alone when I saw those three children coming off the plane. Well in due time, we went through a funeral. I even participated in that part, telling how this good woman, who now lay dead, and I had worked together; how she had been an emotional and spiritual support in particular; how she encouraged me; how at time, she prodded me. I even thought about some of those times when I had been angry at her and when she had been angry with me. I relived a lot about our life together.

Some of it was pleasant, a lot of it was very painful, and it was painful because I was aware, to some extent, that I would no longer have those kinds of experiences with her.

The funeral was over, the children and I went back to Minneapolis. We went through Kansas City where we actually had been living and where we called home. We stopped off for a memorial service for Eulee at the seminary where I was teaching. We were living in Minneapolis that year because I had a leave of absence and was studying there at the University of Minnesota. Back in Kansas City we were home again and a part of that day I felt that life was kind of all right again, but that afternoon as we went on to Minneapolis, the feelings came back again. What I really felt was simply this: Eulee was not there, in fact she had not lived in that house— she had been too ill to make the trip to Minneapolis in the fall in time for the children to be in school, but we hoped that she would be there. For the better part of the year, I lived with many kinds of feelings, sadness, disappointment, at times I got angry. I suppose one of the big struggles I had was with my feelings toward our doctor in Kansas City who had missed that cancer back down the line. Eulee had been under his care for quite a while. She had not been feeling well. He had her hospitalized, tests were run, and he said to me later, "You know, Everett, we can't find anything wrong with her. I'm beginning to wonder if somehow she's choosing to be sick, I just don't know what to do."

Well, after Eulee died, I remembered those things and I said to myself, "I've got to talk with our doctor, whose name was John. The occasion came, and I told him of my disappointment, of my wondering just how well had had taken care of her, and then he told me something. He said, "Everett, your wife's kind of cancer I had seen only once before in my many years of practice, and it had been so long ago that I had really forgotten what to look for on an Xray, what to look for by way of symptoms a person would present. I'm hurt, too – I missed her illness; we don't know whether her life could have been prolonged or whether it could have been found in time to do something about it, but I want you to know that I'm very sorry and hurt about this because she was my friend, too, and I hope that I'll be a better doctor."

JOHN: Everett, how long after her death did this conversation take place.

EVERETT: Oh, it had to be the better part of a year, John, because I finished the year at the University of Minnesota and did not return to Kansas City until September, almost a year after Eulee had died.

JOHN: Okay, then this was a different stage of your grief when you were kind of straightening out relationships with other people.

EVERETT: John, to tell you the truth, I'm convinced that I experienced what is sometimes called "delayed grief." I didn't have an opportunity to grieve like a person could there in Minneapolis, and I was taking care of three children.

JOHN: I think this is the way we respond to grief a lot of times; with a real strong schedule of busyness to overlay the thing. If we talked about this thing in stages, remembering what you've just recounted in your experience, what would you say is the first response to loss.

EVERETT: The first response is shock. We can't stand that kind of loss all at once, John, I'm convinced.

JOHN: Hey, this is the reason some people faint, I guess.

EVERETT: That's right. I felt it can't be so, or I hope it's not so, somebody tell me it's not so, I'm really dreaming or I've imagined this.

JOHN: Yes, I was with a man one time and his response was, No, no, no," and he just walked the corridor of the hospital shaking his fist and screaming, "no." I'd like to say this kind of response is normal as apple in America.

EVERETT: It certainly is normal, and it very well may be that this is one of the blessings we have and don't quite understand. I'm convinced that the human body is so designed, so crated, so constructed that there is the shock producing part of us that does it for us.

JOHN: To protect us.

EVERETT: This is the emotional side of the body that protects us from this kind of trauma and the same way the body has its built-in faculties to protect us physically from serious injuries. That is why a person goes into physical shock.

JOHN: Okay, second stage would be what?

EVERETT: Well, in terms of my own experience, it would be the overwhelming sense of loss and loneliness. I never felt more lonely in all my life. It's possible that I might feel lonely or even more lonely in times to come, but I frankly don't think so. I believe I've had my most lonely moments.

JOHN: This is true in the loss of people, the loss of an animal that's valued, the loss of things. It's possible for a person to go through an experience of grief if he's lost a ring, or a picture, or a book.

EVERETT: Anything that has meaning for him.

JOHN: During the depression when so many people lost their investments, their savings, etc., the shock of that and the sense of loss was so great. I remember in my childhood hearing my folks at home talk about so many suicides after hearing about them on the radio in those days. Okay, what is the next step?

EVERETT: The next step kind of depends on the person, John. The next step is the struggle to kind of let the grief happen.

JOHN: All right, we call this acceptance.

EVERETT: Yes, there is anger, and sometimes there is guilt. There is still a continuation of the feeling of disappointment which I would call acceptance.

JOHN: And acceptance would come in stages, too.

EVERETT: Yes, acceptance will come in stages. In fact, based upon my own experience, I would say that acceptance will take anywhere from three months to six months to work through.

JOHN: Okay, now that's what I wanted to get into. If you are at the stage of acceptance in three to six months, let's say in the event of a death of a close friend. If we could have a schedule, we would say that a person is on schedule, if there were such a thing as schedule. And this acceptance would extend—I guess it would extend indefinitely.

EVERETT: Yes, it will. The more importance the person, or object, (or whatever it was) had on you, the longer it may take you to completely recover from that. I notice in myself, nine years now almost since Eulee's death and with remarriage (and I have a very good marriage and a wonderful wife nowadays), that occasionally I will experience a little tinge of the grief that is appropriately related to my wife's death.

JOHN: Yes, I'm glad you said that. I have been recently having times since my mother died in March, where I have had little flashes and little moments where I remember her with a strong surge of emotion and nostalgia. It just sort of comes like a wave, and then it passes.

It needs to be pointed out, with respect to acceptance, that it is an up and down thing. It comes and it goes. And after you have begun to accept the loss, and are trying to get back into the light, you'll have a few good days and then it will hit you all at once, and you'll say to yourself, "Oh my, I'm right back where I started." But you're not back there really.

EVERETT: Now I want to say this next stage here will be something like readjustment where you're relating to other people or other places or other things that can never take the place of the object or person lost, but do establish new relationships and new experiences. If we could put a time limit on this, we'd say, hopefully, that a person would be in a state of functional readjustment in twelve months. After about a year, normally, an individual can begin to feel that life is really good again, that he or she is beginning not merely to move back into life, but be back into life. My own time schedule is the one I know the best, and because I did experience some delayed grief, I was a little late in working through some of this. I say to people nowadays, give yourself plenty of time, but don't get lazy at your grief work because it's human to try to avoid pain. Grief work is painful.

JOHN: Hey, I want to say here, before we go, that while you are grieving, give some time and attention to your children. It's absolutely essential for a child involved in any loss in a family that the child's feelings be considered, and this this child be given the thoughtful consideration of a parent. He grieves, too, and he ash feelings, too. And if you fail to accept this part of the child, you're missing something beautiful and valuable in the life of this child.

EVERETT: John, You're exactly right in what you say. This really deserves more attention and maybe we can talk about his at some other time.

JOHN: Okay, maybe we'll come back and do this at a later time.

EVERETT: That will be find.

JOHN: Hey, one of the things that I like about this man Jesus, is His humanness. God in Jesus Christ was totally man. And as total man, He was no less totally God. Now one of the recorded experiences in the life of Christ is His grief. His grief over the death of a friend, even when He knew that he would shortly raise this friend from the dead. The tears, the grief was there. And He experienced grief over people's behavior and other things. He grieved over the city of Jerusalem. He looked on them and wept.

EVERETT: Yes, so when you're grieving, you're not being weak, you're being totally human. It takes a strong person to grieve appropriately.

JOHN: Yes, so go on and grieve, and get through with the grief. Move to a new place in life. In the design and the construction of your total self, God has given you time, privilege, and opportunity so that you can grieve. Life will bring grief experiences to you; you don't have to go and search for them. The thing that I'm concerned about is that you know that grief is normal and that you have some sort of program for being finished. And God will protect and guide you in your grief.

August 1975

JOY – DEATH

I had a phone call early this morning at my house, and a friend who lives here told us about another friend who had died. I had known this person for a long time and the conditions under which we met are very strange but very meaningful.

The death was sort of expected but not really expected. And in just a minute or two I had just a rapid flash of the time and the circumstances under which we had been with this person, this woman; and the different places where we had met the two of these friends, the woman and her husband. We had seen them in Alaska and Europe and a lot of places. The one thing that made this friendship special was that they had visited in our home, I mean in my childhood home; and

I had visited in theirs and our lives by accident or design had been drawn together, and the friendship was one of those friendships where you know, you don't keep in touch every day. We didn't have to keep the friendship alive by writing letters and frequent telephone calls to assure each other of love and concern but every time we got together the friendship was there. Whenever they were coming anywhere near where we were living at the time or we were going near them, we always got in contact and had some good times. Lots of laughter, some tears occasionally, sometimes deep sharing, but lots of laughter, lots of fun.

She was a happy person. I was sobered with this news. I wanted to rush back and run to her and say, "not yet, not today." And I realized this was me;, it was not her. I had every confidence in the woman that when the time came she was ready, and that death did not defeat her. It was more my own emotional surge that I knew took over at that time. And if you want to know what I'm talking about–if you will look around you now–if you are with someone–imagine one person in the room who is gone and who will not ever be back and put a blank spot where that person is and measure your feelings. Measure your emotions and relations with that person or if you really want a trip, put a blank place where you are and picture the family or the group of friends—or however you identify with other people. Picture yourself as gone and you'll get something of the feeling that's been sweeping through my mind, and that's sort of where I wanted to start with you.

It was shortly after this that I saw this very, very old woman taking very feeble steps walking down the highway counting her beads. I wanted to stop and say, "Tell me your prayers." But I knew I did not have the right to intrude into the privacy of her prayers. Something in me prayed while I watched and I saw this person whose name I did not know, whose face I had not seen, speaking prayers to a God of my youth, and traveling a road that I knew I had traveled before and might possibly travel again. I sorta felt myself drawn closer to God, to the deceased friend, and to the living, praying friend. I felt myself again a pilgrim, on a road, on a journey that is a part of life. I found myself aware that I could not consider any part of this journey insignificant or irrelevant. That I must measure the time and the distance of my life, giving myself room for joy and for sorrow, giving myself room for solitude and for friendship.

On the last television program that we had or the one previously, I mentioned to you that I was going to a retreat and speak on "Joy." You know the funniest thing happened. There were two speakers. This other guy was from England; I haven't seen him in three years, haven't corresponded with him, and he was just back in the States for a lecture tour. When we got there, we were kind of introducing ourselves and going around the Sunday night before the retreat started. Guess what he said he was going to talk on? He had a Bible study and the subject of his Bible study was "Joy." I nearly flipped my lid and he did, too. But we had a joyful week. We had a lot of fun and a few tears, lots of laughter, a little bit of nostalgia, and crying, but the whole focal point for my work and his work and the thinking, playing, and relating with the people last week was "Joy." I learned some things about myself. I learned that in spite of all of my talking about "Joy," that nostalgia, sadness, melancholy— give it any name you choose—these emotions are very good friends with me and I am with them. Sometimes "Joy" is more of a stranger. And melancholy and loneliness are more of a familiar emotion. I started to say friend, but I changed that word. I think I would rather call them emotions. If I'm going to be friends with any of these emotions, I think I'll choose joy. That's a deliberate, willful choice. The choice of oy.

I've known some people, and I'm meeting more all the time, who know joy and who move toward joy. I know some friends who are experiencing joy, and who have chosen this as a lifestyle. And this friend of mine who just died, knew joy. You know something, she even named one of her children Joy. And we're talking about a kind of joy, just like we said before. It has nothing to do with the laughter and hysteria. It's the kind of deep awareness of peace and purpose and healthy, meaningful relationships that give depth and beauty and spontaneity and freedom to life. That's the joy. This kind of joy that can experience for a while, depression, or sadness or aloneness. And it does not destroy the continuing complexion of joy. I think the word I'm using is closely into co-mingle or almost synonymous with the word "hope," because when you have a real deep and abiding hope in yourself and for yourself and in God and for God then you have this joy, too.

This is what impressed me about the old woman and I watched her feet. I was not observed. I was the observer. I watched her shuffling gait while she more or less sauntered or drifted down the road. Her hands held her beads individually as she repeated the appropriate prayers and as the hands held the beads, the footsteps measured the journey, and I had the feeling—Boy, this is meaningful—this is my life and this is every man's and this is a whole composite picture of man's existence. We're all on a journey, we all have this pilgrimage and every one of us must walk his own single, solitary journey. Now, we must walk the journey—make the journey— and we walk the road as individual and solitary beings and we meet other people at varying stages of our journey, but every one of us is a person and the journey has a beginning, and the journey has an ending in this place we call time.

Hey, let me show you what I'm talking about. This is where you came into the picture on this earth. You had nothing to do with that. It was something completely above and beyond your kin, your knowledge. And if you'll let this be time, here, and this is the line where you're born, this.is you right here.

So, here you come and you break into this world at birth. You enter the world of time here and then you leave it at a place called death. Here's the place where you come into time and this is the measure of your life on this earth. It's the period between birth and death. I'm convinced that the length of years here is irrelevant. Man's life is not measured by the number of years that lapse between birth and death. I'm convinced that it's how deep a man plumbs into the meaning of life, how deep he goes. I'm saying plumb—p-l-u-m-b, or plunge into the meaning of life and I think it is also how high he ascends in purpose and deed and devotion and dedication and this is not an emotional graph. I like to picture my life as being something like this all the way through until at some high point or until at some low point I cross the barrier. I can imagine nothing for me—now this may not be for you, but for me—I can imagine nothing more disappointing and boring than to live a life of nominal existence where I quietly enter the scene and quietly exit the scene, as T.S. Eliot said in, "The Hollow Men," "not with a bang, but with a whimper!" It's alright to cry when you get spanked on the bottom in order to start your breathing as a baby, as an infant, which is what I understand is the way they do it.

I think it's great when a man can leave the scene, you know, not whimpering, not crying, and not complaining but laughing, or rejoicing, or experiencing any kind of triumph. This is the road right here. This is a period of time, here. I do not believe for you and me that your road is laid out and prescribed. To me, God's will embrace the whole picture here: I do not believe God's will is one single, solitary line that eliminates the necessity for your choosing, selecting, responding, and obeying.

But God's will for you may lie in experiencing the depths of meaning and understanding particularly in interpersonal relationships. God's will for you may mean that you will experience some highs that have to do with commitment, with relationships, with experience, and with awareness. Now, if I understand this man Jesus of Nazareth, this is what His life was like. Man, He had some depths and without apology He got into depth. I believe that Gethsemane may have been at some point a depth. I also believe that Gethsemane could have been considered a "high," particularly when He said, "Nevertheless not my will but thine be done." I believe that His experience with the Apostles, particularly when they denied Him, betrayed Him, and abandoned Him could have been with Christ a period of depth. I also believe a period of high could have been when He was restoring them and when He was saying to Peter, the only thing that really matters and the only thing that is really important is, "do you love me? Do you love me?"

This is the journey. This is the pilgrimage. Counting the beads is a symbol of praying. We pray in a lot of different ways. Some people use external means to remind them of praying. But you're counting the beads whether you are plumbing the depths or scaling the heights of life. This whole experience is one lived in prayer, is one lived in freedom and it's one lived in exploration and discovery, but you have to keep walking. The one characteristic of this journey is it moves. Life doesn't stop anywhere along here. Now it stopped one time for—who was the guy fighting the battle and the sun stayed in the heavens?—Joshua. Okay, it .stopped for him. I doubt very much if the sun will stop for you or me. Time moves and this is the way God has designed this particular segment of eternity.

Oh, yeah, that's one thing I wanted to say. Eternity doesn't begin with your birth and eternity doesn't end with your death. Now there are some people who say, "this is all there is of man, man exists totally and completely between these two points." And I'm thinking if that is as far as that man's understanding goes, that's fine. I do not believe eternity begins and ends with my birth and death. I do not believe that eternity begins and ends with me. But rather that I am born out of eternity into time, and that I'll leave time and go into eternity, and this gives me an identity as a person made in the image of God. It gives me direction, the road that I travel, and gives me a relationship which is symbolized in the beads. The beads, that's what I wanted to talk to you about, the praying. Probably, the most significant conversations I will ever have on this earth will be with God. Sometimes they will be with God when I'm alone as a solitary being, speaking out of the depths of my heart into the limitless dimensions of God's own being. We call this private prayer. Or you call it solitary prayer.

I have not once on this program said you should pray or you ought to pray. I think prayer when it comes and there's an overspilling of a full heart, is something entirely different. No,—no, erase that—Whether the heart is filled with grief or joy the prayer is the same. Whether the heart is filled with the sense of one's own aloneness and solitariness or rejoicing with the warmth and intimacy and beauty of human friendship is one and the same thing. The overspilling, the overflowing of a heart that reaches out beyond itself, beyond the dimension of life between birth and death, the heart that overspills and binds itself with the eternal, infinite creator whom I choose to call God, this is prayer. The prayer doesn't have to take on any particular form. Doesn't have to have any particular words.

I heard somebody referring with a particular group of people—and this is an old joke I'm sure—referring to God as the one who liked to be read to. By this they meant that the people in this particular church read their prayers, and I assumed that this was some child's statement that he was like God because he liked to have people read to him. I guess he assumed that the people in this church were reading their prayers to God for the entertainment of God and I'm sure that's not their purpose at all.

But when your life overspills or reaches out in commitment or desperation, either one, and you reach out and touch God, and God reaches in and touches you, this experience is what we call prayer. Now, the way you experience the touch is not prescribed, the way you reach out is not prescribed. I contend that prayer does not have to have a particular form, though it can have a particular form if you choose. 'And while you are being yourself, while you are on the journey in the road, prayer keeps the direction straight, it keeps your eyes clear, your hearing keen, and your sense of awareness finely honed—very sharp. Now, the journey here is not the complete and total measure of your life.

So, at this point, you see, death takes on a different complexion. Well, life does too for that matter, but particularly death takes on a different complexion. Because you can see death not as an end to something, but you can see death as the time when the individual's life is relieved from the limitations of this body and this road and these beads impose on you, and you can see death as a sort of expanding and enlarging, and I even see exploding experience.

What I've really been saying here this morning is something that I learned anew about joy. Because you see, I learned that joy includes sadness. Just like death includes birth. That elation includes depression and that all of these different emotions and different experiences can be molded together and formed into one composite whole. So, to experience joy, you don't have to rule out all the sadness, loneliness, and depression. You embrace it and you include it.

To include joy, you do not deny sadness and tragedy, because all these things together are taken up—are conquered—are molded—and are moved into the whole totality of man's place here on this earth under the purpose and within the circle of God's will. I felt better about my friend who died yesterday morning at 9:00 o'clock. I felt a great deal better about her when I realized that she had lived fully, when I remembered her laughter when I recalled her tears. When I remembered the good times that we've experienced and also when I remember the darker times when with sadness and loneliness we sat and cried. I have the feeling that somewhere in another dimension of existence, I do not know the details of the scenery, the landscape or any of these things, but I am convinced that somewhere she walks another road, not counting beads but living with God.

January 1975

MY MOTHER

Since I talked with you last, I have been back to my home (where I was raised) to attend the funeral of a very beautiful lady–a woman I have known all my life. In the last week I learned some things about myself and about life that I did not know, and since we had a place to talk, I decided that today I would talk to you about her progression—the progression of life.

I had a telephone call Sunday night saying that my mother had died. She was almost 91 years old, and I think if anyone ever lived each of her 365 days of each of their 90 years, she lived them. So, we made our plans and went back.

I was shocked at first. I think this is my initial response at first to pain, whether it is physical, mental, or emotional, and I was stunned. I didn't cry. I was trying to assimilate the truth into my thinking. Everything in me objected to the truth of the message. As the night wore on, before we could leave the next morning, the truth gradually sank in, and I began to experience a little grief.

I had the funniest feeling. I told a friend about this and he made it okay. I had the feeling that I wanted to crawl off in a hole somewhere to hide. I don't think I have ever had that particular feeling before, but it was very real. Everything in me was looking for a place to hide, knowing full well that from this particular truth, there is no such place for any of us.

I met my brother and we drove quite a distance. And I waited at the funeral home to see her. Not long ago we did a hot line here on grief, and that helped me. I did not know this, but I learned a lot about my own grief—It was necessary for me to see my mother, knowing full well she was not there. But since I was not with her when she died, I wanted to see what we politely call her remains.

We waited until we were permitted to see her. I stood there and this flood of memories just washed over me like a tremendous wave. I remember a lot of the happy times that I had allowed myself to forget. I remembered her laughter and when she was young and strong.

My mother taught school. She taught school the greater part of her life. She was teaching before she was out of high school in a one-room schoolhouse, in another state. All 12 grades were in one room—if you can imagine that. Attending in the grades were two of my uncles. My grandfather had insisted that they attend school until they could write their names. After several months they learned to write their names and quit school. She said that they were much taller than she was.

As her own life progressed, she continued to teach school. She finished college, and then, according to the laws of the state, she did some graduate study. I think that every child in the school that had no parents became her child.

We were standing there at the casket and a man came in and introduced himself. I had known his older brother, and he said, "This woman was my mother; the only mother I ever knew."

I looked to see the expression on his face and he was very serious. As another man came and then another, I realized how many lives had been touched by this woman, who, over a period of 90 years, had spent most of her life helping to guide the children in classrooms.

After she retired from the classroom due to changes in the school board, she became a post mistress in a very small town of about 250 people. She kept this job for 17 years, which included the period during World War II. I had three brothers, and at one time all four of us were in combat at different places in the world. It was my mother's job during this time to take telephone calls because one of the few telephones in the city was in the post office. It was her business to take telephone calls in which after she heard. She would accept telegrams that generally came over the telephone where she would hear someone read, "The war department regrets to inform you that your son...."

She told us the feeling that she got when she heard the man start to read the telegram, fearing and hoping each time. Fearing that it would, and hoping that it would not, be one of her own sons. I am thankful to God that she never had to hear that telegram.

After she left the post office in her second retirement, she went back to tutoring children that were having problems in school. One of my college classmates–we were sophomores together–came to her funeral and said that he had just heard of her death and wanted to come by and see me. You know what he told me? "John, I'm a grandfather now."

I was stunned because the last time I saw this man he was drinking a quart of milk sitting on a curb hitchhiking from a larger city back to the school that we both attended, and I thought that same night we both ate a half dozen bananas. For this man to have the audacity to tell me that he was a grandfather was just more than I could accept.

Then pretty soon... I said, "Rudy, I am, too!" Then we shared on a different level. I was aware at that moment that balance in life is a necessity, and not only this, but it is also absolutely imperative that we recognize that life also has a linear dimension which we call progression. You are not the same person you were last week when you viewed this program, nor the same person you were yesterday. You have moved a certain distance along this journey we call life, and your life, as mine, is moving towards its final conclusion.

We have had so much scare talk from the pulpit about the necessity and the nature of death that I think it has not left us entirely free to look at it. I'm not too interested in looking into the movement of life, because if I can copy my life today, I will be happy when the end comes without a lot of unfinished business. There is a progression of life.

I remember when I was a very small boy, a woman taught us to work in the garden. It seems to me when I was small that this was the biggest garden in the world with the longest rows. I felt, as a small boy, that these rows must at least have been a quarter of a mile long. When I go back there as a man and look at the garden, the rows are short.

One day when we were working in the garden in the hot sun, there was a baseball game going on across the fence which made working a lot harder. I decided that if I cut my big toe just enough to make it bleed that I would get to go into the house and Mother would wrap it up for me and feel sorry for me; then, later on, when she got busy, I could get over the fence and play ball. If you are young enough and in the position to try that, I would like to strongly discourage you, because I cut it more than I planned and still have a scare on that toe.

The way things changed with the passing of the years have given me a very sober and solemn insight about my own time on this earth, and my own time here with you. So today I want to stop and say to you, "Sir, that life of yours is moving and you are using up the days and hours and weeks and months and years that have been allotted to you, and no human being on earth knows how many you have. Once these days or hours or weeks or years have gone, you cannot call time back or change one single moment."

In "The Rubaiyat of Omar Khayyam, the Tentmaker," there is a little four verse phrase that reads, "The moving finger writes, and having writ, moves on. Nor all your piety, nor wit can lure it back to cancel half a line, nor all your tears wash out a word of it." So, watch each word you say.

That came into my mind when I was standing there watching the people come and go at the funeral home. We are a large family. in Mississippi I am related not only to the DeFoores but also the Smiths and the Browns, and the Jones, and the Pentecosts. We tried to describe how were related but we finally decided that we were only fifth cousins. I never did figure out if we were fifth cousins, why our families were still kissing.

But the boys that I played with when I was in Mississippi are now men. The people I sat in Sunday school with are now aging, and they are growing, and they will be moving. And what is happening in that group today will never happen again. It is forever and eternally deposited in the vault of time. It becomes a part of history, a part of time, a part of memory.

It is important what you do with yourself, with your time. It is important that you recognize that the relationship that you have with your family, with your wife, with your parents, your husband, your son or daughter is so important, for what you do today is eternal and can never be undone. Yes, God forgives. Thank God. and God forgets. Thank God.

God in his infinite wisdom had told you not to call back one single moment of time, and you will never relive the moments you are living now. Life has a forward movement—progression. Life doesn't regress. Time does not regress.

We had the funeral in the little church where I grew up as a child. It is a little church made out of red brick, Almost square, maybe a little longer than it is wide. I didn't know this until I was a grown man, but I was happy to find out that my daddy had a logging business in Mississippi where he hauled logs on a huge wagon with huge wheels pulled by oxen teams. He went to the railroad where he loaded the brick off a railway car and hauled them to this site where the church was built sometime after 1910.

I went to church there as a child, and the preacher there got so loud and shouted a lot, and he was really hooked on Hell. He screamed and shouted about Hell and the devil and judgment. I never heard him talking much about Jesus Christ, except occasionally. The only way I could get away from this was to learn to sleep in church. To this day I think I can stop any time I have 15 to 20 minutes and I can sleep 13 out of 15 minutes or 28 out of 30 minutes. I can just lay down and go to sleep. I think I learned it from this little church, because with that man talking so much about these fearsome, frightening things, the only way I could tune them out was to go to sleep.

I sat on the church bench again last Tuesday. The casket was down front, and the front of the church was full of flowers sent by caring friends. I thought to myself, in all the years I've been to this church, I have never been to this place before. I looked at my brothers, my sons, and my wife and saw how different we were since the last time we had been there.

I turned and looked at the place where, as a child, I had seen older people in the congregation sit, and they were all gone. I watched a woman play the piano in her own particular way. She used the hymn book part of the time and part of the time she improvised. I heard the minister who had been my mother's pastor during a rather lengthy period of his life. I heard him walk to the pulpit in this non-carpeted church with a floor of white pine. I heard him say, "I am the resurrection and the life. He who believeth in my, though he were dead, yet shall he live."

I wanted to say, "Hurray!" but I was afraid they wouldn't understand. I thank God that I had the assurance that the little span of life we live on this earth is not the full measure of a man's life. You can't take human life, made in the image of God, and contain it in 90 years. There is a lot more to you, Sir, than the number of years you are living on this earth. I believe that when God made man in his own image, that through Jesus Christ, he gives us life eternal, and death is a time in which we change the container that the life inhabits, and death is the time when one body is exchanged for another body. This body is made to last about 70-80 years, and it will wear out. Then, you will need another body to contain the life you have, because the life you have is eternal, and it will last forever. This is the time we make the change.

I did something else I want to tell you about. I have always had responsibility at funerals. I've had to officiate at most of them, but I cried at this funeral. I was not afraid to grieve. It was strange, and it was good, and I was not ashamed. Well, not much. I was embarrassed a little because of these messages in my brain that big men don't cry. We have to be strong, but I went ahead and did it anyway. Before the funeral, I went out and looked at the open grave. I hadn't done that before, and I don't even know why I did it. I guess I wanted to experience the reality. She was buried right alongside my daddy who died when I was five years old. He died when He was in his early 40s; she died in her early 90s. We buried them side by side.

Albert Schweitzer coined the term that caught the imagination and caught the fancy of many thinking people. He called it "The Reverence for Life." To me reverence for life would be an awareness that today is important and time and time being your accumulative experiences on this earth. Reverence of life would be the acceptance of progression of life. To me it would also embody the recognition of the apparent value of every person you meet. The willingness to spend time with family. The concern and care that characterize attentive listening. My own reverence for life means that I must not let myself live in continuing guilt or anxiety or inferiority or anything that destroys or inhibits the freedom to live life at an abundant, rich, and overflowing level. To me reverence of life recognizes that friendship is an essential and vital part of living.

I got a lot of cards from the people in the television audience and I thank you. Some people saw the notice in the paper and wrote a letter. People that I did not know previously and faces that I have never seen caught me up in a warm fellowship of love and transcended personal knowledge. It made me know that I do not only belong to the human race, but also to the family of God. The community of love, the relationship of caring—you blessed me, and I thank you.

I could not help but remember that God himself came to earth and lived out his number of days, and then at the end of his time, God's own son–God himself died. The life left the physical body that he had inhabited his 33 years on earth. His friends took him–with a great deal of grief and sorrow—and laid him gently, warmly, and quietly on a cold slab and walked away—but here is the best part: He did not stay! For death cannot hold him and neither will it hold you.

February 1075

CLAIMING YOUR OWN IDENTITY

It is nice to remember that each one of us has something that is in a very personal, particular way his own. You have your own identity. Nobody else has it. You are once, and in all eternity. You are a one-time creation. You are unique, you are special. You are important. And I think when a person can grasp this, it gives him a different place to star in this world.

I just want to say this morning that God made you, and God made you in His own image. God made you like Himself. God doesn't make any mistakes, and you are not a mistake. You are the way God designed and intended you to be, so go ahead and be free to be yourself. God made you a human being. He did not make you God, so you don't have to be perfect. I can be a growing person, and I can make progress, but I don't have to be perfect.

Here on "A Place to Talk," I have been emphasizing to you the importance of being willing to claim your own lives. It is important for you to recognize that you are a person, and that you have an identity and a place, and an importance, and this is where it all begins. This is where you can declare that I am me and I don't have to imitate anyone else. It's all right for me to be who I am. Here I take my stand. I will be myself.

Here you can claim your ow emotions, Claiming them is a good first step. Emotions are neither good nor bad, right nor wrong. Feelings are natural functions and are resolved by this human body. When you feel angry, it's all right to be angry, and it's all right to claim your anger and say, "Hey, I'm mad, and I'm mad about this and this...."

To deny the anger and to push it back in will give you an uncomfortable feeling in your stomach or in the back of your neck or in whatever place you store it when you don't express it. It is even all right to express joy. Have you ever had the feeling that it was not your right to be happy? That you should feel apologetic about saying, "It's a beautiful day, and "I'm glad to be alive."?

Around some grumpy, grouchy, gripey people sometimes you get the feeling, "Well, I shouldn't be happy because they don't feel well, and I don't want to make them feel bad." That is not good reasoning. If you are feeling happy, express it, share it, and claim the joy that is your very own the same way you claim sorrow.

When you claim feelings, It's all right to claim joy; it's all right to claim hatred; it's all right to claim uncertainty or doubt. It's not wrong or bad to have these feelings. You will decide what to do with them after you have claimed them.

I am talking this morning, not about community or family, but about one person—you—and about your saying, "This is me and this is my life, and I am being myself. I am a human being, I am not trying to be God, and as a human being, I am feeling human emotions. My humanness is okay. It's all right for me to be myself and my emotions are okay."

A person can acknowledge his feelings. We have totally different lifestyles. For a person to say, "I am having some real guilt feelings. I am feeling guilty about the way I've treated you, or about a particular thing I have done, or because I am taking too much of your time." Whatever the feeling is, you can verbalize it. You can speak it out, and you can get it out of where the feelings are stored.

It's all right to say to another person, "Hey, I don't know what you're feeling, and I was wondering if you would tell me." This is coming on straight with a person. This is a request for something. You will find that if you will deal honestly with feelings with your wife, son or daughter, husband, mother, father...you are dealing honestly with the relationship. Honesty in feelings is as much a necessity in a relationship as money is in a business, or as much a necessity as it is in dealing with the Internal Revenue Service or with a human life. Claim those feelings. Make them your own, and then you can deal with them.

There are three feelings I want you to be aware of. They are guilt, inferiority, and repressed anger. These three feelings, when they are kept inside, are very destructive. Some people grow up feeling guilty. Some grow up guilty when they do or don't do something, and this becomes a habit.

If you have a consistent, recurring feeling of guilt, check it out by speaking it out loud to another person, and see what his response is. Find someone you can trust who will help you evaluate this feeling. Then get it out in the open and lay it out and look at it.

There is another feeling I want to look at, and this is the feeling of inferiority. It is a feeling. It is rarely a fact. If this is one of the feelings that have been bothering you, find a friend, doctor, minister, counselor, neighbor, or some person you can communicate with easily and talk to him about it, and get it out in the open.

If he is an aware person, he won't laugh, and if he does, just say, "Hey, man, I'm serious. I really need to deal with this." Usually the person will hear you, and if he doesn't just get up and walk off. Bring it out in the open. Guilt and inferiority need to be out in the open. They need to be expressed. They need to be ventilated.

The next thing is repressed anger. One of the normal, healthy, human functions of the body is to get angry. If your body is functioning, there will be times when you will feel anger. When you express it and handle it responsibly, then it is not a threat. If it is kept inside, anger can go into an ulcer, hay fever, and a lot of other things. Repressed anger will tear you up inside, but expressed anger is rarely as destructive. Will you get it out in the open and look at it? This is really a freeing, liberating act. When you get anger outside and hear yourself speaking it, and you ask the other person involved to deal with the anger along with you, this is great.

Man, God made you and you are valuable, and you are important to God. And if you are valuable, for God's sake, acknowledge it to yourself. You don't have to prove it to anyone else once you acknowledge it to yourself. Claim yourself, claim your life, and then claim your feelings. Claim them, deal with them, and then get on with the show.

Beware of the person who says, "I have never been angry. I have never been sad. I have never been jealous, or had my feelings hurt." Beware of that person. He is not telling the truth, and if he doesn't tell the truth about those things, he probably won't in other circumstances. Anger is as normal as joy or happiness or delight or ecstasy. And when you get these things out into the open, you can deal with them.

The next privilege I want to remind each one of you of is that of asking for whatever you want. Nobody can read your mind. You can't ready anybody else's mind. So, when you want something from me, ask me for what you want. When I want something from you, I must ask for what I want.

If I want you to notice that I have on a new suit, I can come on straight and as, "How do you like my coat?" or if I'm not sure about our friendship, I can say, "Hey, I'm not sure about where I stand with you and I wonder if you would tell me how you value our friendship." Then you might want to know the same thing about me, and you can ask where I stand with you.

This is especially good in families when we have a tendency to withdraw from each other. Sometimes the husband withdraws when he is thinking about business, and the children go to their mother and ask what is wrong with Daddy. Then the mother intervenes and serves as a go-between, and this destroys family solidarity and family unity.

Another way to handle this is for either mother or the children to go to the daddy and say, "Hey, Daddy, I want to know what is bothering you. I'm not sure about what is going on in this house." If he is worrying about his job, he can say so. And if he is resenting something that the children have done, or if he is unhappy about something that is happening in the household, then he can come on straight and let the other members of the family know what he needs and what he is feeling.

As for what you want from your wife. Say to her, "I want you to express your love to me in this way." And the wife recognizes the fact that you are honest with her. Then she should ask for what she wants from her husband, such as, "I want you to compliment my cooking, see that I have cleaned the house, or that I have spent the whole day making the house attractive and colorful and appealing so that when you come home you will have a pleasant atmosphere."

It may be easier for women to ask for this, for what the woman does is a lot more visible most of the time, and it is easier to call attention to it. It may be necessary for the husband to ask, "Do you appreciate the fact that I bring home the salary that pays for the utilities, that makes the house payments, that provides the car and make it possible for us to take vacations? If you do, I wish you would tell me." Then the husband can get what he wants by asking for it directly.

This is especially good when a little child can come up to a daddy and say, "Hold me" or "kiss me," or "Mommy, can you tie my shoe?" I watched one day in a church meeting when there was a little girl, very obviously neglected but very cute, and she had on some new shoes. She untied one of the shoes and went to her mother with the shoestring flopping and asked her mother to tie her shoe. The mother bent down to tie the shoes, but never stopped the conversation she was having with another person.

The child had wanted attention. She had wanted to be loved and affirmed, but she didn't know how to ask directly for what she wanted. The mother filled the request, but missed the deeper needs of the child.

Sometimes we do this in families. It may be when your wife is in the closet and says, "I don't have a thing to wear." When she says this, she may mean she doesn't have anything to war...or she may want her husband to notice that she has a new hairdo.

And when the husband sits down at the table and says, "Is this all we have to eat?" he may be really saying, "I'm tired and have had a long day and need to be nurtured and acknowledged." You can ask for what you want. Just give the person the option of giving you what you want or refusing to give it. But until you ask for what you want, you never give the person a chance to grant your request or deny it.

I mentioned the little girl with the shoestring. I believe children generally make their needs known until they learn that that doesn't pay. When a child says, "I'm hungry," I have heard myself say, "You're not hungry, You're sleepy. Go to bed."

We say this, we are denying them the freedom to express their feelings and calling them a liar. One thing that will help is when the child asks for what he wants it to give it to him and acknowledge this as a true expression of his feelings and needs. Do this without erasing his request, and putting our own interpretation as an overlay on top of it.

When a child comes in and is tired, it may be that he is trying to verbalize something that he has learned he cannot express safely. Sometimes, we adults pout when we have needs and cannot ask directly for what we want. Now when our needs go underground, they come out in the form of what is popularly called today "a game."

A lot of games can develop when one person does not have the courage to ask that his needs be met. This is where we get busily involved with requiring another person to read our minds and we set ourselves up to be mind-readers.

The same God who made us in his own image gave you and gave me the emotional mechanism that deals with our needs on the inside, so it's not only okay for you to be who you are, but also for you to have the needs that you have. It's okay for you to express these needs, and it's okay for you to ask for what you want.

When you are working in this direction, you have a real good hold on life. One of the things that I like about this man from Nazareth is that He was just as human as He could have possibly been. He was himself. I get the idea from reading about His life that He was probably the most authentic person that ever walked the earth. I like the fact that He experienced anger.

I like the picture of God in the Bible saying that He is a jealous God. Jealousy to God is not a sin. I like the loneliness of Christ and His need for companionship–His need for friends. I like His fatigue and His joy.

He had the same emotions that you and I have, and He dealt with them honestly and honorably. He asked for what He wanted. He asked the disciples at times to be with Him, and at other times He asked them to go away. He recognized that if others didn't know what He needed, there really wasn't any way they could fulfill His need.

Nobody ever accused Jesus Christ of being untrue to Himself. I'm glad He wasn't. It may be then, that your calling in life and my calling in life is to be ourselves to be true to ourselves by being the self that we are.

I have purposely avoided the statement, "Who am I?" because for most of us, it isn't a real problem. The decisive issue is not, "Who am I?" the decisive issue is, "Am I willing to be the self that I have already decided I am?" Here is the decision that will guide and direct your past, present and future.

February 1975

YOUR PERSONHOOD

You know, there are a lot of people who have influenced my life that I've never known personally and when I talk with other people, when I talk with some of you and some of you talk with me, you've talked about the influence that people have had on your life in very strange and different ways. I'm thinking of two of the people who have meant so very much to me, and I want to tell you this morning some of the things I've heard them say.

I've always wondered if after reading a man's works, (and I've had this experience once or twice) but I've always wondered how it would be after you had read his works to sit and talk with him and see how much real understanding you had; how much real understanding of what he was saying came through in his writing and how much of our own interpretation is superimposed on what we read.

One of the men who has helped me most I think in understanding what I had always felt, is a man named Martin Buber. I think if I could draw a picture of Isaiah, the old testament prophet, the way I saw him, I would put Martin in the frame and walk away and say this is Isaiah. He had a profound trust in God, a deep penetrating insightful understanding of man and God: God's relationship with man, and man's relationship with God. There are two very simple things that this man wrote about and talked about at length that I want to say. One is, he used the phrase "I"—"Thou." What I'm going to say is "Thou." He said that every human being is a "Person." That every human being is "I." And when you are talking to another human being, he also is an "I," but since he is not you, you call him a "Thou."

He used the words "I" and "Thou" to distinguish relationships from an "I"—"it" relationship. A thing is an "it." A person is never a thing, a person is never an "it."

You're always "person" and the person that you are is always your primary identity. And we can never say of a man that he is just a carpenter, or he is just a preacher, or he is just a doctor, or he is just a plumber, or an electrician. He is always a person. He is a person who makes his living in a certain way, or he may even be a person who is paralyzed, but he is never just a paralytic. He may be an alcoholic, but he is never just an alcoholic, he is a person who has a problem of alcohol. He is never just a drug addict; he is a person with a problem that is related to drug addiction. He is never just a Mexican or a Mississippian or a honky. You are never just a Texan; you are always "person" and the identity of person always comes first. Now this is the meaning of the "I"—"Thou" relationship. When I say "I"—"it," I'm talking about something —an inanimate object, something that doesn't live, I say "I"—"it" l refer to me and this couch or "I"—"it" is me and the carpet, or me and the car—car is an "it."

Now, there are some people that will disagree with that. But to me a car is an "it." My pickup truck is an "it." It's a good "it," and I like "it," but it's not a person. And in the "I"—"Thou" relationships we give to the other human being his true value so we can see him as he is and let him be the person he is. And we do not ever assign to things a value that is higher than the value that we put on persons.

I think this is the way we sometimes get in trouble when we value things more than we value persons. One of the ways to check yourself out on this is to look at the way you relate to your wife and see if she to you is a person. One of the ways to check this out is to look at your children and see if this is just a son or just a daughter. When you assign to another person a role or a relationship there's a real danger that you've lost sight of the person. I hope and pray for myself I will never let anybody be just a friend. However, we value that word that maybe this person will always be to me a person with whom I have the relationship as friend. That this man will never be just my doctor, or this man will never be just the clerk behind the counter, that he'll always be a human being with infinite worth and value—with problems, yes, with handicaps, yes, but always a human being, anywhere in all of eternity like you. Your worth and your value is both infinite and eternal. If you do not give this, if you do not claim this for yourself, no one can give it to you. Once you claim it nobody can ever take it away, and I like that. It's yours—you claim it and you accept it and, man, it's yours forever, and nobody—nobody on this earth—can take it away.

Oh, by the way, I don't know if I mentioned this or not but there are two Sunday school classes that are meeting and taking a television set into the classroom and are listening to this program and then discussing it. When I first learned that I got really up tight and said, "I'm going to have to work hard to make this thing good enough, you know, for you people to use it in your Sunday school class." In fact, I had a hard time imagining that you could take a sinful TV set into the church without the church burning up or exploding, but I guess maybe you worked that out before you did it. I'm glad you're doing that and I hope, as you go along, that you'll write to me and let me have some feedback from the whole class. I'd really be interested in that. I'm flattered. I'm glad you're doing it. Hey, I got some real nice letters too and that helped. Part of what I'm saying this morning came out of the material of some of the letters. I got a letter from a man and he said he felt like I talked down to the TV audience. When I do that, I'm not talking down, I'm talking best about on my own level. I always try to communicate with about an eighth-grade vocabulary. I get sick and tired of people who work hard to convince others with a wide vocabulary and the ability to use words that are obscure and rare. So, if this gives you problems, I'm sorry. I'd sooner communicate with children than adults anyway.

Now, where was I? Oh yes, "I"—Thou" relationship means that you're a person whether or not you agree or disagree., Culturally, socially, ethnic background similar to mine or not. Whether or not you live in the same country that I live in or whatever. I think I mentioned that we lived in a foreign country for a while.

At one time when we were living in another country, I had to go down every six months and register. The office where I registered had a sign up over the door that said "Narcotics, dangerous firearms, and aliens." That's where I registered—me and the dangerous firearms all lumped together. I went there every six months. A very unsmiling man handed me the forms, asked me what I was doing, and looked me up and down. I felt like I'd been thoroughly examined. I know what it's like to be a stranger and an alien in a foreign country. I also know what it's like to be in a foreign country where you can't speak the language and lose part of your family. My family got separated one time for about 24 hours in Germany, and, Boy, that was something else! I have lived during the war and since the war, too, with primitives, Aborigines in New Guinea at one time. I've lived with the Eskimo and I've lived with the Indians. I've eaten their food; I've slept in their houses, and I've stayed with them for days when I could not speak their language. I'm more than ever convinced after these and other experiences that the human being is made in the image of God, that the life of every human being is sacred and holy, that the value of a human being is inborn, that is, built into the person, that value is not something you earn, that it is something God gives. The way other people value us may be earned, but your inherent value is God-given. That is the reason you must always be "person" reflecting God's image, never a thing. I've heard and I'm sure I've said it at different times, "Well, that doesn't make any difference, he's just a so and so. He's just an ex-con, he's just a jailbird, he's just a drunk, he's just a—oh, he just works for the IRS—he's just a policeman or he's just a Baptist preacher—he doesn't count." I was not saying nearly so much about the other man as I was saying about myself.

Martin Buber, our present-day Isaiah, though now deceased, has given us some deep insight into the nature, worth, value, and I'm convinced, beauty of man. There is something else I want to show you. There is a guy who is still living in Switzerland. His name is Paul Tournier. He's written a half dozen books. He is a brilliant man. I met him one time, and I was so excited I just stood there and dribbled. He had a flock of hair, he did then, stood out more then, now he's gotten old and kind of round, but he wrote quite a few books. He wrote *The Meaning of Persons* and *Grace and Guilt* and *The Adventure of Living* and some books on how to grow old or something, I've forgotten the title to it. If you are a reader, you'll enjoy his books. Now though he never acknowledges that he got this idea from Martin Buber, I think he's picked up on Martin Buber's idea. I'm going to show you one of the diagrams that he uses, I think he does, but if he doesn't use it I got the idea from him. And he uses the idea that you're a person and you're made into the image of God, so we'll let that circle be you. Over here, this is a person and your worth and value is in who you are not in what you do, okay? If you're the husband, over here is your wife. You're a person and she's a person. When you stand before her you become more than just you. You have the role or the relationship of husband.

Now look, here's what I'm saying this morning. I'm saying that you're a person; she's a person—you're the "I"; she is the "Thou." Okay? Now, the relationship you have is where you share your life with her and she shares her life with you. In that moment you're more than person. You become husband, but you do not lose your identity as a person—You become a husband when you stand before your wife and this interchange of life is called your personage. It can also be called your role. Then you have a son here, and when you stand before your son, you're not a husband, you're a father. But you will share your life with him; he shares his life with you and the interchange of life, the intercourse of your life with your son, gives birth to this role of father. If your mother is still living or your father or either of your parents, when you stand before the parent, you're not a husband or father or your son. Okay, now you share your life with your parents and you're a son, and there is a giving of life and there is a receiving of life, but you never give this up. You never lose this identity. You always remain person. You always remain yourself. The same person, before the wife is a husband. This person doesn't change but before this person you are a father, and before this person you are a son.

Now, this is a constant. This is you. You have infinite and eternal worth and value and you don't ever sell yourself. Don't ever sell yourself to be just a husband, or just a father, or just a son. Okay; one more deal over here. This is your employer. When you go to your employer, you become an employee or whatever your occupation is. You don't sell yourself here, any more than you sell yourself here or here, or here. You always retain this. You don't sell your soul or relationship or for any role or for any other person. You go downtown and you talk to a salesclerk, who is more than a salesclerk and you're a customer. And there's one more relationship I want to show you here. When you go to your doctor, you are a patient. Now there's always a give and take in every relationship. You don't lose yourself, and you don't give up yourself, you always hold on to yourself and hold on to your worth and value. Even when you become sick and you're a patient. You don't give it up. When you're with your wife, you're still a husband but you don't give up yourself.

When you're doing this you're doing one thing that is very important. You're claiming what is your own, claiming the fact that you are a human being with infinite worth and value. And here you become husband and here you're father, son, employee, customer, patient, and you never give up the self in any of these roles.

Let me tell you the good thing now. Life has a way of changing relationships and I think this will help you to understand the meaning of Job, the book in the Old Testament. You can lose your parents and you can lose this relationship: you are no longer a son if you don't have parents. You can lose your son and you're not a father. You can lose your job and you're no longer an employee; outside the store or business you're not a customer. It is possible, hopefully it won't happen, but it is possible for a man to lose every single relationship and still survive as a person. I hope it doesn't happen, but this is what happened to Job and this is what that Old Testament book is teaching. That the person, the self, can survive because this is the way God relates to us primarily. First God lives in us. The kingdom of God is in us. Then He communicates Himself to us through other people. But Sir, you can survive if you lose your wife, your job, your son, your daughter, your mother, or father, and, Lady, you can, too. This "I" is made in the image of God, the person you are. This "Thou" is made in the image of God, the person that God created so that you could have a relationship here.

I want to show you one more thing. I've known some people who live kind of like this. This is the job over here. Some people put so much into their job or their profession that pretty soon all other relationships were crowded out. The man's whole self is poured into this relationship. When you ask him what he was, he said, "I'm just a doctor, lawyer, counselor, electrician, plumber, or carpenter." That's all he was and when he lost his job, he lost his soul. There is a better way to live. And the better way is to be the person you are, and to go through life claiming the personhood when there are a lot of forces in our society that move to de-personalize or take away an individual's worth and value. There are some people in our time who will minimize your worth and value if you allow them to, but no one can take it away from you unless you allow them to.

This is one of the fascinating things to me about this carpenter. He was always a "person." His profession at that time was a carpenter, later on He became a preacher. He was called a healer, revolutionary, fanatic, a liar and finally condemned as a traitor, and then He was called a martyr. Some people have called Him a fake. He's even been called a myth. He always stood firm in a conviction—in His own identity as a person of infinite worth and value. He has the capacity to give personhood—this is Jesus Christ, the greatest person who ever lived and taught us about our own greatness.

October 1975

PERFECTION

The "be perfect" drive is present in a whole lot of people. It's present particularly in the people who have ulcers, heart trouble, some form of hay fever, and there are a lot of other evidences of any inner drive to be perfect. So, one of the things that I thought we'd do this morning is to work on finding a better way. I talked with a lot of you who listen about this, and it's been sort of a common problem to a lot of us. I think it starts out when a person is convinced in childhood that there's something he needs to compensate for in his own understanding or it may be a message the parents unintentionally transmit because of some of their own inadequacies. One of the mysteries and wonders of this succession of generations in families, where you have parents and children...parents and children...generation after generation. One of the questions is: Why, in the wisdom of God, did He arrange it this way?

The answer is simply because He saw it best, but there's a tendency on the part of some parents to expect their children to do everything they could not do, and be everything they could not be. This imposes on some children an impossible burden and instead of thinking about your children, would you think about yourself and give yourself some sort of understanding of the goals and standards you've set for yourself? Do you have to do your job perfectly while you work? Do you have to keep the yard perfectly? Do you have to run the store or the service station perfectly, keep your books perfectly, or whatever it is? And when I say perfect, I mean without any error or without any question there, and without any single mistake or inadequacy in your whole system of performance.

When you set this kind of goal for yourself, the first thing you're doing is guaranteeing that you will fail. I'd like for you to consider not failing and setting yourself a realistic goal that you're capable of accomplishing and capable of achieving. So, the first thing in looking at the "be perfect" goal is, and incidentally, I'm going to talk about the scripture in just a minute. The first thing, however, is the way this is used as a compensation. A child finds out very early in life–most of them do–that he is not perfect and there's an area of inadequacy that he discovers in himself. Here's where he gets punished for something, he's criticized for something, or he goes to school and he doesn't make all "As," now there's a tendency on a part of a lot of us to do something that we call over-compensation, and instead of making up for this much of an inadequacy, we make up for this much and we over-do it. It's almost as if we owe ten dollars and we pay back fifty. It's almost as if we wasted ten minutes of time so we have to work double-time for two hours in order to pay back for the ten minutes of time that we consider we've wasted.

So, the first think I want you to look at is how much of your life you spend making up for things you feel you've done earlier to somebody. Now I'm talking particularly about children who have spent most of their lives making something up to their parents. Well—I hurt my mother and daddy when I was sixteen, or I hurt my mother and daddy when I was eighteen, and now that I'm sixty-five, I'm still paying them back. That's ridiculous! There isn't any way to pay back a person for an injury that you've done, and the only way to heal the pain or to bridge the gap that the injury caused is to go and say I'm sorry—And accept the forgiveness if it's offered, if not offered, you forgive yourself. But a far as paying back, making up for, atoning, or compensating for, that is not a realistic way to look at your relationship with other people. It won't work and it won't help you and it won't help the other person. Don't spend your life compensating or making up for something that you consider some sort of injury that you've done. I know some men who spent years making up to their wives for..., or some wives who've spent years making up to their husbands for...some or the other. And there isn't any way you can do it. Some people who have gone through an experience of divorce work extra hard or accept certain kinds of behavior in order to compensate for the fact that they're divorced. Or sometimes they work real hard to compensate the children for the loss of a father or mother; you can't do that. When you set yourself up to do this, if you'll stop and look, you'll probably find that there's some reason you need to make yourself fail. And might be a better way. I say there might be. Sometimes I'm facetious when I talk like this, and a lot of you hear and acknowledge it, and I'm glad. There is a better way of course. When you try to pay for a debt incurred earlier in life—and I mean an emotional, social, and, I would say also, a religious debt—you are arranging your life so that you hurt yourself. When you try to make up to someone for something that you have done or someone else has done earlier, you're setting yourself up for failure and you'll never change this other person's mind.

There are two statements... three...four—four statements that I would like you to look at briefly in passing, and these statements are not true. One statement is "I can make you feel better." That means that I can conduct myself so that I can relate to you in such a way that I will determine what you will feel. I've said before on this program many times, we affect each other and we influence each other, but making someone feel is something we can't do. I can't make you feel better unless you allow me to. I can't make you feel worse unless you allow me to. Turn around. You can't make me feel better unless I allow it, and you can't make me feel worse unless I allow it. So, compensating for an injury done earlier is unhealthy. I've heard people say, "Well, I never wanted to do this, but my mother wanted me to," or "I hurt my husband or I hurt my wife, or sister or brother and so I've been doing this for years to kinda pay back for what I've done." And that's not fair, not honest; it's not healthy, and it's not Christian. So, don't spend this part of your life compensating for what you've done earlier; you'll miss the meaning and the joy and the beauty of life that is available today.

Now the next thing I want to talk to you about is something Jesus said, because I hear this a whole lot from people. One day when Jesus was talking, He said to a group of people, "Be ye therefore." This is what I want to talk to you about. Now I want you to look at these words. We read it like he said ..."do ye therefore perfect." and He didn't. The answer is in the being not in the doing. This is what I want to talk about. Be the person that God created, then you don't have to break your back doing something that you are not constructed to be. Here's an accurate interpretation of "be perfect." It means be human, it means be the individual made and created in the image of God. It means be an individual who lives a 70+ years on this earth; it means be the individual who makes mistakes, who does some things right and some things wrong—be the individual who sometime succeeds and sometimes fails—be the individual who both needs forgiveness from others and extends forgiveness to others. Now that is the part of a perfect being. And when Jesus of Nazareth was talking about being perfect, this is what he meant: He meant that through this life you have available to you all the essential necessities of a right relationship with the creator of the universe and in this beingness, in the acceptance of this, you experience the fulfillment of being.

And it's a gift. You don't have to earn it, or deserve it or, work your way up to it. Some people call it grace, and I like the way some of us call it "love." To Martin Luther it was summed up in one word, "forgiveness." Some call it patience; some call it kindness; to some it is gentleness. Regardless of the name you call it, it's the same thing; it doesn't change because you call it another name, but in the understanding of this, you will lose some of the compulsion that you might have picked up as you try to compensate for earlier wrongs.

You see, I must accept the fact that in the eyes of God I am perfect. And the more I accept my perfection, the perfection of creation, the perfection of a right relationship with Jesus Christ, with God through Jesus Christ, the perfection of being the man I am–who I am–living in the world where I live, doing the things I do, then my ability to do is increased as a result of my being. Then, when I can be perfect like Jesus meant it, I no longer have to do perfect, and I can do normal instead of breaking my back to do other things. Now this "be perfect" is a drive, commandment, or an attitude you can discard—and you can discard it today. You don't have to live like this any longer than you plan to keep on failing. So, you'll give this up, take for yourself a whole new set of standards, and decide, as far as you and your job are concerned you don't have to over-compensate for something that was done to you earlier in life, and you don't have to achieve impossible goals set by a God who was devoid of understanding.

Now, I want to say for the benefit of one or two people who listen, that I realize there same some groups—religious groups—who believe that they live morally, and ethically, perfect, and that beyond a certain point where they meet God they never sin. If you are one of those, I tip my hat and say, "God bless you, and may you have a good journey; may the wind be always behind your back, may the road stretch out before you...." But I do not know anything about this kind of experience. When you achieve this, that's fine. I hope you'll teach the rest of us. I want to come back to say this I understand the teaching of Jesus Christ, that what He meant for us here was to be the person He's created, to achieve our own perfection for good works—but accept our own perfection by His good grace, and then the good works will follow as an act of natural obedience when we accept the gift He's given us.

Now, the better way—here's what I want you to consider—when you work in your yard or in your flower bed or when you build something, or whatever you do—even some people work at this in speaking. Would you consider—instead of being perfect—would you consider being realistic and learn to live in a world of reality rather than fantasy.

I notice this particularly when people talk about keeping house. There are some women, I used to know some—don't think I know any now—who had to keep the house perfect. It had to be completely clean and spotless, and everything had to be straight and neat in every dresser drawer and in every closet and everything polished and clean and some women became slaves to the houses. When the house is out of order or when something is out of place, this person becomes intensely uncomfortable and cannot really function. Now, this is part of the drive of a perfectionist; this is a part of a drive of a person who decides she has to be perfect. The house becomes for her then, not a place in which she lives for her comfort, enjoyment, relaxation, rest, and peace. It becomes a monster with a long black whip that drives her. And she is never through, and she is never finished, and she cannot find one single place in the house to rest because the house for her has become a harsh driving merciless taskmaster. This woman has moved out of the world of reality and has moved into the world of fantasy, setting for herself an impossible task she is incapable of achieving to guarantee herself she will be failure.

Now the difference between living in this world of fantasy and living in this world of reality is nothing more than a decision. You have to sit down and say, "What is my house for?" It doesn't hurt to remember that someday somebody is going to come along and wreck that pile of junk that you live in and the one I live in—it has a lot of meaning, worth, and value for us today, but it's not always going to have that. And if you spend your whole life keeping a house clean, neat, and straight, then after you die, somebody comes along and wrecks the things and hauls it off for junk and paves the lawn you've worked so hard on for a parking lot for a supermarket. You'll feel kind of silly standing up in heaven looking back to see what you've done most of your life and what you spent most of your time on this earth working on.

I've known some men—and I am at times one of them, but on my better days I've quit it— who feel that they have to get all the work done at the office and everything in good shape that somehow, some way, and by some miracle they're going to do everything that needs to be done. And I know—and you know—that there isn't any way to do this, but we find it hard to go home, leave the office when there's work remaining to be done. We drive ourselves, and—even when you get it finished at the end of the day—tomorrow morning when you get there and the mail comes in and the telephone starts ringing, everything you had completed the day before will be undone.

Now, this kind of need to do perfect is one of the things that kills men, particularly if you have a position of responsibility and you feel, well, "the responsibility is on me and if I don't do it, nobody else will do it." One of the things that has really impressed me since I've been a pastor, I have watched quite a few men retire, and I have seen men who worked zealously and faithfully for a company all their lives. Their work was their very life, and they sat at this desk and wouldn't take a vacation and would work extra hours and do extra things and were very valuable and faithful employee for an individual or company or a large corporation. They considered themselves absolutely indispensable and couldn't take any time off for the wife and kids, because "if I take time away, I don't know what will happen."—I mean, that is what they said. And one particular person—I watched him retire. Went by that day to visit him in that shabby little office that he had occupied for more than thirty years. I was there when he got his gold watch with engraving on the back, and then he went home to "prop his feet up," he said, "and retire and loaf." By accident, I was back in that same office about a week later. The office had been expanded and enlarged; the office had been completely redecorated. There was a beautiful new carpet, new desk, and new furniture, and the new man in it had a salary substantially higher than the man who had retired. And all the glowing speeches I had heard about this man's faithfulness, and about his years of long and faithful service to the company—it didn't mean a thing, because there was another name on the door, another name on the desk, and there had been a lot of changes. It was almost—when I walked into the newly decorated office—it was almost as if the previous individual had never been there. If I ever saw a human being try to do a job perfectly, that man did. But in doing so, he moved completely out of the world of reality and into a world of fantasy. The world of fantasy that says, "I'm indispensable and no one else can do it like me." The world of fantasy that says, "If I don't do it, it won't get done." The fantasy that says, "Everything depends on me, and I've got to do it, even if it kills me." The fantasy that says, "It's got to be done this way because this way is right, and I've got to do it perfectly this way every day—I've got to do it perfectly." That's fantasy—it's not reality.

It's not healthy; it won't make you a better person; it won't make you a happy person to live with; it will finally break your back. Reality brings you to a point where you say, "I will do my work today, and I will enjoy the experience of working, but I will not do it perfectly." "I will clean my house today" or "I will cook this meal today , and I'll do it, and I'll enjoy it, but I will not do it perfectly—I no longer have to." "I'll work at the job and I'll sell eight hours of my time today to the individual, company, or corporation for whom I work, but I will not sell my soul."

That's living in a world of reality. And that's the way that you will get a lot more fun and a lot more enjoyment out of life. When you have broken your back or your heart, I think it probably breaks more hearts than backs trying to be perfect, people will pass you by, feel sorry for you, and seek out an individual who is bigger than his job and has confidence in himself. They'll seek out a woman who is bigger than her house and can enjoy her life, and therefore, is an enjoyable person.

We talk a lot about being a Christian and about this man named Jesus. One of the most attractive and beautiful things about Him is that He lived in reality. The things that He expected of Himself were reality-based—In fact, probably based more on reality than edicts or principles that ever govern the life of any man. He did not require impossible things from his friends, and He did not require affection in behavior from any of His disciples. He left them room to make mistakes; He gave them the freedom to be human. He took on humanness—put it in the context of reality—and dealt with them there. I would like you to consider that this would be the best thing in the world that you could do for yourself. Treat yourself like He treated you.

March 1975

PRAYER CAN CHANGE YOUR LIFE

It's not possible to know every object in the universe, but it's possible for you to know real, continuing, understandable communication with God.1 Now if this is really true and if you and I are fully capable of contacting the creator of the Universe, then it's worth our taking time. I'll be right back.

When the whole universe consisted of nothing–in fact, less than nothing–not only were there no planets. or stars or galaxies or mega galaxies, there was nothing, there was less than a vacuum. And the Creator, in His original act, brought forth life, existence, being, entities of various kinds here in ·the universe, and this One who originated all things, we call God. And before any things existed, God existed. That's a big God. Now, if this is not true, then you and I are god. If there is no intelligence or being in all of the universe higher than your intelligence or superior to your being, then you and I are gods. And if we're the gods, then as far as I'm concerned, this universe is in trouble in general, and this planet in particular. But I won't try to explain, defend, or justify God's position. I live and move and think and act with my life predicated on the fact that God IS and I am. My primary concern is my communication with Him and the establishment and maintenance of a channel of communication in an interpersonal relationship such that I can both speak to Him and be spoken to by Him. And that I be enabled or empowered or ennobled to carry out His will so that my life is in harmony with the universe, with the plan that the Creator has for the universe. We call this the Divine Plan.

Now, the one thing I want to talk about with you here on this program—and a lot of you have written in and asked for us to talk about here—is for us to discuss prayer. In talking about prayer, I simply call it communication with God. I think that communication is a clearer term. Prayer, like a lot of our religious symbols, has become clouded and the meaning has become obscured with both use and disuse across the years.

The best book that I've touched in the past ten years has been a book called *Prayer Can Change Your Life*. It's very beautiful, very well-done. I don't have any copies for sale and don't get a commission. But if you haven't seen this book and you're interested, probably your bookstore can get it for you. It very clearly sets out a pattern of prayer. Much of what I will be saying this morning will be taken from this book. It's been a real help to me in my own personal growth and in my own personal pilgrimage.

In this business of communicating with God, let me say this about prayer: Do you know what a lot of my prayer time was in the beginning? I spent a lot of time in prayer rehearsing my sins, almost fondling them, reinforcing my guilt, and beating myself up. I spent so much of my time confessing my sins! In talking with people who are not satisfied with their own conversation and communication with God, this is one of the things that is nearly always characteristic of their praying. Prayer is not meant to be a continual period of time where one beats himself and chastises himself and hates himself for the wrong that he has done. I have, myself, earlier in periods of prayer, gotten up from my time of prayer feeling more guilty than I was when I started to pray. And I have left periods of prayer more guilty and with a deeper feeling of condemnation than I had when I started to pray. So, I'd like for you to look at your own feelings about prayer–and your own concept of prayer–and observe what you do when you are in communication with the One who made you, gave you life on this earth, and wishes the best for you.

If this has failed, have you spent a lot of time beating yourself and chastising yourself for the things you have done that are wrong? So, to begin with, I want to say that it's necessary to confess your sins once, maybe twice in prayer and that anything more than that is a waste of time. Then you spend the remainder of time thanking God for His forgiveness, and thanking God for His love, not rehearsing and recalling over and over and over the same sins. Hey, I want to ask you something, particularly those of you who are parents—now this is a hypothetical situation, this is a make-believe situation, but I want you to listen— Suppose your child did something wrong. Okay, that might not be hard for some parents to suppose but suppose he did. And suppose he came in and said, "Hey, Dad, I did this and it was wrong, and I feel terribly guilty and I'm sorry, and I want you to forgive me." Most parents would say, "All right, Son, you're forgiven. Thank you for being considerate of me and being considerate of yourself. You're forgiven."

Suppose the son came back and hour later and said, "Hey, Dad, I'm still feeling guilty about this and I'm sorry that I did it, and I was wrong, and I want you to forgive me."

Some parents, maybe most parents, would say, "Thank you. We've discussed this already and I have forgiven you. It's all over; It's done with. Now, forget it and go on about the business of living."

Suppose he came back two hours later and then again two hours later and suppose he came back the next day and said it all over again. "Oh, I did this and I'm so sorry, and I feel so guilty, and I'm so ashamed." and he went through the same speech and the same routine beating himself, hating himself, and condemning himself, and the parent said, "Hey, we've already talked about that, I've already forgiven you. It's over; forget it, son, and go on about your business."

And then suppose he came back the next day again and he did this for weeks and months and even years. Any loving parent would finally say, "Hey, Boy, what on earth is wrong with you? I've told you over and over and over that you're forgiven. Now forget it and go on about the business of living." Do you get the point?

My point is that some of us treat God as if God did not have even as much kindness and as much capacity to forgive as you have and as I have. God is a loving, kind, and gentle heavenly Father. And His willingness and capacity to forgive is a thousand times greater, ten million times greater than yours or mine. And if you would forgive your child, know well, and know clearly that God will be a million times quicker to forgive you. So, I'm saying that time spent agonizing anguishing and carefully rehearsing our sins and our faults in prayer is wasting time. I want to suggest a better way to us the time when you are in conversation with the Creator of the universe. I want to say: instead of rehearsing your guilt and instead of rehashing your sins, (and really, I think what we do is just enjoy all of the sins all over again)– so, instead of doing that, I've got some positive suggestions for when you are praying or getting ready to pray, or when you hare having your time of devotional, whatever you call it. I want to suggest that you confess the sins once, and say "God, thank you for your forgiveness." And then move on.

The first and most important thing in prayer is your willingness to accept the fact that God loves you. Now, I'm talking about praying and that prayer is acceptance of this. You can start a prayer, if you want to, by saying "I accept the fact that you love me. I accept the fact that you love me right now, right here, as I am; that I, through Jesus Christ, am acceptable to you, and I am accepted by you, and I accept the fact that you, God, love me now!" No buts. This is the most important thing that can come out of prayer.

Then, the second thing is this: It's all right for you to say that you love God, and let it stand. First, God loves me. With all the strength that I have, I love God in return. I do not wait until I get better, or until I get good, or until I achieve a certain level of moral and ethical behavior or accomplishment. I love God now as I am, the same way God loves me. Now, this is praying, and this is more important than my reciting what I want or calling out a long list of names. Prayer is probably the time of greatest personal spiritual growth when properly used.

The next thing that I can use—or you can use if you choose—is the decision that I will do several things: I will be loyal to myself; I will be self-sacrificing; I will be forgiving; I will adopt a principle of loyalty, self-sacrifice, and forgiveness, I will listen first to myself and then listen to others. When I accept a principle of loyalty to myself and self-sacrificing for myself, putting the person who is loved by God, first, and forgiving myself, being loyal to myself, and identifying myself—then, I'm ready to be loyal to you; I'm ready to be self-sacrificing to you, and I'm ready to be forgiving to you. You see, it must happen in me—this love; before I can be loving towards you, I must be loving towards God as I accept his love. Then when this happens, I am a new and different creature. You know why? Primarily, because my world is no longer lived with me, the self, as it's center. God becomes the center of my world.

When God, the Creator of the universe, is the center of my world, then His plan for my life is my road map and is my guidebook, and God's plan includes you. If I'm the center of my universe, my plan doesn't include you. But when I start here and when I get down on my knees to pray, or stand, or kneel—or whatever position you or I assume—the most important thing is that I see myself accepted by God, that I love God in return, and that I establish the principles of loyalty, self-sacrifice, and forgiveness.

Now, the next thing here that's important for me is that I accept the love of other people. I accept your love, this makes you important, it makes you significant, and it gives us a relationship, and as I have accepted God's love,

I accept your love. And this means that the relationship I have with God is duplicated in relationship with you. So, I accept your love, and I give you my love in return, and then these principles govern my relationship with you so that I neither have to hurt you nor be hurt by you. Incidentally, I accept your love and I see in it the picture of God's love. I recognize that the love you have with me does not begin with you anymore than it ends with me. It's almost as if you and I both are caught up in the eternal and cosmic plan for man in the universe and there is interplay. There is a giving and taking, sharing or receiving that takes place between my life and yours.

Now the next thing I want to say about talking with God (and I'm saying that if you will pray this way your life will change) is that when you make this a conscious thing, it begins to make a difference in your behavior. Consciously giving yourself to prayer mentally and emotionally will make a difference in the behavior that you experience each day.

The next thing I want to say is that prayer must be regular and it also must relate your life, so much so that I give myself reminders during the day at different times, different moments to remember in the hustle and the bustle and rush of life, that I'm loved by God and that when I go downtown into a store to go shopping, I'm loved; when I'm talking with a friend or with a stranger, I'm loved by God, and I'm not a lonely, wandering, lost, unidentified stranger of the universe. This gives me a continuing, conscious knowledge that I am somebody and that the Creator knows where I am and knows who

I am— and I don't get lost in a crowd. It's necessary sometimes for us to reinforce this.

Now there is another step in prayer, as I learned in this book, *Prayer Can Change Your Life*. It has been a real big thing to me. I have gotten more personal comfort and relief from this than I guess anything that's happened to me. Prayer, for me, must be an act of surrender. When I come to pray, I give up the burdens, and I take them out of all my anxieties or concerns or blessings or praise or thanksgiving, whatever it is. I lay them down before God. To the limit of my capacity to surrender, I give them to God. And when I surrender these things, I'm willing to be made into a whole being. I'm not going to be made into a whole being by my own strength or the power of my intelligence. I'm not going to be made into a whole being because I convinced or persuaded God, but simply because I take things out of me and I put them into the hands of the One who made the universe whose plan guides my life, whose will I continually seek to know. Then the change is further implemented, the change which began when I said I accept the fact that God loves me and I accept the fact that I'm loved by God. I make loyalty, self-sacrifice, and forgiveness the way that I relate to myself and the way I that I relate to others. I accept the love of other people, and I accept their love not only as just what's happening between this person and me. I accept the love as evidence that the Creator of the universe is loving me through that person; Man, that will keep you from feeling insignificant, worthless, and useless. Then when your prayers become regular and the way you relate your life, and you use time and reminders to bring your mind consciously back to this place, then it becomes more clearly and completely integrated into your life patterns. There is a real relief in being about to surrender and being able to say simply, "God, I can't handle this; I give it to you"—and to be able to say at time out loud to a friend, "God, this is bigger than I am," and say to the friend, "Hey, I'm not dealing with that anymore. I've given it up."

Now in discussing this, some people have said, "Well that can be a copout. That's true; any part of this can be. But the person I'm speaking to isn't interested in copping out as much as He is interested in tuning in. So, I'm talking about tuning in: this is the surrendering or release of this to God and giving it up. This can give you the freedom that you as a person want and desire, in order to know the fullness and richness of life. This is what I think we all are supposed to know as Christians and as human beings. I can't ever really make myself believe that Whoever put us here has gone about His business in some remote corner of the universe with only an occasional, over-the-shoulder glance to see what happens back on planet Earth. I have a real deep conviction that Whoever made you, Sir, is intimately involved with your life and has a deep concern for your welfare and your well-being. I think He cares about your wife and children or your husband and children. I think he cares about what's happening at your business. And the only barrier to your availing yourself to all the strength and beauty which God means for you to have—the only barrier— is your unwillingness to enter consciously into a continuing communication with the Creator, which we call prayer. The greatest man who ever lived is Jesus Christ. The secret of this man's power, characterized by gentleness, is His prayer.

September 1975

MOVEMENT

The amazing thing about life to me is its constancy. I've talked to you some about this river in Mississippi that ran right by my house and has been a significant influence, I guess as much as any single thing, this river has influenced my life. The continuing movement, the continuing flow, the continuing change; its depth and the fact that I spent a large part of my earlier years—the formative years of my life—by this river. And to me it's always been a picture of life. It's been a picture of the way a man starts his pilgrimage on this particular earth and moves from birth to death.

What I said in the introduction sounded a little pessimistic. That's not supposed to be pessimistic but rather explanatory. If you look at your own journey—and that's the thing I'd like for you to consider—**your** journey and not anyone else's, just your own. Start here with birth, let that be your point of beginning on this earth, and then move to the place we call death, where you leave life in this sphere and move into life into an eternal sphere. Now, there are some significant places and one is at five years—simply because here, school starts—For some it starts earlier, for some it starts later. There's another place that's significant, It's at twelve years—this is puberty, onset of menstruation for women, puberty for men. And there's a period at nineteen , where marriage occurs for some.—Incidentally, Telle and I have been married 30 years, last Friday. Had a long, serious talk, decided to try it thirty more and then evaluate—but we liked it. Let's see 5, 12, 19 years. Do you know that grandparents are getting younger? I've forgotten what the age norm is, I believe it's 37, for grandparents. Then somewhere here, there's and age called 65, which is changing, too. That's theoretically the age of retirement. Now what I want you to consider is where you are on this progression here. You may have started school early or later. You may have been in puberty early or later. May have gotten married early or later, that's not the thing. But you can look at this line and you can place yourself on this and know generally where you are. I am particularly interested in a group of people who are in this bracket right here. I know a lot of you consider you exciting and attractive people, and most of the people I know who are growing and finding challenge and thrill and excitement in life, but it really doesn't matter where you are along the road. Talked last week to a beautiful little gentleman, just seven years old. I was amazed at this young man's grasp of life and understanding of himself, no beyond his years. Not understanding, but appreciation. I think probably that this came because his parents had the capacity to appreciate life. But wherever you are, here, I'm especially interested.

I met with a group of people the other night in another city, and they all had children under eight, that's one of the characteristics of the group. And these people are interested I the kind of lifestyle they can discover for themselves that will give not only them a greater freedom to experience and enjoy life, but will also give to the kids. And kids under eight, I don't mean that kids over eight can't grow: I hope some over fifty can grow. But kids under eight, you still have a lot of time and a lot of exposure and a lot of opportunity with them.

And this time, between grandparenthood—or whatever you want to call it and retirement is significant, too. Now, I'm interested in this time between retirement and retirement and the time when you check out of existence and life as we know it here on this earth, and you enter into that other place where only one person has ever gone and returned—that was Jesus of Nazareth—no, two. Jesus raised Lazarus from the dead, but we have no account what Lazarus said or did after he had raised or how long he lived. I read a story one time about a Russian author. And the name of the story was "Lazarus." He used a lot of imagination, but after I'd read the story I was not sure what kind of life Lazarus had and was not promising.

But this is the point here, where you leave this planet but life does not cease. The life that was given to you by God when you were created in His image and born on this earth is eternal. You do live beyond the grave and all the promises we have and the greatest promise we have of this is "Hope." A man who lives without hope is all—man, most miserable thing, I think—I'm sure. This hope is an essential ingredient in our life.

Now the journey. The first thing I want to say here is, "Sir, and Madam, This thing moves. And if you think that it's not moving, you haven't looked in the mirror and you haven't looked at the calendar. We say, "One year ago, I was...Ten years ago I was..." and we even say, "Next year I hope to be...or five years from now..." or "I'll be through college, or I'll be through high school, or I'll have reached retirement or I'll have moved." That simply means that you're further away from this point and you're closer to this point. Now without the scare and the shouting that you hear from a lot of people, I would like to say–as gently and as kindly as I can–that your life is moving today–that it will end. One of the most beautiful memories that a person can have when you come to the end, is that you have lived it well, you haven't left a lot unfinished business. It's nice to keep your business current—your business with yourself, and your business with other people—and not have a day terminate with a lot of loose ends not tied together, and a lot of business not finished.

This is one of the things about good movement, when you can flow with the stream, when you can move with the current and take both the ebb and flow of life, then I'll guarantee you that you'll have a different quality of life from the people around you. One of the things about this river was that it was a challenge. I don't know how fast the current flowed–I would guess about two, three miles an hour– but one of the challenges was to get out in the middle of the river, and you could swim against the current. And if you swam real hard and real fast, you could hold your own against the current. That way you expended a lot of energy, but you didn't get anywhere—either upstream or downstream. I guess it was sort of a thrill or gave you some sense of elation, but you didn't go anywhere. It was a different journey when you got in the river, like we did sometimes, and started moving with the current and swim downstream, two, three, four miles, like kids do in some areas.

That seems like a long swim for me today, but the current did the work. But you moved with the stream and you saw new scenery and moved from one point to the other. I know some people who have been able to flow with life, to move with the stream of life, and who are experiencing and discovering an ease and gentleness and, incidentally, people who have achieved a productivity in life that seems to be denied to some. And when you meet these people, they have something that is lot of others don't have. One thing is that they can take the highs and the lows in the normal course of a person's life. There're going to be highs and lows, there're going to be days when you get up, you, and things don't go well at all. And some people are able to ride with the current and say, "Well, I've been here before, and I'm not particularly concerned about it, because this, too, shall pass away."

I was reminded the other day of a poem that I read and I think the name of the poem is "Even This Shall Pass Away." It starts something like this:

"Once in Persia reigned a King,
Who upon his signet ring
Graved a maxim true and wise,
Which, if held before his eyes,
Gave him counsel, at a glance,
Fit for every change or chance:
Solemn words, and these are they:
Even this shall pass away!"
Do you remember this in school?

Okay. When a person is able to experience the highs and lows in life—the good and bad, the times of health, the times of illness, the times of progression and the times of regression—and remember that this is not an eternal and constant thing, that even this shall pass away (both the positive and the negative, the good and bad) that man is equipped for living, or that woman.

The other day, a very, very pretty person walked into the office—I think her name was Mary. She said, "Hey, I haven't met you, but I'm in a Sunday school class that listens to your program"—one of the nicest gifts I had all week. We did not talk long, but she said she listened, had heard what I said about freedom and responsibility. And thank you for hearing. Then a lot of others did, too, and I like that. People who live with the ebb and flow of life, who move with the stream, have a capacity to hear and—I'm convinced—a deeper dimension of comprehension, than some of the other people.

The human body is so constructed that as it moves from birth to death, it changes. One reason that I'm convinced that death is not a stranger or alien—one of the reasons is because of the progressive changes that take place in the human body, and the body is not designed to live forever. It's designed–the body– to house your life for that period of time. I know some people make it a hundred years, my grandaddy did—a hundred and two. Some make it a hundred and ten, some a hundred and twenty—I guess. But as Carl Sandburg says, "Everything that is born–dies." And eventually your body will wear out and the best techniques that the embalmers can employ will not do anything to prolong the life in your body. Now to live in a state of harmony and peace with your body and to move your body along in the stream of people who surround you in any working pr playing day, and you will experience a different quality of life as compared with the quality of life a man knows who fights the flow, defies the movement, and stays in a state of turmoil and antagonism and hostility with himself and the people around him. One of the things about the ebb and flow of life, or the highs and lows, sickness and health, richness and poverty,

That's what I mean about ebb and flow—One of the things about people who stay there is they have more energy to give the creative and productive experience of living, and they don't waste as much energy of fighting against the stream—they don't fight windmills, they don't spend their times fighting phantoms. Gert Behannah, who's known by a lot of you, has an expression that is just beautiful. She talks about "crossing the river at its narrowest point." There's an old cliché which is more characteristic of the West than it is of a lot of other places in the United States. There's an old cliché about crossing the river. I mentioned this last week, I guess. But I had a good friend, who said, Sometimes there's nothing left to do but cross the river." Didn't understand this, but I talked to people who live in the West and I think it had to do with the early traffic and travel across the Western Plains. When you came to a river you could move up it, or you could move down it for a certain length of time. And then, there was nothing else to do and at some point than the cross the river. Gert talks about crossing the river at its narrowest pint. But some people choose to cross the river when it's at its highest, flooded stage, and they fight the current, and they risk the injury that comes from debris that's moving down the river during its flood tide. There are others who—in quieter, gentler, easier time—choose to tackle the more difficult tasks of life in an atmosphere of calm and quiet. And that's great—I am glad there are people like that! I've known a few, have even—sometimes on occasion—experienced this myself. One of the things about the movement here of the life span that you experience and enjoy on this earth, one of the things is growth is possible at any point, and it's possible at any place, and at any time. The body is designed to wear out, but one of the beautiful things about life is its designed to (with proper employment) recreate itself constantly and continually as you give yourself the opportunity for new experiences, new information, new understanding—and this is the basis of growth. Life doe move from the birth to the grave. But life is so designed that the grave cannot contain it.

Let me say that differently. You are designed in the image of God, that the grave cannot contain you. You're a life, there's no life apart from you, I mean as far as you and I are concerned. So, hold on to this fact, that you are so constructed and designed that you'll not spend eternity in a state of non-existence and non-being. But that you will spend your life in existence and eternity in the place of your choosing with the person of your choosing, and I think this is great. This is where the freedom comes–in that area of choice–this is where the authenticity comes in the area of responsibility when you live on this earth. So, I'm saying that the periods of time— that we outlined here on the board in the beginning— that these are significant growth places, can be for you and for those around you, and instead of being obstacles and hard times, they can be occasions and situations where you experience growth.

There's another thing that I want to say here, this movement includes the death of some, it includes the birth of some, and the constant that characterizes this journey—the only thing you can count on–is change. The capacity—I believe this is true—the capacity to accept a debt and capitalize on change, maybe the real secret of the people who have experienced the optimum, the ultimate in living. Fighting against change and trying to keep things as they were, the unwillingness to experience the joy of the present and the longing of the good old days characterizes people who are perpetually unhappy and continually dissatisfied with themselves.

Ther's a picture in the book of Revelation about a river. This picture describes the throne of God in of its magnitude and immensity being a symbol of the authority of God and the sovereignty of God, and the unlimited identity that God has as sovereign of the universe. It says a very strange thing—at **first** it's strange. It says that out from under the throne flows the waters of the River of Life and the waters are described as "living," which means they are alive and bubbling, not stagnant, they are opposite stagnant. Waters that give creative, vivacious, exciting living to the person who experience the relationship of God that puts him continually—listen—in contact with life at its source.

I believe that the source of life may be touched in its movement and may be experience in its change. If I understand this Man, Jesus of Nazareth, this was one of His secrets. He was always in contact with the source of life, and He was always in contact with the movement. I never see Him anywhere fighting against the movement or the progression of life and the source. He was not burdened by change, and He was not overly concerned—either with birth or death —except as it influenced His friends around Him. Stop for just a minute, and place yourself somewhere on the continuum–on this line–or one that you will draw. And then, if you look carefully, you will know exactly how much movement you have experienced, willing or unwillingly. And I want to say, Sir, whether you like or don't like it, it continues —whether you flow with it or fight against it, it continues–You have no control over this. It may be a step forward in your growth. To accept it as a fact, and to learn to live with it, and flow with it, and experience a different kind of inner peace and a sense of inner direction and a different kind of purpose. Jesus Christ got in the stream; this was God in the form of man. He got in the stream. He moved with it. He started here and moved to here, and then He moved beyond. So can I, and so can you—as did He.

September 1975

MEMORIES — HOPES

I want to talk to you about "memories and hopes" here on a "Place to Talk."

I kept those Christmas cards and kept them in a little basket in my study—I put it off— and I've started several times to go through it and last night was the time.

It was really something different. I felt like I had touched base with people and some of them in distant places and some nearby. I felt that I had spoken to them and had been spoken to. Some had written notes and I think that I'll do the same thing next year. I've done this for a couple of years. Christmas seems to be a rush season and we have a hurried, frantic pace; so, the cards do not register with me then like they do with me at another time. So, I thought that I would have Christmas in September (but I didn't put up a tree). But I really enjoyed them and I discarded them, and it's necessary for me to put them aside after I enjoy them the second time.

I said that I want to talk about memories and hope because this is where I spent some time specifically enjoying some memories. When the memories are selected by you and or by me, then that makes it a whole lot different ball game, and it gives you something, and it gives you control over what you remember. And it gives me control over what I'm remembering. And the memories can be joyful and sad.

One of the capacities of being a human being is selecting what you remember from the past. This is the beauty of being human and this is the beauty of being in contact with yourself. And knowing what capacities and faculties that you have for thought and reflection and reasoning, and so you take your time that you want to remember, and you pick the experiences that you want to remember, and you use this as a time for reflection and for celebration and for enjoyment, and for excitement even. Now I want to draw a diagram on the board because this "memories and hopes" is something that I have been working with and been enjoying, and I have been doing it in a context of what we call a "norm."

If you take your life and have it functioning between these two lines and we'll put up here this will be a high and this will be a low. We will refer this to an "emotional high and an emotional low." If you want to use other words, it can be "excited and depressed," it can be "thrilled and dejected." But if you will look at your life as the time you live between this line which will be—we'll call these two lines a happy, helpful living and this is the "norm" right here. You notice that I didn't say "normal," people usually say normal, but it generally applies to something that a person has not achieved. I wish I were normal in this area, or I think that I'm abnormal. (I think that we over-work this word.) It may be that being normal may not be living on a straight line here, like this. It may be that life for most of us is a series of experiences where we experience life somewhere within a given framework, and I do not mean that it has to always be bound by these two lines. But somewhere here, maybe your life for a while goes on like this and some people reach a plateau. It may move up like this and sometimes it may make huge deviations like that, but the freedom and the experience of living life within a framework, where you function safely for yourself and happily with other people and this is what we call a "norm." I want you to think about the "norm" of your life and the ways that you preserve it while we're talking about it this morning.

Now I want to say at the beginning, I believe that this man Jesus Christ established a "norm" for Himself which regulated His life, but did not limit it or restrict it. Because He found a "norm" that regulated His life, anything was possible; He was a free man. Because He respected the limits of His "norm," He had no limitations. That's true of you and true of me, and it's true of every man that lives in the world as a person and who functions in the presence of other people. This is important, know the "norm" is here and the memories that you select within your "norm," memories move back this way, your hopes project into the future.

I submit that your ability to live within your "norm'" may be in part be the way you determine selectively and when these memories are selected, they are memories that enhance and enforce you as a person. Then you're living within the "norm." When your hopes for the future are realistic and when you set goals that are within your reach, when you give up the idea of perfection for yourself, then you're living with the "norm," and I want to say again that Jesus said, "**Be** ye therefore perfect," but He never said **do** perfect. And there's just a whole lot of difference between His word and His meaning—being perfect and doing perfect. I do not believe that in any sense of the word, that Jesus expected you or me to be morally, ethically, spiritually, socially, perfect in every way. Growth, yes, and affection, no.

I have a group of friends who has a slogan, "The program is a program of progression, not perfection." So, if you are progressing in this life, you are –in the sense of the word– are already perfect. This will set you free from a lot of failures, a lot of anxiety, and a lot of ulcer work. When you give up the idea of being perfect and if you 're one of these individuals who says, "I'm a perfectionist," it may be time for you to stop kidding yourself. A perfectionist not only succeeds in making himself miserable, he, generally, makes the people around him miserable. Now, this is what I want to talk to you about living in the "norm" and giving up the whole idea of perfectionism.

Selectively using your memories and your hopes in order to enhance the style of life that you have chosen. You choose your lifestyle; it's not thrust upon you. You are in charge and you can control the quality of life that you experience each day. One of the first problems here or one of the important things in living within the "norm," and choosing the lifestyle; one of the important things is when the person gives up the idea that he has to do perfectly and that he has to speak perfectly, that he has to achieve the ultimate in his profession. I do not mean that he will not grow and succeed, (I'm not talking about that), but when you set for yourself goals that are impossible for a person to achieve, what you really do is to guarantee yourself unhappiness.

Now, you can start at this point, you can say that I realize that I will never be loved and respected and admired by every significate other person within the circle of my friends and acquaintances. Everybody won't like you, you will not be admired and trusted and revered and respected by everyone. Jesus Christ Himself wasn't. If you have everybody liking you and not one single enemy, you've done one or two things: You've deceived yourself or you have achieved a goal higher than that set by Jesus Himself. It is very good for me to remember that He chose twelve, and two flunked the course. Well, I don't know if you say that two flunked the course, they did at one time. In fact, at one time all of them flunked. And if He could not pick twelve friends—or **did** not pick twelve friends and all of them remain faithful, then the possibility is that you won't do any better than He did. (He was a pretty successful man).

I do not read anywhere in scripture that he beat Himself up for choosing Judas.

I do not read anywhere in scripture that He said, "How could I have been so stupid?"

I don't even read where He said, "How could you hurt me like this?" I'm submitting to you that He lived within the "norm," that He had hopes and memories and that He did not entertain either the reflections of His past or His anticipation of Golgotha . If He did not entertain either of these, I'd cite the "norm" of reasonable living and reasonable expectation. I'm speaking primarily of people, this morning, who are hung up on this business of being perfect. Instead of requiring impossible goals for yourself today—instead of requiring impossible goals and standards for yourself today, how about requiring two things of yourself today? Maybe something like friendliness toward the family. Maybe something like adequate rest and food for myself. That may be simple and that may be basic, but you watch and make a check on the wall to measure the number of days that you adequately take care of your physical body, and that you adequately take care of those around you emotionally, socially, mentally. Know that's living within the "norm" and that's reasonable expectation for you in one 24-hour period.

Then, on Monday morning when you go to work you might decide that today I'm going to work eight hours at my job, I'm going to give myself mentally, physically, and emotionally—if your job is a kind of job you can give yourself emotionally to. And I'm going to make my work today an extension of myself; I'm going to make my work an expression of my creativity—the capacity to make things, to create things, to bring forth ideas, to evoke responses in people—I'm going to make my eight hours on the job today a time when I really give myself creatively and productively to the world. This is living within the "norm."

Watch to see the points to where your line swings up here and you achieve above your "norm." You experience emotions, responses, and awards beyond your "norm." Watch the times where you really exceed and out-do yourself—and these times come to everybody. It's good that they come, it's the time when in memory you look back and say, "Boy, that was a great day! It was when I was crowned Homecoming Football Queen (and they gave me a dozen roses). It's the time when they called me in and said we are proud of you, and it's the time when I got this telephone call or when a friend rang my doorbell. Or when my wife said to me or my son or my daughter...." It's a high moment in a person's life and you take this moment and you store it up and you make it a memory. You probably will not remember the smaller experiences in ever day living. You can selectively put that in your memory bank and look back on it when you have need to reinforce yourself as a person.

The capacity for selective memory is rarely used, but it is a valuable tool and I highly recommend it to you. Now, if you have one or two or three of these in your life—and if you have more than three, sir, you' re rich. This is also the basis of hope. When you selectively remember that there have been good times in the past and that there have been good moments. Then you can take this and project it in the future and say, "I have the hope that there is more hope for me ahead than there has been in the past.

One of the friends that God has left me with had gotten a 20-year loan on a home when he was sixty-five, bought a new house for himself for his new bride—and he bought a red convertible. And they spent a lot of time in this red convertible in front of their new home—(I mean going to and from it, not in front of it). But, some people might have called him a silly old man. But he's got more living. If I could measure another man's life, he has experienced more qualitative joy from 65 to 80 than a lot of us experience the first fifty years of our life. His goals are realistic. I think I mentioned one time before, he decided that he wanted to play the piano and started taking piano at 65. I don't know how well he played, he never played for me. He decided after he had been taking piano that he had abilities as an artist. So, he started painting, and I have a painting in my house that this man painted and gave to me, and I have been very grateful for it. In fact, I have two and one is a new friend.

This reasonable expectation for oneself and one's future. Reasonable, realistic goals. I want to use another word for reasonable. Goals that lay within the norm, so that one can accomplish and achieve these goals without sacrificing the basic essentials of life. The basic essentials of life to which I refer. Adequate care for oneself physically, mentally, emotionally, and spiritually (and stay with that just a minute), when you are taking care of your own body and your own needs physically, mentally, emotionally, and spiritually, first. Second, when you are taking care of the physical and emotional needs of those for whom you are responsible. An emotional responsibility is just as legitimate as physical responsibility. You haven't been a good daddy when you just feed your children, clothe them, and house them—animals do that for a whole litter of them. Not until you have provided for the emotional needs of your son or daughter, have you really been a father and have you really been a mother. Some parents let their children starve to death emotionally and call themselves good parents. I think another word for it is mental cruelty. And I would like you to hear me if you hear anything I say. The main thing that your child may need is some love and affection and some touching. If you do not know how to love and touch a child, for God's sake learn—and I say that reverently—and for your sake learn and for the child's sake learn, and for the sake of all humanity learn. Don't let your ·child grow up untouched, unloved, uncared for, and if you do you, are rearing an emotional cripple in your home, whether you're the mother or the father. Caring for your own needs first, caring for the emotional needs around you, second; then you can produce and create within these lines by still doing and still doing these other fixing things. Say, you can take care of yourself and take care of those who are around you and function in this line easily.

Now, you have to watch and everybody has to decide for himself because you can't speak with authority about what goes on in every person's life, but it may be here that when you are high here in levels of achievement, that you are neglecting the people around you and neglecting your own physical, emotional, spiritual, and mental needs. It's also true when you're on a real low, down here, that you are neglecting the needs of the people around you.

There will be times when you will be here, there may be times that you are here. The important thing is where the swing takes you back you don't worry too much about being here, you don't worry too much about being here. These tentacles of achievement, experience, accomplishment, hope, and joy: that's the icing on the cake. That's the good part of life and you enjoy it, thank God for it, and experience it. These low times of depression, fear, anxiety, grief, doubt, uncertainty, or whatever form that they make take in your life. They will pass. You've probably been to places like this before and it will pass—it will pass and you will have better times and better days like this. The willingness to make the choice, and it **is** a choice, to live within the "norm;" it is a decision that lies in your grasp. This is one of the privileges that God has given you. Animals don't have it; animals have instinct and they have been driven and motivated by this instinct. But you have intellect and motion and you have the capacity to make this decision and that's one of the beauties of life and one of the beauties of being a human being.

When you're taking care of yourself and your own needs—when you're taking care of your needs emotionally and physically required— the needs of those around you, you're in business, then you're free to be creative and productive. You're faced sometimes to exceed the limits of your "norm" in achievement or in sadness and grief and you'll recover. And you'll find the guilt and take the ebb and flow of life within the bounds of your health and your happiness and your security that's the "norm."

At this point you'll find yourself free to be selective in the events and experiences which, in the past, gave you comfort and hope. You'll also find yourself free to anticipate good times in the future and to look forward to moments, events, and experiences which you cannot get in point in time and place, which you know will surely come. That way you don't have to grasp the past and always hold onto something that must, of necessity, slip your grasp. And this is why Jesus Christ could live on this earth 33 1/2 years without anxiety, without worry and depression, could live with death looking Him squarely in the face. I heard an old country preacher one time say that Jesus lived his whole life looking down the barrel of a loaded gun. And He did, but He never lived frightened. He was never controlled by fear and anxiety. He, on the other hand, possessed a certain sure, quiet confidence in Himself, faith in God and an almost child-like trust in His fellow man, knowing that some would do him in, but that others would love him.

July 1975

RELATIONSHIP

Rebuilding the patio, I talked to you about and the bricks that I moved, I put back in another form. I've done a lot of work in the alley behind my house, moving sand and moving dirt, and I've learned something about myself I didn't know: the same thing applies to human beings in other situations. There's a fellowship, There's a closeness, and there's a unity of some kind that exist between human beings in similar situations. I was dressed in my jeans and work clothes and most of the time wet with perspiration, and people stopped and talked with me and smiled and waved. They would not have done it, if I had been dressed another way, or in a different situation downtown. I was hauling some dirt in the back of my pickup, and a man driving a larger truck had been going up and down the alley. I had to move each time he came; he stopped and apologized for interrupting my work. I thought this was a very thoughtful gesture, he didn't have to do it but he did, because he had the right-of-way. He had the right-of-way simply because of the fact he was the biggest, you know.

On the lake, fishing, there's sort of a spirit of kinship or oneness that exists between fishermen. You speak to other fishermen, and you wave at them, and you respond to them simply because of the fact that you're doing the same thing at the same time. And they know who you are and what you 're doing and know where you are. I've noticed that the same feeling exist very strongly among schoolteachers. I don't know what it is you schoolteachers think you have in common, but it's there. n also applies to construction workers, it also applies to construction workers, it applies to business and profession men and men who are in the same profession or professions related to each other. I've noticed that housewives and mothers seem to have a common feeling and a common language that binds you together when you are parked in front of the school picking up children, or when you are taking them downtown shopping and places like this. People in doctors' offices, too, seem to have a closeness. This is sort of an unspoken thing. When I've waited in a doctor's office to see a doctor, I see other people there; they respond to me, and I respond to them in a different way. We—each one of us—know why the other one is there. I don't know if human beings change with these particular situations, but there is an acknowledged oneness of purpose that ·gives people a closeness and intimacy that we don't allow ourselves to have at other times.

I think the way we dress has a lot to do with this. I've been amazed at the way clothing identifies people. The kind of clothing a person wears gives him a -sort-of identity in our society, as much or more so than any of the other countries that I've visited. Not long ago—no it's been about three or four years—I was fishing one summer on vacation, and I was with my family, I was living on a small island. There was nobody else on this island, just the family and I went into town one day to get some groceries. I'd run out of money; so, I'd wired home for some money, and got a Western Union check, and went into town to get groceries we needed. I had on a pair of blue jeans cut off just below the knees, and I had on an old shirt with the sleeves torn off it, and the sleeves were raveled and ragged. And I had on an old floppy hat, and I was bare footed. I didn't expect to see anybody I knew; I hadn't been wearing shoes all week on the island anyway. I had some identification, had a driver's license, and credit card, when I went to the check-out stand. A woman looked at me and she looked at this Western Union check, and she said, "I can't cash this."

I said, "Well, I have identification. A car with a license plate on it,—it matches my other identification, and she looked at me again, looked at the way I was dressed, she didn't look in my face, she didn't look in my eyes. She looked at the way I was dressed and she said, "I can't cash this."

I said, "I want to speak to the manager."

She said, "The manager's not here."

"Well, somebody's in charge of this place and I want to talk to him;" I said, "furthermore, I know the man that owns this whole chain of stores, and if you don't cash my check, I'll call him then."

She said, "I don't care whether you call him or not, I'm not going to cash your check." She let me speak to the manager or whoever he was, and he looked at the check and he looked at the way I was dressed and never looked at my face, or my hands or anything.

He looked at the check and he looked at my clothing, and he said, "No Sir, we will not cash this check." And I said, "I know the man that owns this chain of stores, and I'm going to call him on the phone."

He said, "Go right ahead."

I called and the rascal wasn't home, he was probably fishing, too. But I had to go back to Western Union, which was quite a distance across the city, and get that check cashed and get cash in my hand, before I could buy what I wanted. I've noticed that people who are suspicious of the way we're dressed when it comes to cashing checks are not suspicious of taking cash, if you have the cash money, your clothing is all right. But I was made aware all over again, I became aware of the importance of dress and the identification of persons in our society.

Now, I know it shouldn't be that way, but that's one of the ways we measure people. I think in a lot of businesses people wear uniforms simply to identify them as a member of a business, or a member of an agency or school. Some no longer require the kind of uniform that they used to. Is this simply in your opinion is this simply to avoid facing the individual is it because we want a quick—being in a hurry— we want a quick way of identifying a person and in our mind, placing him in a category, or putting him in a box. I think sometimes it is.

The one thing that I wanted to talk to you about directly is there is a fellowship of suffering. Generally, it's most obvious in a hospital and people in hospitals have a closeness and a warmth that you don't find in other places. This fellowship of suffering brings people closer together, and it allows our compassion to surface. When people have similar pain, ,similar affliction, similar handicap. It draws them closer together. I wondered a lot of times, why was it necessary for Jesus Christ to suffer—Until I look at the suffering that takes place in the world on this earth, and then I know. I don't understand why, but I know it happened in a very real way for a very real purpose.

People in mental hospitals don't have the kind of fellowship that people have in other experiences where they go through periods of suffering. One thing about mental suffering is, it does not draw you close to other mental sufferers. But I've noticed that after people have gotten out of the mental hospital, when they find someone else has been there, there's immediately an identification and a smile, a laugh, and a nod or something like that: A fellowship is established. But the trauma of mental suffering is destructive and it separates, and it drives us away from people, rather than to them. After it's over, and the person has emerged from this period of trauma, then it's a different matter entirely.

Grief seems to draw us closer together. Grief has a way of bringing families close together. And the pain sometimes draws us close together. But I noticed physical or mental pain rarely brings us closer to other people unless we are in a position where we can help a person in pain; or where the person who is near us can help us. It depends on whose bearing the pain. After the pain is over, and after the immediate crisis has subsided, then there's a fellowship, there's a closeness, and warmth. There is a fellowship of worship 'that exists between people who are drawn together in a common experience of worshiping God. And this fellowship most of the time is experienced in corporate worship. I think we make really too big a thing of this denominational bit. I've chosen a particular denomination and I've chosen to worship there, and I like it, it's mine. But if the particular form of worship I choose separates me from other Christians, then I have to come to the conclusion, that either this other person's wrong and I'm right, or the other person is right and I'm wrong. What I'm saying is, that anything that comes between human beings and separates them, creating doubt, mistrust, fear, and suspicion, is not the work of the creator. It's something that's anti, that's opposed to everything that God had In mind for human beings when he put us on this earth and made us members of a of family. You grew up as a child, with a mother and a father, and probably brothers and sisters. You belong to this family and it was your physical identity and your physical ties with these people that made you a member of this family. You had a father and a mother and you owed them authority, and you had maybe brothers and sisters and you owed them allegiance, now after you became an adult, you no longer owe obedience to that father and that mother: respect–yes, honor–yes, love–yes, obedience–no. This is hard for some parents to accept. it's hard for some parents to take. But, one of the earmarks of the successful parent is that children grow up and move away and become independent.

> Man, if your child is still clinging to you at 21, 22, 25 or 30 years old, there's something wrong with you. And one of the ways to find out what it is to sit down with a friend and see why you haven't let this child go, so he can determine his own particular lifestyle and make his own .choices. The way— you were probably making yours by the time you were this age. The fellowship of this family is affirmed only if the individual members of the family

can move away from this fellowship and establish their own family and another fellowship of their own choice. If a person can only move in one fellowship, a fellowship of a fisherman, or a fellowship of the working, or the fellowship of the suffering, or the tennis players; if you can only move in this circle, your life stagnates.

Mental health, as I understand it—happy, productive, free living—is measured by a person's ability to move, from one fellowship, or from one group, or from one activity to another. So that you today from 8 to 5 you have one identity. After 5 you have another identity; you move into a new group, you are a carpenter from 8 to 5, but then after 5, from 5 to 9, you're a friend who goes to a home and you get together around a piano and you sing, or you do something like that. or you go home and you belong to the fellowship of the television viewers. But your identity changes. It's the same way Sir, with the members of your family. When you are willing to allow your children, or when you are willing to insist that your children become independent, autonomous, self-supporting and experience the freedom of knowing choice, then that child is about to live happily, helpfully, and productively in society.

Now, one of the things about belonging to the human family is that we have a choice of coming into another family. A man has a choice of belonging to the family of God. And you can, if you choose, and it is a deliberate choice, I think—I'm sure it's a deliberate choice. You have a choice of belonging to the family of God, and you take the life that is yours, and you give it to God thereby identifying yourself as a member of a new and different family or fellowship. You move from the fellowship of the human family into the fellowship of the family of God.

Here's what happens. You make God your father by choice. He was your father in creation, and He made you, and He is spiritually your father. And, He is your heavenly father now by choice. When you do this, all of God's other children become your brothers and sisters, and you now belong to a new and different family.

And do you know what? The family in which you are with your human father and mother is built to self-destruct; the family of God is built to last forever. The family into which you were born is a temporary family and the relationships are temporary; and you are there only until you can find enough strength emotionally, physically, and mentally to be on your own.

The family of God is so structured and so designed that you in this family retain your freedom and your own integrity, but you don't leave the family. And your relationship with your brothers and sisters is strengthened by love, forgiveness, a common hope, a common acceptance and a common experience of forgiveness and sharing and caring. Now this fellowship is creative, and it's productive. It is the most healing, hopeful fellowship you'll ever have on this earth. It's stronger than the fellowship of fishermen, the fellowship of schoolteachers, the fellowship of law enforcement officers, or the fellowship that exists between members of certain professions. This fellowship is the only relationship you can have on this earth that will last beyond death. This fellowship is the only common relationship you'll have with other people that lasts beyond this life. This kind of fellowship is one where you experience the awareness that you belong to God and that God belongs to you, and you belong to every other person who belongs to God. And every other person belongs to God and belongs to you—those who are already dead, and those Christians yet unborn, you belong to God, and you belong to them, and they belong to you. And this gives you a special place on this earth, it gives you a special identity in the universe. It means that now in a whole, totally different way, you matter. It means so very definitely that other people matter.

Now here's where relationships change. You see, if you and I are brothers and sisters in this new fellowship, then I have to care about you, I have to forgive you when you make mistakes, and I have to accept you in the areas where you are inadequate and incomplete as an individual. If I belong you cannot treat me with scorn or condescension, or prejudice. If you belong to God, and therefore to this fellowship, and if I belong, then I matter to you and you matter to me. And when I acknowledge this, and when you acknowledge this, even though we don't wear a particular uniform, I have a deeper feeling of oneness and intimacy and closeness with you. Then when I see you working in the alley shoveling sand or dirt, I've a deeper feeling of closeness and intimacy with you, then when I meet you in the hospital and say, Oh, do you have someone here?" Or have a deeper feeling of closeness and intimacy than one person has with another, when they're both hitch-hiking down the road going from someplace to somewhere. This is a fellowship that transcends, exceeds, and surpasses every other fellowship that two human beings can know.

And this is a fellowship that is strengthened as each individual establishes his own independence. This kind of fellowship does not foster a sick, helpless dependency. This fellowship, the fellowship of God—which is called, incidentally, the Body Of Christ—This fellowship encourages a person to be independent and autonomous as a person. And the more independent and autonomous he becomes the closer he is able to come to his followers.

There is no relationship that you can have, that exceeds the relationship, which comes when two individuals–each of them independent, self-governing, free, and self-confident—stand face-to-face and choose to share—choose to love, choose to care, choose to trust, choose to believe—when these two people stand in this fellowship and they make a conscious decision to leave the other person free, each of them makes a decision to leave the other person free, and they make a conscious decision to give to the other person the respect of trust, to believe his word, even when there's a disagreement, to believe in his worth and value even when there's a difference in race, or culture, or ethnic or social background. This is the way that Jesus of Nazareth dealt with people. He had an identification with a lot of people. But his strongest identification was with the individual with whom he stood face to face, in a spiritual deep communion that bound him to them.

August 1975

MARRIAGE RELATIONSHIP

One of the relationships that I've had most exposure to in the past several years is the relationship that two people find when they come to a place of impasse; there are places in life between people in almost any kind of relationship where things just seem to come to a stop. We call this "a standoff," and it seems at this point the relationship cannot go any further.

Sometimes it happens between husbands and wives. There's a sort of strange silence or deafening silence. The husband stays in his position and decides he will not give another inch, and the wife stays in her position and decides she will not give an inch; sometimes they feel that they've done all they can. It happens sometimes between parents and children. And I've seen them say, I' can't go any further, I will not go any further." Sometimes we say, "I will not stand for this another minute; I've had all I can take; I'm fed up to here." It happens sometimes between employers and employees. I don't mean just angry people. I'm talking about people who really have had good relationships in the past or who desire to have good relationships, but the press of schedule or routine or the intensity of emotion at other times the burden of performance, the limitations of a contract, all of these or some of these things work together to bring relationships— between the husband and wives, parents and children, and employers and employees, between friend and friend, between customer and salesman— bring these relationships to a halt.

The question that I hear most frequently in this particular situation is "What can be done?" Initially— this is kinda funny — initially the one or both persons want to fix blame which is one of the ways that you just intensify the problem. Ther's no good that come from fixing the blame. One person becomes right the other wrong; one person is justified the other person's condemned so there's no virtue, no value there. and the more you, at this stage enter into the

"It's his fault. It's your fault, It's not my fault" conversation, the more you intensify the problem or the more you escalate the relationship.

I want to deal with some solutions and talk about some tools that you can use if you are at this place, and I especially would like for you, sire, if you are in trouble with your wife, or ladies, if you are in trouble with your husbands. I'd like you to give some attention to what's said here. It may help, though I'll never know you and you'll never know me personally, there's a real possibility that some of these things which have been tried and proven in other areas can change the course of your life and possibly prevent some real tragedy. Now if you watch this and give it some sort of credence and understanding, it may be that you'll have a different place in life. This will be particularly relevant for parents and children where an impasse has come about. And if you are interested in a better relationship with your son or daughter, it might be worthwhile.

The first thing that's necessary is to face up to the facts or acknowledge where you are. Now this is calling it like it is. Let's deal primarily with husband and wife right now. If this is between you and your wife, you want to move toward a solution, sit down and say, "We're in a bad place." Or it might be best when you acknowledge it to use the word "I"—do not use the word "You." Use the word "We" sparingly and one of the ways to open this is to say, "I feel that we are at an impasse, I feel shut out, I fell unloved or I feel unwanted," or whatever you feel, and then come to grips with it and say, "We're at a bad place and my feeling is..." or "I feel that the marriage is not going to last."

More marriages are failing today than at any time in the history of our country and the failures are on the increase. One of the ways to prevent a failure in your marriage is to start here, acknowledge that "I'm in a bad place, I don't like this thing and I don't see any hope for it here." Honesty is the cornerstone of the relationship where you moved to get beyond it. Tell it like it is and call it, not say

"You," but say, "I feel, I want, I need, I wish, I like." Now after you acknowledge where you are, you can begin to move beyond it.

After you acknowledge that the automobile is out of gas, you can take some steps to go get some more gas. After you acknowledge the car is stuck or the motor is burned up, or it has four flat tires, then you can begin to do something about it. The next thing you can do is to ventilate. Now, I want to be very specific here because you can be hurt unless you use this with caution. When I say ventilate, where you say up here where you have acknowledged this and where I feel we are. Down here you say these are my feelings. Here there's a definite need for honesty in the first person and you stick with the "I."—"I feel lost, I feel unloved, I'm angry, I'm sad, I'm depressed." It may be–I say this very carefully and very cautiously– please use it this way, it may be that there are times when you'll need to say, "I hate, and "I resent," if you'll use the word "I" and leave off the word "You," you may possibly be able to clarify the relationship at this point, instead of muddying the waters.

The basic requirement for rebuilding a relationship is honesty on the part of both parties. And when you're willing to be honest about your feelings with the other person and the other person is willing to be honest about his feelings about you, this is the beginning of the solution. It's the first in chopping your way out of the jungle. So, acknowledge where you are first, then express your true deep feelings; it really doesn't matter what they are. Now you may have a tough time believing this, but it doesn't really matter. If you're having trouble with your school principal or one of your teachers, if you're having trouble with an employee in your organization, or if you're having trouble with an employer.

Now there are situations where this will not work, and I expect you to use your own judgement because it would be impossible for me to know everything about everybody who's listening to this telecast. If you're angry with your employer and he's very volatile and doesn't like to talk and doesn't want to discuss anything, this will be of no value. I'd suggest you find you a better job and better employer regardless of the pay, because you are probably not making enough money to compensate for the personal loss that the job is inflicting on you. I know some people who stick with jobs that are destructive because they think they have to make a living. In this country there are other jobs available. One of the saddest things in the world would be for a person to spend his whole life working on a job he did not like, performing a task he did not approve of— you spend your whole life, and your life would be over, and you've spent your whole time here on earthy doing something you didn't enjoy. So, there are exceptions to what I am saying. What I want you to consider is that if your job is healthy and if the relationship is healthy you can probably acknowledge with your employer or employee however valuable he or she might be to you, acknowledge that you're in a bad place and then say, "These are my feelings about it."

Again, let the feelings come out, let them be honest and bring them out in a clear articulate straightforward manner. If you or the other person needs to say, "I hate you; I'm angry with you; I wish I'd never started this job; I wish we'd never gotten married; I wish I'd never entered into a contract with you." That's all right, it doesn't really matter because this is just a beginning and this must be brought out in the open.

I keep wanting to cover up my tracks or be cautious, here you'll have to use your own good judgment about this and use it cautiously. I know this works I've seen it work with people. Now, but when you do this and you keep saying, "I feel and I don't feel it the word "you," leave it out. That's where the trouble starts and every time you use the word "you" you're getting back into the problem instead of moving into the solution.

At this point it's good to remember a slogan that a group of people I know have, It's where you say, "The winners live in the solution; the losers live in the problem." You might ask yourself, "Where am I living? Am I loving in the problem or am I living in the solution?"

It's not polite to talk about hogs or pigs because we don't generally consider this a very polite topic of conversation, but we used to have pigs when I was growing up. Then they go bigger, they got to be hogs, one thing about pigs is they like to wallow in the mud. It seems to be a part of their life. I don't know what you do when pigs are raised in a different manner today; I don't know what they do about a wallow. But there are some people who wallow in problems. If you don't know what wallow is, it is a mud hole that the hog gets out of and gets dry, then he come back and gets back in. I guess it's one of the ways he keeps himself cool. There are some people who are this way with their problems. They never get too far from the problem.

Some of you might in your acknowledgment need to recognize that you like the problem, and if you didn't have this problem you really wouldn't know now to live. This could be one of the ways to ventilate and you honestly say, "I've lived with this problem so long, I don't know that I want to live without it." If your husband is drinking excessively and you're being a perpetual martyr, you might not really want him to quit drinking, although you say you do. If you have a child that's a behavior problem and you talk about it all the time and you pray about it all the time, it might be that you don't really want to give it up. Either you live in the problem or you live in the solution. The winners live in the solution; the losers live in the problem.

Now that's the prelude, hold it. This is the way you go about the change. With two or more people involved this is your part. Incidentally, you can do this in some situations whether the other person changes or not. Here's the first step in living in the solution. How can I change? Now the emphasis is on the "I." It's not an "if you change, I will… and if you don't change, I will…and if you don't change, I will not… and if you do change…I will not."

That's not the thing. If you're working on a solution and you're looking for some way out of the wilderness of an impasse or a misunderstanding, then the first question for you is how will you change? I mean **you** there. If it's where I'm involved, I've got to ask myself "How will I change?" No, I don't mean some change in feeling, but I mean something specifically—"I will stop… and I will start…"—now that's an example.

You might say, "I will stop screaming at my husband or my wife or my son or daughter. I will stop nagging."—There's another word for nagging, I've forgotten what it was but you might know it.—"I will stop criticizing. I will stop spending too much money. I will stop going int debt. I will stop overdrawing the bank account. I will stop sleeping late. I will stop going to bed early." …Whatever is necessary to bring about the change that will build a new relationship between husband, wife, son, or daughter or whoever is at an impasse.

This is the first step. It's necessary to say, "Okay, I'll stop doing this," and the second step is "I'll start." Usually the "start" can be identified from the "stop." Now it doesn't have to be done in this order, and these two words might not be the way you make your change.—These are examples.

So, if I decide to stop nagging, or criticizing my wife, I can start complimenting her. In Transactional Analysis terminology, we call it stroking. So instead of coming home and saying, "Is the all we have for supper?" I'll make up my mind before I get to the house that I'm going to say, "Gee, you look pretty," or "Gee, the house is clean," or the lawn is mowed or the house has been vacuumed or something, and I will find something positive and I will make this change even though I do not feel the change. I will change the behavior and the change in feelings will come later.

First change the behavior and the feelings will change themselves. If you wait for the feelings to change first, you'll be here until the world looks blue and nothing will happen. I will stop criticizing. I will stop nagging. I will stop mistrusting; I will start trusting, even when I fear I will be wrong. Fear is a real detriment to change. I said in the beginning of the program, one thing is constant; that is change. One thing is certain, everything will change but God, thank God. But everything else is in the process of change. So, when You get ready to work yourself out of this impasse or out of this dilemma, the first thing is, how can you change and there has to be willingness here. But even if there isn't a willingness, you could just be gambler, you could take a chance. What have you got to lose? Go ahead and try it.

The second thing in the solution—and living in the solution—the second thing is after you change, you ask the question, "How will I be different? If I change, how will I be different?? Now, this is the way you measure yourself, It's not the way you prove it to anybody else or it's not the way you check anybody else's change. This is the way you check yourself; you see all I'm talking about really is you. Because you're the only person whose life you change, the only thing you change on earth really, is yourself. You can't change another person, and as long as you try, you're sentencing yourself to a lifetime of confusion, frustration, and turmoil. When you change and you stop this and you start doing that, how would you be different?

Here at this point, it's necessary to be realistic. One thing–it's very simple. How about this: "well, I'll smile more." You may have to work on that; some people haven't had a lot of experience and haven't had a lot of practice. "I will laugh more." I know many who decided he was going to live more in the solution and this man kept a small metal pad that he made out of aluminum with a spring clip on it, about the size that would fit in the palm of his hand, and he carried a pencil in a shirt pocket. He actually tallied the number of times a day that he laughed and in the beginning nothing was on the pad at the end of the day. Now this man is known as a jolly, happy person who worked at it. He laughed even though he didn't feel it, and his laugh at time was hollow and empty and almost embarrassing, but he changed his life, by not following these steps but following a similar program. If you change how will you be different? Visible, observable, tangible ways: I will smile more; I will laugh more. I will listen when people talk; I will play golf once or twice a week, or tennis, or swim, I will work in the yard, or I will help my wife in the house, or I will start going to church, or I will stop drinking excessively— These two things here will also work in this area.

I have seen people change what could possibly be considered an impossible, hopeless relationship. I've seen these relationships change. I know some marriages where the husband and wife have a new quality of love and a new depth in their relationship that they never had before, and they've moved to this point from a place of absolute hopelessness and despair.

Hey, you can do the same thing if you're willing to work at it. First you acknowledge where you, can't move anywhere until you do, then you express your true feelings using the words "I feel." Then you ask yourself, "What am I willing to change?" Then you say, "After I change, How will I be different?" I don't think it's a mistake that God in His infinite wisdom saw fit to put us in a world of change. One of the shocking things that happened to us recently is that we discovered how truly infinite this universe is, although it's still finite.

We've discovered, too, that if we could travel with the speed of light, we would never live long enough to even explore the universe in which we live, much less populate it, or conquer it. We have a different concept of the world in which we live, with this we have a different concept of who we are, and who other people are. The concept of change is one of the constant factors in understanding the human personality and particularly in understanding yourself.

God made you this way. I's not an accident, and change works for you. You see, God created you as a creature of change, living in an environment that is constantly changing, it's a part of God's plan. It's a part of God's purpose. Aging is change, and aging is a part of God's plan.

Changing of the seasons—the passing of time is part of God's plan. Jesus Christ, Himself, lived in a state of constant and continuing change. He grew. He aged. He changed. You're in charge of your life, as you choose you can change what is necessary for you, what is good and positive in your life, all these changes you can make.

July 1975

MARRIAGE RELATIONSHIP WITH GOD

Hey! I was writing down a few things that I was wanting to tell you about, and I thought of a story. I told a story a couple of Sundays ago and I don't have the source for these so if you have the source, I'd be glad to hear it and write it down. But this story was told about a pleasure boat in some corner of the earth remote from Texas, it's a pleasure boat that ran aground on a small island near the mainland. It seems that the fog had been heavy, and the night had been dark, and the pleasure boat had run aground. Next morning when all the passengers had all gotten safely ashore, they discover two priests living on the island there. Except for them the island was uninhabited. The priests could not speak, their clothes were in rags and some of the passengers were indignant, and it seems that they concluded at least that years ago that the priest had taken a vow of poverty and silence and they lived on this island to minister to the villagers who have moved along with the migratory movement of the fish.

The primary occupation of the island was fishing and the priest not being able to communicate with superiors or the communication not being effective, had remained on the island faithful to the vows that they had taken and faithful to the charge and had lived in the level of existence just barely above starvation. So, when the travelers were rescued, one went back to the mainland, talked to the bishop and the bishop came over personally and investigated the situation with the two priests. He stayed with them several days and released them from their vow of silence but was unable to make a change in assignment without the approval of his superiors. (Oh, he came over in a rowboat, I forgot to tell you that).

And after he talked with the priests, he and they learned to say a few words. He taught them the Lord's Prayer just as an exercise for their vocal chords which had been silent for so long. So, the bishop went down with the determination, with the responsibility of two priests, and the bishop went down and got in the rowboat and the hired man started rowing him back to the mainland. Now, a strange thing happening about midway between the island and the mainland, the bishop looked up to see the two priests walking on the water coming toward him. They walked up to the boat stepped into the boat and sat down, and one priest said, "Your excellency, we're very sorry but we have forgotten the words to the prayer."

Now, what this means, these men did not remember the proper words or proper prayer, but their life was so powerful that they could walk on water. Now, how that relates to you and me is what I want to talk about. I will not be held responsible for the accuracy of the story or the authenticity of the reporting, but that's the way it was told to me. The thing that I'm most concerned about relates to you how much harmony and the consistency there is, between what you say and what you do. I hope, decidedly, those of you who listen regularly, are out of the rut of feeling guilty or calling yourself a hypocrite.

I talk about inconsistency in between speech and action, the primary thing that I try to get across here on this television program, is that God loves you and through Jesus Christ you have complete and total forgiveness for your sins. Jesus Christ paid for your sins on the cross, and you're no longer guilty; He bears your guilt and you get credit for His perfect and righteous life, so before God you're forgiven, and when God forgives, God forgets. I speak this to primarily Christians, and if you are another faith, I respect yours and I respect your right to believe and to experience life and God in any manner that you choose; I do not mean for this to be offensive to you. It's my faith and I respect yours and I leave you free to respect mine. So, I'm not dealing with guilt, and I do not need to project or reinforce guilt. There is a tremendous area of growth that is open to you and me and to anybody who wants to experience it simply by looking at something that is very close to life and it's also very near the surface. Let's talk first about your relationship with your wife which is pertinent to a lot of us, and if you're not married, make it a close relationship with a friend or family member, if possible.

There is one thing to say, Oh, sure I love my wife. It's one thing to tell her that, and I noticed most wives like to be told, well not you know an extreme number of times...Just 40 or 50 time a day. I think would suffice for most women. But the words, too, are important in addition to the action. I want you to consider, you men, treating your wife as if she were the most important and valuable employee you had, or the employer who could give you a raise, give you a better job, or give you a vacation, as if you were a person in a functional position could benefit you financially, socially, profession and economically or some other way. I think one of the things that happens to some wives is they starve to death because you do not pay enough time and attention or give enough consideration and common courtesy to your wife, and you might check this out. Would you consider treating her as you did when you were dating and courting, I do not mean all the time, but I mean showing her the small acts of consideration, courtesy, and love that you showed when you were courting.

Sometimes when you've been married for a while, we tend to take each other for granted and when you take a person for granted, you have already minimized their value, you minimized their relationship and you have sat yourself up for trouble in the future. It's one thing to say I love you and it's one thing to say, sure I love you; it's an entirely different ball of wax to demonstrate by your behavior on a regular and consistent basis the fact that you love her, that she is valued enough to merit your time and your consideration, your thoughtfulness, and your generosity. I've been amazed sometime at my own selfishness, when I say selfishness, I mean putting myself first ahead of other people and finding that for me being unselfish is almost as mechanical as changing a tire. I never did like to change a tire. Well, I didn't mind changing a flat, if it comes at a convenient time. But it's a very mechanical process for me, and it requires me to get out of the car and do something that I do not want to do and do not enjoy doing and do not like to do. Now, although the car may have pretty good tires it's not going to run very far with one of them flat. I'm saying that most of us regularly do things mechanically, that we do not want to do, or we do not enjoy doing, but the doing of these things is a necessity, for the enjoyment of life.

You may not want to show acts of consideration, courtesy, kindness, and love, it may seem at first to be a mechanical act. I want to say that the car will work better, your marriage and your home will function better if you are considerate and kind and thoughtful of your wife and if it were reversed, this is also true. Especially where there are children in the home, particularly small children in the home. I think women get swamped with a lot of small children in the home. And the washing and the duties around the house, the cleaning and the cooking, the taxi driving, the wiping noses, bathing, putting to bed; it's so demanding on the mother's time and that when the father comes in and you might check this out, this is nothing more or less than another interruption.

Now, when the time schedule reaches that stage, you watch, you're going to lose your spouse or your home. Because nobody likes to be considered on a continuing basis as another interruption. One of the beautiful things about our society and our culture, I like America and like these United States and I'm glad we're nearly two hundred years old; I hope to have two hundred more.

But one of the things about our country is the opportunities provided for mothers to schedule and organize and conserve time in the home. I'm saying that one of the ways that you can show your love, other than using words is by organizing your time schedule—for at home and becoming an efficient homemaker or housekeeper, or whatever you call it. So that you'll have time to demonstrate to your husband the love and affection that you feel and if you are at the point where you are past feeling,–it may be where you think you are past feeling–it may be that you're really not past feeling–you're just fatigue and exhausted. Sometimes when people say my marriage is in trouble, what they're really saying is that I need some rest. And I doubt very much that you can pick up and go on a two-week vacation in the Bahamas. I don't think that I could afford it and not many people can. Well, I don't know if some people can, but if you can't afford to go for a two-week vacation in the Bahamas, you might consider rescheduling your time at home. To do this; it is an act of love, saying I love you is one thing and doing it is an entirely different thing. To be a loving, caring person means you organize your time, and you arrange your schedule and to include that person in the circle of your activities and the circumference of your failures. When you schedule a person out of your life, it communicates one thing and when you schedule a person into your life it says something different.

I said scheduling and I mean planning, and I mean awareness, action, and behavior (wait just a minute), the process of living and making a home for the man, the husband. The process of having a home and making a home for the mother, the wife, can be a very demanding, stressful situation, it can also be a cop-out. "When the child grows up" is a myth, and "when I get a promotion," it's never, neverland. "When I retire" is never or forever, and if you do not do these things today, you will probably not do them when or if. I'm saying that the time to demonstrate "love" by behavior, is now and the real power in your life is channeled into behavior, the real power in your life is rarely channeled into words.

Sometimes I've listened to a speaker, and I've spoken some myself, and some people have listened. But someone said, "How did you like that guy. I mean, how did you like that man?" I have almost a time-consuming desire when I hear a man speak on marriage in the family, to go to his wife and say, "Does he know what he is talking about?" or go to his children and say "Does he know what he's talking about." Now of course I wouldn't do that, but I probably resent someone saying this to my wife or children, my sons, after I had spoken. But it would be nice to know how those closest to him see him, how his own life measures in terms of action compared with words.

I think it would be interesting to go to a church–any church–where churches talk about God's love. I think it would be interesting, if you check out your church, a lot of your church people and some of you have your television sets in the church right now. Sit down, and when you talk about God's love and "God so loved the world that he gave..." and you use your cliches including the thirteenth chapter of 1st Corinthians where you talk about love suffereth long, we do and I do, I'm a man. No, I'm not, I'm a Christian, thank God.

When you talk about love being long suffering and kind and patient and that sort of thing. Sit down and make a list. Hey, I challenge you to do this and make a list of things your church does for people in the community that demonstrates love that you have for the world and the people.Then sit down and another way to do this is kind dirty, okay? I'm going to throw you a curve, now watch it. Put dow the dollars that you spend for others. Now I mean outside the church fellowship, not people who are going to join your church and not a group of people who would in anyway whatsoever profit throught love and action of church, and I mean "grace love," like when we talk about God's grace love. How much grace to expend in your community.

How many of your dollars and how many of your man hours are spent right there in the church. Now, if you are an average church, you know what the ratio is. The ratio is 100 to 1.

We spend and I'm with you here in the church family, the body of Christ. We spend a hundred dollars on ourselves, this is characteristic of the American churches, it's not, thank God, characteristic of churches all over the world. We spend a hundred dollars on ourselves and when we spend one dollar on the person completely and totally outside. Now, I don't mean trying to make a convert, I mean I read somewhere one time, where a man said, "I was hungry, and you gave me meat. I was thirsty and you gave me drink. I was naked and you clothed me. I was sick and imprisoned, and you visited me." That's what I mean, it's not the man who will join your church and be a fruitful and productive tithing member, it's a man who is starving to death. Who has never heard of or experienced the love of God with an unselfish motive. It's the man who is starving to death for a cup of cold water.

It's the man you help and will turn around and betray you or deny that he ever knew you—will sell you a love for thirty pieces of silver or less or more. Now, that's what I mean about love that acts rather than love that talks. I think sometimes in talking about God we have emersed the world in an ocean of words. And the world starved for and clamored for some demonstration of the love that we speak of so carelessly.

When I was a kid in school in a competitive group of boys, we had a little cliché:"you've got to walk the walk, not just talk the talk." In the family, to be a loving father, you've got to do it, not just talk about it. To be a loving mother you've got to do it, not just talk about it and I think that children will learn it from us, and I think they will learn it from you, and I think they'll learn it from me. There's a world of difference, between walking on water—I'm speaking figuratively—a world of difference between walking on water, Sir, and praying a pretty prayer. One of the most difficult men to get along with—one of the men most difficult for me to get along with I've ever met— prayed.

A prayer worded so beautifully that when he prayed, I and those in his presence were left breathless. But he was an obstinate, unloving, (well I'm trying to think of some nice words, it's not the normal way I describe him). So, I hated to be around the guy except when he was praying. I used to say to myself, that guy is a hypocrite if I ever saw one. I was wrong, he wasn't. I decided since we parted company years ago, that maybe I heard the real man when he prayed. I heard the frightened man when he talked to me. Maybe that's when our real selves come out when we pray. One of the most brilliant and intelligent men that I have known, was this professor that I had, when I studied in Scotland and his name was Tom Torrance and he was a beautiful human being. When he lectured, he was arrogant, positive, assertive, and I really did not like the man, when I first heard him speak. And then—at the end of his lecture—he prayed as he always did, he prayed just like a little child. His whole voice, his face and everything changed, and I felt like I was witnessing a little bitty child coming in with a long night gown and kneeling by the side of the bed at night, saying, "Dear God." I think probably that was the true man. For praying is action, it's not just a word. You've heard the words, "not everyone sayeth unto me Lord, Lord, shall enter the kingdom of Heaven, but he who will, doeth the will of my father who is in Heaven." You've heard the words, "in as much as you have done it unto one of the least of these"....He said, "one... it."—"You've done **it** unto me." That's what I'm saying, Man, if you love somebody show it, plant it, act it, take the time, use the energy. To demonstrate your love and affection and your care by acting. There is some risk involved, lots of risk, but I want to assure you it's worth it.

May 1975

FAMILY

There's been a lot of talk about the family and the nature of the family, I say recently, In the past twenty, twenty-five years. Most of the time during the pilgrimage and progression of man across the pages of history, we've more or less taken the family for granted. And there's been a lot of talk done recently about the nature of the family particularly here in the United States because it seems that this is the place where the family is breaking down. And more and more as the family breaks down we are seeing the necessity for having a family unit, not only for the rearing of children, but also for preserving a happy, healthy, secure environment in which a man and a woman can grow and mature as individuals. I think the idea that families exist for the good of the children Is erroneous. The fact that adult men and women need family structures in which to grow Is equally significant.

Now, I want to say in the beginning that I will be talking about a family unit which consists primarily of an adult female and an adult male and there may or may not be children. And I'm not saying or implying that everybody has to be married or that you can't be happy unless you're married, what I will be saying Is you can be happy and married the same way you can be happy and unmarried. But the understanding of the family background out of which you came will give you a better understanding of yourself so that you can have a better life today.

Here's what I want to say in the beginning, first, here's a man, he meets a woman, we'll call him "male" and her "female" and they're attracted in any one of a dozen or more or five or more different ways, and the attraction may be healthy and the relationship may be healthy, and it may not be healthy.

These people may be ready for marriage or they may not be ready for marriage. This man and this woman, this male and this female get married or they decide to live together, and then pretty soon a child is born into this family and this is child number 1. Now this is the only child that will ever be born into this particular family, because when this child #1, is born this man had never been a father and this woman had never been a mother and so this ls the first experience for them and this is the first experience the child ever had because this child had the experience of being the first child in the home these parents are learning how to be mother and daddy parents. They're learning how for the first time. They're probably young. Let's make them twenty-one years old. Now, when this child ls born this man is learning his way in the world, he ls building a business, or he's getting promotions in his company, but his interest ls definitely in getting ahead. He may or not be interested ln being a good father. She may be a working mother, and she may or may not be interested ln being a good mother.

He may or may not have the capacity to love a child. Sometimes when a little boy is born into the home the man feels threatened without really knowing it. Or without really knowing why, the man feels threatened because there's another male in the house. Sometimes when the first child is a girl the woman feels threatened because there's another woman ln the house and she feels maybe the husband doesn't have enough love to go around, not for the two of them; it's sometimes the man gets threatened.

Now, when this first baby is born and the parents are both twenty-one years old, the years three to five are the most important years of this child's life. During this time, a large part of the personality ls formed, during this time he learns something about his personal worth and personal value. And this ls the way he learns it. This child looks at his father and he decides how acceptable he is to the father, and this tells a child what he is worth. This is where the child's self-image is formed. When you were between the ages of three and five, or four and six or something like that, you decided what you were worth by the way you thought your father and your mother felt about you. It may have been accurate, it may have been inaccurate, but one way or the other you reached the conclusion. This child looks at his mother and he sees the way she treats him and he decides what he's worth by the way his mother treats him. Okay, Now this ls the way you got your sense of worth and personal value and sometimes a person grows up with what we call a feeling of inferiority. It may have started here, a lot of things develop, help develop, the feeling of inferiority later in life. But your feeling of inferiority may have started with your mother and your father.

Now, again for the record, I'm on the side of the parent, I'm a parent, primarily. I'm not saying it's anybody's fault; I like to talk about responsibility not fault or blame. So, a child gets his sense of worth and value from the people directly to him. Now, here's where he gets his sense of security. The child learns to be mature in proportion to the amount of love he sees expressed between this man and this woman. If the child—particularly when he's younger—if he sees mother and daddy are loving and kind and thoughtful and considerate and gentle with each other, that child grows up with a feeling of security. He is a secure individual. Because he sees himself in a secure setting. Mother and Daddy love each other and he concludes, this is a safe family; this is a safe home, and I can relax and rest and be safe here. If he sees his mother and daddy fighting all the time, or he hears the loud, screeching, screaming voices late at night, or he sees his mother crying after his father has beaten her, the child will not be secure. He'll be frightened and afraid probably throughout the greater part of his life.

Some of you watching this television program can remember childhood experiences with both parents, the good and the bad, maybe some can remember the ugly. But, here's this child and by the time he's five years old, you see, he leaves these two persons, and he goes to school, or he starts playing with friends and he's introduced more to a larger, social world, he's introduced more to a larger social world. He's introduced more to a world of his peers, and he learns things from his peers, but his basic life position is probably pretty well set here. It can be changed, but it takes work to change it. He can grow beyond what he learned by age five; it takes some discipline and a directive program of growth to change this.

Okay, in this family there's a second child. Here he is, this ls child #2. We'll let the first one be a boy, the second one be a girl. Now, this second child wasn't born into the same family because the family he was born into already had one child and she came into a family of three. And so, her mother and father had already had one child and they were not nervous about her coming, not nearly as nervous as they were with the birth of child #1. And when the little girl was born, her father was twenty-six years old and the mother was twenty-six. Later on, if there's #3, he's born at a later time and he's born into a different family because this family has one, two, three, four people in it, whereas the first child's family only had three. This child is in a family of five, this child was born into a family of three, this one into a family of four. So, the parents are different, the family structure is different and the whole relationship is different here when this third child comes into the family. When this third child was born his mother and father are both thirty-one years old and there's a lot of difference between a father who ls thirty-one and a father who is twenty-one, I won't begin to tell you what it is. Now, this happens sometimes, death or divorce or sometimes a job traveling takes away the father, and it leaves all three of the children relating to the mother. Now let's let this third child be a boy. This means that this boy has no pattern for a model; he doesn't know what he's supposed to be like when he grows up. He is loved by his mother and he's cared for by his mother and he know what an adult female is supposed to be, but he doesn't know what an adult male is supposed to be; so, sometimes for a little boy, there's a lot of groping.

I know something about this; my father died when I was five years old. There were two younger brothers in my family and my mother did the very best she could. I knew and even remember when I was very small; I knew that this woman was a mother and that she was an adult and that that she was a parent. But I knew when I grew up I wasn't supposed to be like her. I mean, you know, in most—in a lot of ways—I guess the father is like the mother, but they're different basically. I think the mother provides something for the child that the father cannot provide. And the father is to provide something for the child that the mother cannot provide. Sometimes right here, now, when the father is missing–or sometimes it's the mother–sometimes we have substitute parents. A substitute parent can be a grandparent, and thank God for good grandparents. They have saved the lives of a lot of children. Sometimes it can be an uncle, or if the mother is missing, sometimes it can be an aunt. Sometimes the schoolteachers have served beautifully as substitute parents. I know of some instances where doctors–medical doctors— have been beautiful substitute parents. Of course, you can't be a substitute parent to an unlimited number of children. I know of one boy who said his life was saved because every six months he had an hour visit with his family doctor and got to ask him a lot of questions; this physician did more than care for his body; he cared for his total being. This man has lived a very successful life and has made a tremendous contribution to the world simply because he was cared for by a loving and understanding doctor. I think a lot of pastors served, and priests and rabbis served well in the role of being a substitute father. Substitute mothers, I think are harder to come by than substitute fathers. School teachers serve as substitute mothers, grandmothers do, sometimes you can find a neighbor or an aunt or somebody like that. Mothers may be harder to replace. I think so, it may be a lot harder to replace the mother in the family than it is for the father—it doesn't mean they're more valuable. Now, this is the female, sometimes when there's a divorce the man leaves this woman and he marries another woman. Okay, and this woman later marries another man. So, here's a child related to a stepfather, and he sees his real father over here and he's married to another woman, and this child needs a lot of interpretation because particularly a younger child has difficult sorting out the parents.

In working with family life conferences, in the church group in Tennessee a couple of years ago, I asked how many kids had one parent. I meant by that one, that one of the parents was out of the home by death, travel, or divorce. Several hands went up. And I asked how many had two parents, and several hands went up. Then I asked how many had three parents, and one hand went up. The I asked how many have four parents, and about half the kids in the room held up their hands, which meant there had been a divorce and that each of the parents had remarried. There are some people who had as high as eight fathers, and some who had a large number of mothers. Here's where the family structure begins to get very complicated, and it's very difficult for a child to sort out all the personalities. One of the best things you can do for your child is to interpret to the child what is happening to the family. If you are in a serious place in your family, and you're going to get a divorce, the child needs to hear from you exactly what's going to happen. If you're not planning a divorce, it's important when you disagree with your husband or wife—it's important for the child to hear from you that you're not planning a divorce because a lot of children decide their parents are—they see it on television all the time and they hear about it from their friends. And some children live in mortal fear that their parents are going to get a divorce.

Now, I want to show you something here about the family when the children grow up. I think the greatest gift a parent can ever give a child is when the parent interprets to the child the meaning of being an adult. The father can say to the son or the daughter, "You're no longer my child, you will always be my son, you will always be my daughter, but now you're an adult. You have a father in heaven to whom I have introduced you by personal example and personal instruction. Now, I commit you to His care and to His keeping; I relinquish my responsibility as your parent, and I give you to God. I assure you that your father in heaven will be the kind of parent I never could be on this earth, and I give you to Him. I will forever remain your friend, will forever love you, but I relinquish the role as your father, and I give you to your father in heaven I stand alongside you; I stand equal with you but not superior to you. You no longer owe me obedience. I earnestly ask for your love, but your obedience belongs to God as does mine. And I, here this day, say goodbye to you as my child and I welcome you as my brother." Now, that's the way for a father to say goodbye to son and welcome him as a friend. I hope by this time that the child has been introduced to God, to his heavenly father. Whether or not he chooses to worship the heavenly father would be, of course, his own decision. Tragedy comes later, if not sooner, where the earthly parents try to maintain control or authority over children after they're grown. When your child is eighteen or nineteen or seventeen—at some point—it varies with different children. He has the right to be free, he has the right to make his own decisions, his own choices and you do not have authority over an adult , even if he happens to be your child. If your child has not learned responsibility and duty by the time he's eighteen or nineteen, the chances are he probably will not learn it from you. However much you love your child, this love cannot be expressed any better than through release.

I want to digress here just a minute, and say if your child is on drugs, alcohol, or any other form in which drugs are used, if he's in trouble with the police, he deserves the right to pay for the mistakes he's made, to get himself out of his own mess You have no right to overrule the freedom he has to make choices and decisions because you were there. In fact, your efforts to do this may only intensify or aggravate the dangers and destructive decisions that he's made concerning his own life.

The church is called the family of God, and a lot of people who have never known a real family structure on earth have found a place in the family of God. Hey, I heard something which to me was very beautiful recently. I heard a woman give to a group of people an invitation to be her family. I thought it was one of the highest compliments I had ever received as a member of a group. I think this is God's invitation to us to come into his spiritual family, the church. If the earthly family—the family of your mother and father and brothers and sisters—if your family is successful, it will dissolve. If you are a successful parent your children will grow up and leave you; if your children don't leave you, you haven't been successful. But the family of God does not dissolve, not even death dissolves the family of God. So, when you come into God's family this is a relationship which will last forever.

Hey, one time Jesus was talking to a group of people and somebody came to Him and said, "Master, your mother and sister and your brothers are here and they want to talk to you."

And Jesus said, "who is my mother and who is my brother and sister?" Then He pointed to the people around Him and said, "They that do the will of my father in heaven, these are my brothers and my sisters." What He was saying was that the people who shared His work on earth and who do His work on earth—they were His family.

Whatever you may or may not have had in the family of your childhood, whatever you may or may not have had in the family that came about as a result of your marriage—now this we cannot change. For some people this is gone; it's gone forever. But the good news is this, the good news is that you can come into the family of God. It's necessary for you to come in as a little child, and you can enter this family as a child and you can know the warm friendly presence of God through the person of the Holy Spirit—I think this is sort of a mother figure. You can know the parental care and strong love of your heavenly father, and you can know the supportive, continuing, forgiving love of other Christians as your brothers and sisters, and this is your family.

March 1975

PARENTING

Sue J. is here and we were just talking real fast about what we're going to say on the telecast this morning. Sue and I work together at Pastoral Care and Counseling Center, and Sue, I'm really glad you came.

SUE: Thank you, John. I watched the program last Sunday and I thoroughly enjoyed listening to your talk.

JOHN: Thank you. Today we're going to talk about the older teenager, and the two years that we have been working together we've mostly been listening to the children and young people and sometimes listening to the parents. Today I want to talk about some of the things that you can do as a parent, some of the things that you can do as an older teenager. I firmly believe that with one or two members of the family working together, Sue, the majority of the conflict at home can be eliminated. Some parents will disagree with me on this statement. I have seen some of the families do it.

SUE: Yes, that's true.

JOHN: In that little crib sheet that we were going to use, the first thing that we said is that every member of the family needs—this is not just for the kids, this is for the parents, too—every member of the family needs a safe place. The mother and the father need d a safe place; you need a bedroom where nobody will go rummaging around. This is your bedroom and your bed or your drawer, or your chest of drawers, or your bathroom, or whatever the structure of the house allows. Everybody needs a place where he can keep his things and the parents need this. What about the children?

SUE: Oh, very definitely! The same is true with children, and especially teenagers because a lot of new feelings and a lot of new things are going on in their lives. They've got to have a safe place and even some secrets.

JOHN: What about a child when he doesn't clean up his room? Does he have a right for his room to be messy?

SUE: Yes, he has to have a place where he can be messy. If he chooses to do that and if it's annoying to the parents, shut the door. That's my feeling about it.

JOHN: All right! shut the door and stay out of the room. How far can the parents go in allowing the child to have secrets?

SUE: When it becomes obvious that the secret or withdrawal or behavior pattern indicates that he is hurting himself or herself, that is when it's time to reach out and help.

JOHN: Suppose you smell smoke?

SUE: What kind?

JOHN: Pot smoke—and that's not a laughing matter. But when you're smelling pot smoke.

SUE: Okay! I hear that, and that's an infringement on the rights of the other people in the family. That's when the home becomes an unsafe place for the parents, for the children, and that's when a limit needs to be set. Hey, if you choose to smoke pot, you choose not to live in my house.

JOHN: Here, we're going to talk about drugs just a minute. A sixteen, seventeen, eighteen-year-old, and nineteen-year-old of course, and twenty— sometimes a fifteen-year-old—the specific age cannot be defined for different children. When your child decides to use drugs, it is for the most part, impossible for parents to prevent this in a particular child, it's unfortunate, but drugs are easily available. They are so available that it would be shocking and most frightening to most parents, if they really understood how easily accessible drugs are to most of our children. When your child decides to go on the drugs, you cannot prevent it, unless you lock up the child and tie his hands and feet, particularly if your child is in school. Know, the use of drugs, or your child's decision to use drugs may mean that he decides to leave home. It's unthinkable for a parent to supply money that your child is using for the purchase of drugs. Let's get back to the home, you have no right to pack the dynamite by putting dynamite caps and sticks of dynamite in the home and endangering the lives of the whole family—play with guns, or play with other kinds of explosives, or fire, or anything that endangers the lives of the entire family. The home must be safe for everyone. A parent cannot endanger the lives of the entire family by smoking in bed, for example, that's one of the ways that you endanger everyone's life. Neither does the child have the right to endanger the welfare and the safety of the other family members by bringing drugs into the home. So, in the child's room the child can find a place of privacy as long as he does not endanger the entire family, and if the child chooses to have the room messy, the cure for messiness is a closed door, and the parents stay away. That's hard for some parents.

SUE: Yes, I'm aware of that, and if they want to change the behavior and to be very aware of it, the thing to do is to recognize any time a child does picks up a shirt and keep his room tidy for one day, then recognize it, praise it, affirm the child, the teenager, the young adult. Hey, last week we were talking about some kinds of developmental stages with children, and I think it's important to remember the developmental stage with adolescence is really a need for independence and, on the other hand, a desire to be dependent.

JOHN: This child wants to be independent or autonomously free and he wants to be dependent on his parents. He wants to be dependent and he wants to be independent and free, and he still wants to be the child at home. This is a necessary stage of growth and the parents can recognize this, you know I keep saying recognize, it and then what do you do?

SUE: Let the child know you recognize it is the next step, I think.

JOHN: All right, tell me that you recognize that I want to be friends, that I still want to be mommy's little boy.

SUE; Okay! I'm aware that there are a lot of things that you would like to have control of in your life; You'd really like to be free and you would like to have some choices about the things that you do.

JOHN: Hey! Let's role play this.

SUE: Okay.

JOHN: Yes, I'd like to be free and I'd like to have my own car and my own money and my own house and my own place. I want to make my own decisions, and I'm tired of you making them for me.

SUE: Hey! I hear that, and it's tough when you feel grown and I'm still telling you how to do things, when to do them, and what to do. However, if you choose to live in my house there are some things that you cannot do to infringe on my rights, for example.

JOHN: Hey, Mom, it sound to me like you are threatening me when you say, "If you choose to live in my house;" are you threatening me?

SUE: Do you feel threatened by that?

JOHN: (That was a good answer.) Yes, I feel threatened and I don't like for you to tell me either "ship up or shape out——wait, either shape up or ship out."

SUE: You know I don't like hearing that.

JOHN: No, I don't like hearing that. I get angry. I get mad at you when you say that.

SUE: Yes, really mad. What would you like to hear from me?

JOHN: (Would you say that loud again?) I want you to respect the decision that I make so I can feel like a man sometimes, instead of a little boy.

SUE: Okay, I hear that. I will respect the decisions that have to do with your problems and have them relate to your friends and your lifestyle, and when your decisions infringe on my rights as a person or my safety, —like if you come in at three, continually, and I don't get enough sleep and I'm really tough to live with— see, you can't do that, and I will respect the decisions that have to do with you and what's going on in your life. When your decisions affect my right to live, that's when I need to draw a limit. Does that make sense?

JOHN: Yes, did I wake you up when I came in last night?

SUE: Yes.

JOHN: A lot of children cannot see this particular point, and I'm glad we stopped to cover it. I like the way you responded. I want to stick to what we said we were going to do. That every member of the family has the right to a place of privacy and a child has a right to arrange his room as long as it doesn't damage the whole family structure. This is hard for some parents to do and you may be wondering what my friends will think, but the way you get along with your child is more important than what your friends think.

SUE: The second thing was a place for privacy. and the third thing the we said was affirmation and praise.

JOHN: Yes, praise. One of the things that Sue and I talked about, and Sue, you do this well, is affirming the child for what he does well, rather than focusing on all the things that the child does wrong. Will you talk about that?

SUE: If the child was feeling of no worth and no value or is not feeling successful in some areas, then they're going to give up or choose a symptom and then get sick or an addiction. Addictions are pretty easy to get into these days.

JOHN: To get drugs.

SUE: If you want to change behavior, you look for something successful in a child, even if it's five minutes staying in the room doing homework, or one good grade, or one grade brought up. You recognize it. (I keep using the word "recognize," but it is essential.) Then, the child is aware that you are aware of what's going on .

JOHN: Okay. Let's work on this finding something in the child to affirm, to praise, to compliment. Give me some instances.

SUE: I had an adolescent's mother talking to me and she said, "I want my daughter to cook. I think I'll have her prepare a meal next week. I really want her to do that, you know. And got to thinking there's too much of a chance of error in preparing a whole meal for a large family."

My thought about that was to begin with a salad. Say, "Hey, come on in herd, Hon, it's your turn to do the salad." and beginning with one thing a child can do successfully. Then it is really important to say that the salad was really fantastic.

JOHN: Yes, and how old do you have to be to make a salad? That's the point.

SUE: You'll have to help me with some things.

JOHN: Wash dishes. No, that's too creative. People don't compliment that everybody eats the salad, but when you're washing the dishes, everybody is gone. It would be hard.

SUE: Unless you walked into the kitchen later and said, "Hey, you did a really good job."

JOHN: Okay, I was thinking about one of the things that a parent can do is say, "Hey, Man, I like your smile; I like the way your hair looks after it's washed," and the length of the hair is not significant anymore.

SUE: "You're fun to be with."

JOHN: You're fun to be with, too, and that's true. IF he's not fun and he's a grouch and a drag, you don't want to mention it. Maybe comment on "your hair and your smile and your eyes!" Look at your kids' eyes and that is really a beautiful way of being honest, affirming, and complimentary.

SUE: Like with boys, you say, "Hey, your arms are really filling out or your legs are looking great."

JOHN: Not "You're really getting big." Don't tell your oldest teenage son that he is getting big. Say, "You look like a full-grown man." And another is your arms, I think it is good when a parent, mother or father recognizes that your son's arms are big. That's for the little boys. Or to an older son, you can comment on his muscles.

Another thing is if you have a child who will not allow you to touch him. You start by beginning to talk with contact just within his safe space but facing him. One way to begin the touch of a child is to catch the end of that little finger. You can touch that finger, hold it a moment and say I'm glad you're home and that's all, nothing more, and this may take you months to move from this position to touching his little finger. But believe me it's work the effort. It's better than money in the bank. Another thing you can do here is you can kick the child's shoe very softly and say, "I like you." Just gently, briefly, just, "Hi, I like you." or you can say to them, with a gently touch on the arm, 'Hi, Man!" It's all right to call him a man and this is sort of a little term of closeness, and sort of a form of flattery. Most boys will respond well to this. What would you do with the girl, Sue?

SUE: I think I would start with the non-threatening kinds of contact. Another good one for a girl is to compliment her hair. "I like the way the light touches your hair." Another thing about adolescent girls and the insecurity that they go through, I think it is important that they hear, "Hey! you have a nice body." You know they need to know that they're attractive, womanly, and feminine.

JOHN: This is for a boy or a girl. You can say, "Hey! I really feel good standing next to you." and when you say these things, you don't' stand there and smile, you say this and move away until the child decides that you're safe and you're not doing this with an ulterior motive or getting the child to do something.

SUE: And if you feel your child feeling resistant, withdrawing, backing off, you're getting too close— ease up a bit. You can tell that there is communicative.

JOHN: Wait and take time. Say, I want to do something here. Your child may decide not to live at home, may decide to run away. When your child decides to do this and today's world over 18,

17—or whatever the legal age is—he can leave. It's impossible for you to keep him at home when he's of legal age, and I want to say that not everything we say here applies to every child or every family and there will be a lot of exceptions. Your child needs to know that he has a place at home, he also needs to know that if the time comes, and he makes up his mind he can leave and you will respect his decision. Does this sound all right to you, Sue?

SUE: Yes, this does.

JOHN: That's a hard one.

SUE: That's the toughest. It seems to be tougher sometimes with girls, or "How can I let my baby, my daughter leave?"

JOHN: And "she's going to be out on the street at night alone, and how can I live?"

SUE: But it's possible to love and it's possible to make your home a safe place. If the child is destroying it –and you emotionally– it is not safe.

JOHN: Your child can leave home, your child can get involved with drugs, and he can become an addict. God forbid not for you, Sir, or you, Madam, but it can happen. When it does the child needs medical care, and the child needs medical help, and he needs the assistance of people who are familiar with drugs. The parent cannot do it for the child any more than the parent can operate on a child. Professional help is necessary when the child get addicted to drugs.(not when they're playing around)

SUE: I've got something else to say about the drugs, were you going to say anything about the drugs? I think it's very important. A parent asked me, "How do I get my child to communicate and how do I get him to hear me?" I strongly believe, and I'm convinced that the degree in which you listen will be the degree in which your child will listen. And your capacity to listen is really limited if your child is not going to talk to you.

JOHN: Yes. The first rule for getting the child to talk is for the parent to shut up!

SUE: You said it simply.

JOHN: Shut up! and shut up for a long time and keep shut up until the child begins to talk. If you'll stay quiet long enough, you'll blow his mind, he will talk, his first sentence may be, "What's wrong with you?" Children do not consider preaching from their parents as an expression of love. Preaching comes through as critical. It comes through generally as unlove.

SUE: That's true.

JOHN: Hey, Susie, there's another thing I want to talk about. We mentioned running away from home. Your child can abuse alcohol and he can get addicted to drugs. There's another thing: your daughter can get pregnant. I hope she doesn't, but if she does, what do you do?

SUE: I think that it is really important to help with the choices of an adoption or possibly they could choose to get married. I want y'all to know that there are some choices and that there are some alternatives and it's not the end of the world.

JOHN: I want to be kind of elementary; first she goes to the doctor and gets a pregnancy test by the doctor; second thing, I want you to go to a counselor; third thing, let the child know what choices that she has and let her be in on the choices. (have the major choice). The child cannot choose to have the parents to support her baby.

Hey, today is Easter here in Abilene, and it may seem that this is not exactly an Easter theme, but to me it is. I didn't say at the beginning of the program that this is Easer, but what we're talking about is the resurrected life of a human being who has found a new relationship with God that gives to him a new respect to his child and the child has found a new relationship with God. That gives him a new respect to the parents.

I mentioned this last time, but I can't help but remember that one time Jesus Christ was a 17-year-old who had hair down to his shoulder. It may be hard for some of you rigid traditionalists. It may be hard for some people to accept but he did have long hair, probably a beard very young. (That's what the Hebrew boys would have had.) So today, when you are looking at this older teenager, remember that God himself was once at this same place.

June 1975

SAFE PLACES

This is one of the beauties of life, you always have a new starting place. I'll be discussing this here on "A Place To Talk."

Hey, I want to talk to you. I've just had the nicest conversation with a very good friend. This friend and I are fairly new acquaintances and out of the conversation there came a new understanding for me, you know, you see you live by a lot of ideas; but they don't always surface and come out verbally. But I've found after talking with this friend, that there are two things I've decided to give myself this year. One thing is a safe place inside, the second is a safe place outside. I believe that if you have a safe place inside you and you've got another place— a room, an office, a hideaway, an escape—if you have a safe place outside where you can put you; even if only for brief periods, I think you can make it. Not only do I think you can make it, I believe that you can enjoy, and I can, too, and not only can you enjoy but you can witness life getting better and better and better as days go by.

The first thing I want to talk about is the safe place inside—Inside—I mean you can call it your heart, mind, or however you can picture yourself. This safe place inside would be a place where you are protected and free. That's not supposed to picture your insides, but to give us something to work from. Inside, I mean safe from guilt, safe from condemnation, safe from belittling, safe from criticism, safe from anxiety. And we've talked about this on this program before, but you, and only you, can give this to yourself. This kind of safety can only be given to you by yourself. This safe place inwardly means that another person can be angry at you, happy, sad, or glad and his feelings do not determine the way you feel. Now you can choose to be angry if he is angry with you or with himself. You can choose to be happy if he is happy with you or with himself. You can choose to be sad, if he is sad, glad, if he is glad, or you can say, "I'm responsible for my own emotions, I'm responsible for my own feelings, and I will not allow you to take charge of my life." And when you do this, this means you have created for yourself an inner safe place. You can't get depressed if you have an inner safe place. There's not any way. You can't stay angry over a long period of time if you have an inner safe place. You can't stay guilty over a long period of if you have an inner safe place. You can't really stay—I think this is right— you can't really stay lonely if you have an inner safe place. Now, the important thing here, this is you and it's also me. The person that I have to protect this place from is not the outsider. The person that I have to protect the inner safe place from is really myself. It's when I inwardly condemn myself and I inwardly criticize myself, it's when I inwardly, because of habits I've picked up, it's when I inwardly belittle myself.

And I decide, and this is a decision—it's almost as positive and deliberate decision as raising your hand, or stretching out your arm. I decide that I will be safe with me. I may not be safe with you, I may not be safe any other place, but I will be safe with me so when I'm alone, I will know peace, I will know tranquility, I will know safety and security. Now, it goes without saying that this is because I know myself is loved by God. This is because two thousand years ago, a man lived named Jesus Christ who lived a perfect life, died on the cross, and paid for my sins so that I don't have to be guilty, and I don't have to carry the guilt or the burden for my sins. So, it's all right for me not to be guilty, to be loved and accepted inside me. Now, once I have made the decision to be safe inside, I need a safe place, and this is one of the things I wanted to talk about today—the home. Now, here's the important thing, I need a safe place in my home, and I want to say particularly for families. Every member of the family needs a place in the house that is safe for the individual. The wife needs a safe place so the family cannot just barge ln and storm ln and take over her life. The father needs a safe place. and each of the children needs a safe place.

We Americans are very strong on cleanliness and neatness; we have the world's largest market in personal items—deodorants and things like that—because we are very careful about being close together. But one of the things that happens in a lot ·of American homes is there is no place of privacy for the individual members of the family. One of the nicest things you can do—Dad or Mother, one of the nicest things you can do for your child is to give your child his own room. And, as long as he does not do anything in that room that endangers the family or the house, or endangers himself let the child have the privacy of his own room, and let it be his safe place. Give him freedom to close and even lock the door if he chooses. Now, you have the right to knock on the door and ask for admission. But children at various stages of life, and most adults, need a place of privacy where for a while they enjoy the experience of just sort of being, and have a reasonable assurance that someone will not barge in and take over their privacy. A lot of husbands have never felt that the home was really theirs. A lot of wives have never felt that they were really safe in the home. And if you are interested in them and getting better acquainted with your spouse, sit down first, and see what your own feelings are, and then ask your wife if she feels safe and secure and free in her own home.

And if you're brave, enterprising, and growing, wife, ask your husband, how safe and comfortable he feels in his own home. It may be that both of you will get some information here which you've not had before. Now, I promised you when we first started this series of television programs, that we would deal more with solutions than we dealt with problems. Although, I have very carefully avoided you know, quick, easy, over simplified solutions.

This I think is a tool. I had the nicest experience in the past two years of meeting some people that I feel are making it, they're happy, they're enjoying life, and they're in contact with reality. The best, most useful, usable tool that I've run across is an open mind. And by' an open mind, I mean the ability that a person has, to see things in the present tense, in the present setting without reaching way back into the background and picking up a lot of bad memories and bad feelings, garbage and dumping it on to the present tense. Wouldn't it be nice if you could get up in the morning, or if you could leave the television set right now, and go to your wife and see her as if for the very first time. Now, I know this is not reasonable, but be unreasonable for a minute. Man, look at this woman, experience her, and enter into a new relationship of openness where you are willing to allow her to reveal herself to you. And where you, Lady, are willing to allow your husband to reveal himself to you. And then enter into a new experience of getting acquainted as if for the first time, like water in two tanks finding the same level because they're connected down deep.

Now, this is what I mean by an open mind. It's where you're willing to live in the present tense, in the present situation, with one person, and allow him to reveal himself to you as he is today, rather than the way you have perceived him in the past. Now, suppose—just suppose—you found out he is like you thought he was, you haven't lost anything. This might require that you let your guard down a little bit.

possibility that lies in the experiment is worth all the risk that's involved. You might find yourself entering into a new area, of a relationship with your wife and a relationship with your husband. One of the happy things about some marriages is, husbands and wives learn to talk after they've been married ten or fifteen or twenty years. And sometimes they really get acquainted after they've been married that long. I mentioned it to you once before; the best way to talk to a wife, or best way to talk to a husband– that I know of– is to get them out of the house and go for a ride in the car. While you 're riding and while you're talking let your conversation be limited, almost completely, to the words, "I feel," at the beginning of every sentence. Tell your wife your feelings.

Stay away from the word "you." Particularly avoid, "you should,... you ought to,.. how could you,... how dare you,... when will you,... why don't you ..." and let your wife know you. And, Lady, you be willing to know your husband. And then, you are dealing from the standpoint of an open mind, you 're dealing with the possibility of really discovering the person of your mate, maybe for the first time. More, more than that, I want to know if you would consider—Dads and Mothers—if you would consider looking at your child with an open mind. One of the good things about my job is my exposure to people and exposure to children.

JNot long ago I spent half a day with a child. We had a delightful morning together. We went to a restaurant and had breakfast, we hauled some dirt, we went to a toy store, bought a toy, and then we went to a wedding. You see I didn't have any background, not much experience with this child, and I spent the entire morning letting him tell me who he was. And I was open minded.

Now, the nicest gift God gave me was four sons, one of the nicest, after he gave me that wife. I am continually surprised, pleasantly surprised, as I discovered these four men now, and they're willing to let me know them. And I have two daughters-in-law who let me know them to. This cannot happen in your life or in mine, until I'm inwardly respective.

Until I have erased my mind of my prejudices and my fears—Now, stay with me Just a minute, and listen—until I expect nothing, require nothing, and demand nothing of the other person and I willing to let you be free to be the person you are, then I say, I'm willing to know you. I don't mean that you verbalize this, surely you understand that, and I don't mean that you sit down and you spell all this out. That would be terribly boring. But, I do mean that this is communicating from one person to the other.

In talking with children and talking with families, one of the familiar repetitive phrases we hear is—I hear the child say to the father or the mother, "You never listen to me." I think if I met this father downtown over coffee or if you met me and you asked me, "Do you understand your children? Or do you know your children?" I'd say, of ·course, I've been living with them twenty years, twenty-five years.

And l think If I asked you if you knew your kids, you'd say "yes." But if a friend of your child—of your son or your daughter—talked with them personally, and if your son or your daughter were asked the question, "Does your father really, really, really know you?" I wonder what your son would say, or I wonder what your daughter would say. Now, Man, the willingness, to let each day be a new day and start at a new place with old and familiar friends, family members, associates, might possibly be the opening of a new door for you in life and maybe even one of the greatest experiences you've ever known.

I've a prayer, and my prayer–one of my prayers is, "God let me see every person this day with new eyes, as if I'd never seen him before, as if I would never see her again, as if I would never see him again."

Then one day, I was telling somebody about this and he asked, "Do you ask that for yourself?" And I hadn't thought about that, but since then I have been praying to God let me see myself today as you see me—and I like that.

I know God sees me with more kindness, gentleness, patience, and forgiveness than I could ever have toward myself, so I pray to see myself in a manner similar to the way God sees me. This is what I mean by an open mind, an open heart.

You know what closes a person's mind? Prejudice, anger, fear, suspicion, jealousy, mistrust. And sometimes we keep very careful records of all these negative emotions. And we assign these things to people and we decide, I'll never trust them again. We decide this about other members of our family. Sometimes a parent has decided that he will never trust his children again as long as he lives—trust a particular child. Children change, so do adults. Children grow, so do some adults, so when you say, "never ever again," what you're really saying is that that son of yours, or that daughter of yours has reached the end of the road and that life is over for him— and that's just now true.

Now from the past program, we've talked about the necessity of setting a child free. Particularly when a child chooses a lifestyle that is contrary to the style of the parents. Now, I'm not contradicting that statement—still saying the same thing. One of the ways I will have an open mind about my son or daughter, who has come of age—and some children come of age at 15 and some at 16, and some older. But, one of the ways I have an open mind, is to leave myself open to setting them free to assume the consequences of every decision that they make good or bad. It may be that one of the results of my having an open mind about my son or daughter would be that today I'd get up and I'd see that this child of mine is no longer a child; he's now a man. And this daughter of mine is not my little girl anymore, she's a woman. My open mind might lead me to say to my son or daughter,

"The time has come for me to give up the role as an authority person in your life. I commit you to the care of God, I release you from all responsibility of obedience to me, and I now take my place alongside you and with or without you I bow to the authority of my Heavenly Father. I release you from any responsibility of obeying me. I will forever be your friend. You will forever be my son, but I will no longer look upon you as a child."

This is one of the ways that a father or mother with an open mind can see a child, when the time comes. Particularly, I think, It's necessary to see a son or daughter this way when they get married. The worst thing—not the worst thing—no, hey, Man, It's not healthy for you to interfere with the marriage of your son or daughter. If they can't work it out, you certainly can't, so stay out of the way. Have no opinion; if they need help, let them go and get it just like you would. The father or the mother cannot help in the marriage of their son or their daughter, however well-intentioned you might be. There are people who can. Don't propose any kind of surgical procedure on your son or daughter, and don't fix their marriage. Don't fix their inflamed appendix and don't fix their marriage. An open mind sees other people with respect, with courtesy, with care, and with caution. This is not anything new, and it's not anything original. One of the nice things I like about talking with you who view the program here, is that some of the time you are already one ahead of me. What I have been talking about is what I've learned from reading the New Testament.

Jesus Christ had a peculiar and wonderful capacity to always view people with new eyes. Man, when He met this prostitute, she wasn't just a prostitute, He saw her as a person, and His mind was open to her. So was his mind open to Zacchaeus. So was His mind open to Matthew. So was His mind open to Peter, after his denial. So was His mind open to all the disciples after they abandoned Him and ran away. So was His mind open to His own mother, when He said, "Mother, I'm grown, no longer your child. What have I to do with thee, woman?"—I think those were his words. So it may be, one of the best gifts you can give yourself this day or tomorrow, is to give yourself the privilege of an open mind with an inner and outward place of safety.

July 1975

SEEING WITH THE INNER EYE

There are two kinds of seeing, one is an inner seeing and one is an outer seeing. l would like to discuss this with you here on a "Place To Talk."

ln Edinburgh, Scotland, and it was spring. The people in Scotland are walkers, they spend a great deal of time walking, particularly in the spring and summer months. I think partly because the weather is so disagreeable at certain times of the year, and the habit is kind of catching. Beautiful parks, beautiful streets, beautiful flowers; and so, I did a lot of walking there. One spring after a particularly cold, wet, dreary, dark winter when the grass started turning green and the flowers were coming out, I was walking in one of the parks near the university where I was going to school. The sky was clear blue there was no smog or fog and the sun was almost straight up in the sky, straight overhead. Shortly after noon, and walking through the park I was approaching a bench, aware that there was a man sitting on the bench, even though I had not looked directly, you know how your eyes pick up things in the corner. I was going past the bench, not to it, and I realized as I got closer that the man was not moving, and that his head was back and he had his arms stretched out on the back of the bench like that, it was a long bench, he was the only one on it. But he was looking directly into the sun, and I stopped when I got close. Without trying to be too obvious, I turned and looked, I couldn't imagine why he was looking this way, and I looked him full in the face and both of his eye sockets were empty. He had no eyes. Just empty sockets there. There were tears pouring down his cheeks and I was startled. I know he heard my footsteps; I was aware of him and he was aware of me, and I knew this and I'm convinced he knew it but neither of us spoke. I wanted to say something, felt that something should have been said, but I did not have any words. I was not uncomfortable, I do not think he was either, but I want to tell you what I heard him say, or what I said to myself to him, though neither of us spoke a word. I stood there for a few minutes, and I heard him say with his silence, "My sight–the sight is gone from my eyes, and I cannot even see the sun; so, in the absence of my ability to see the sun, I choose to feel the warmth." He said further, "With the loss of the sight of my eyes, I have chosen to see with my heart, and though I do not know the dimensions of your face, I do know the meaning of your presence." I felt this conversation. And I saw this man, and I felt that I had been seen.

We lived in Scotland about two years, met a lot of people, heard a lot of great theologians and philosophers speak. No encounter that I had with any person was ever more traumatic and significant to me than the encounter I had with this man, who with no eyes, spoke not a single word, but left me forever changed and for this I am grateful to God and grateful to him. I wish sometimes that I could go back and recapture the moment, you know how it is when these things are all over and you say, "Why didn't I?" I think that I would have liked to have knelt by his side and poured out my gratitude to him, for the gift he had given, but when I reconsider I know that is not necessary. I'm glad that human beings are not limited to words or conversation, but because of that man, what I would have said to him, I will say to you, and what I learned from him I want to share with you.

Theodore Reik—and I mentioned this recently—Theodore Reik is the person responsible for giving us the expression "the third ear." He says we have two ears on our head and one ear in our heart, and true listening is when we're listening with the third ear, when you're listening with the heart. He could also have said that we have three eyes, two eyes in our head and there's a third eye in the heart. And maybe the eye and ear and the heart are one and the same.

It is so much a gift for a person to be able to see with his heart. You might use another word for heart, you might say seeing with the soul or seeing with one's own being and I guess that would be a matter of choice. But, if you follow me and if you understand what I'm saying you might even be living in Midland, or Odessa or someplace like that. I want you to consider looking at yourself with the eyes of your heart and seeing yourself in a new and different way. Now this is difficult, and not everyone will want to do this, but some will and some have already. In fact, some of the people who listen have shared with me, and I've shared with you what we're talking about.

One of the things about seeing yourself with your inner eyes, not just the image that you see in the mirror, but the self that you see when you look at yourself with your inner eyes and your inner being. I have heard people talk about experiences they've had that were very significant. I've heard people say, "When this happened to me everything was different." I've heard people talk about the experience of being a Christian. when they said, all of a sudden the faces of people changed, the room changed, the situation changed, I don't think that's a physical change and I don't have any need to call that a miracle, particularly I think the miracle takes place inside the person rather than outside of him. Now, if you're looking for a different experience in life, you might consider the willingness to remain open, just seeing yourself in a new and different way. You might see yourself as one single, solitary being. I want you to look at yourself with these inner eyes, to look at yourself and be willing to see yourself in a manner completely different from any way that you've ever seen yourself before—to be able to see yourself, first of all made in the image of God, and I want to say that of all the beings in the universe, that you're the only creature in the universe made in the image of God. God made every one of us persons—no I won't say it that way— made you a person. And gave you a worth, and a value—and this is important—an identity that no other human being in all of the universe has. What I'm saying to you is there isn't another you anywhere.

You are infinitely valuable, and you have immeasurable worth. This is inside you; it doesn't have anything to do with your position in life; it doesn't have anything to do with educational, social, or economic achievement. It's just the fact that you're made by God, you're made in His image and that God has written His signature inside you and the signature of God is in the total person that you are. So, would you look at yourself that way? Close your eyes so that your inner vision is not obscured by seeing things outside, close your eyes and see yourself as a person made by God. I want to tell you something else: made for God, for yourself, but also for God. And God didn't make you just to do His will and do His work, God made you to enjoy yourself and to live in this world. So, look at yourself with your inner eyes and be willing to see yourself as you are. Now, made by God, and this is where the action is.

"God don't make no Junk, you're not Junk," you have worth and value and you matter to God. Okay? Now, and the worth made by God and the worth, I'll write the worth is inside; you don't have to earn your worth, and you don't have to buy it, and you don't have to deserve it, and you don't have to prove it. Your worth is an eternal thing, and it is given by God. This means that you have the right to live, you have the right to be who you are, you have a place in the universe as one of our popular writings so beautiful lays out. And you have the right to be yourself, you don't have to pretend to be anyone else, you don't have to mimic or ape or copy anyone, and you don't have to have anyone else's approval. I mean in order to be worthwhile, sure, we want the approval of other people, but your worth and value does not come from what people think or say about you, or what they do to you. This does affect us and influence us. But look at yourself, close your eyes and open your inner self to see yourself as you are: here's the beauty of you. It would be good, I think, for me and for people that I address as friends, if we could see ourselves as having the gift of life, if you could see yourself as living.

I was going somewhere the other day and came to an intersection, and there was a long line of cars, and I realized that this was a funeral procession and I stopped. I did not know who it was, but I prayed for the family there in that lead car, and then I wondered what they were thinking. We value life so lightly, and we're always in a hurry going from one place to another, doing one thing and another. We take life for granted until there's a threat of losing it, and then everything takes on a different perspective. You see, we're busy, and we don't have time for anything until we realize life is playing out—then all of a sudden we've got time. Now, we can't see life with these two eyes, but if you close them, and look with the eyes of your inner self, you'll see yourself as living. And this is the basis for your richness, for your wealth and for your awareness and your strength. Hey man, you're alive, did you know that! Some people are dead, some are dying, but you're alive.

You'll probably going to live through the day and so will I. And for the capacity and the ability to see this, and to focus on this rather than focus on the problems and the difficulties and the nuisances and the little petty annoyances that creep in and bother us. This will give you a different focus and a different meaning and a different direction in life when you can see yourself as just living. There is —I was trying to remember when I was coming out here—one of the Shakespearean plays there's a king whose daughter, Cordelia, I think she died and I've forgotten his name or the play. And if you remember it, bully for you, but I don't remember it. He's stagger across the stage with the limp, dead, lifeless figure of his daughter in his arms and he says, he asks, the question, "Why should a dog, a cat, a rat have life and you—no life at all?" I remember at the funeral of a very close friend, watching a very small bug of some kind—an insect—craw through the green matting that the funeral home had put down there to cover the scarred earth, and I was struck by the fact that the insect had life—he had what my friend had lost. And the insect is a different kind of life, a different quality of life, but the insect was alive; my friend was dead. So, I'm saying to you: you have this; you have life today, and if you look at it and see it, all of a sudden it changes the perspective of the whole world around you.

Another thing you can do with your inner eye, you can see others, other people. I mentioned this one time on this program. Hey, I like it when you write and when you respond, but I talked one time about looking at your wife and looking at other people, and a man wrote in and said, "I looked at my wife for the first time in five or ten years and discovered again how truly beautiful she is." He said, "The sixty-seven years I have been graciously kind to my wife, they've made her more beautiful every day, but," he said," I hadn't looked at her for a long time. Thanks to you, I love her."

Close your eyes sometimes when you're with somebody, and you can see them better. You don't even have to be with them, you can close your eyes when you're away from them and you can see them. It may be that to see your wife, your husband, your son, or daughter with these inner eyes will lead you into a new relationship with the other person.

What I want to say about the other person, and looking at him is when you open yourself up to see another person, when you see this other person, you'll see him made by God, and you'll see God's work inside him, too. Now he has infinite worth and value just like you do, and he's made in the image of God, and he's loved by God and he's cared for by God, just exactly like you are. That doesn't mean he can replace you or you can replace him. It means that God is big enough and gracious enough, and gentle enough to love all of His children without neglecting any. There are what?— three-and-a-half or four billion people on the face of the earth— God is not limited and loves every single creature that He's made.

And when you can see yourself made in the image of God, then you're really free, and I think the shades are pulled off of your eyes, scales. So, you can see another person as he is, with his own worth and value inside him, rather than trying to identify him by what he does, or where he came from, or the color of his skin, or the particular accent or dialect with which speaks. If you can do this, man, you are unique. A lot of people cannot see this.

And the next thing–and some of you are already ahead of me–when you can see with your inner eye this other person, you can see his inner worth. You stop measuring him, and you stop comparing yourself with him; you see this other person is unique because you see yourself as unique. And when I say unique I mean that you have a place, and you have a face, and you have an address, inner address, and you have a home inside you, and you have a place, not just on this planet, but a place in eternity. You are greater than infinity and you are greater than eternity because you carry inside you, resident, the life of God. God has vested—God has deposited—His life in you, and you carry in yourself the very life of God. Hey, look into the mirror: try that. Then close your eyes and look into your heart. God's life is resident in you, and He Is also resident in me, and He's resident in the person there in the room with you right now, He's resident in your wife, your son, your daughter, your neighbor or your enemy, or the stranger, or the service station attendant, or the waiter at the table, or the waitress, or the service man who comes to your home, or the man who comes to collect the rent, God is there. You can also see this other person as living. The thing about this other person's "livingness" is a lot of times we use this as an excuse to postpone improving our relationship with him.

You know I've been a pastor—as I told you—for about twenty-seven or twenty-eight years and I've conducted a lot of funerals, I never know whether to say, conduct a funeral and perform a wedding or perform a funeral and conduct a wedding. I guess that depends on the people involved or something. But when you can see this other person as living, then all of a sudden it changes the relationship. I have heard so many times, family members and friends and relatives say, "Oh, if I'd only known, I would have done things so differently and I wish I could go back and change things." One day, I went one afternoon about four o'clock with a man to select a casket for a very small child. It was a bitter heartbreaking experience, and we made it through. I don't know who had the toughest time, the father or me; the mother was in shock in the hospital. But while we were going through this agony, he said, "if I had known when I went to work this morning that I would be picking out a casket for my daughter at four o'clock, I would have gone out of my mind." Then he turned to me and he held on to my arms and said, "This morning my child was alive." Now, you can't see this with your eyes, with these two eyes. But you can see it with your inner eye, if you look, the persons around you are alive. It is so very important to see that. Man, you're alive and the other side of the coin reads I'm alive too, but I'm alive just for a time, and you're alive just for a time. Don't wait until life is over for me before you decide that things could have been different between us. And don't wait until life is over for your husband or wife, son or daughter, mother or father, or for your enemy, or your friend or the stranger, don't wait until it's over before you're willing to see the person and if you are brave to be seen by him. But we'll talk about that later. The most important thing on earth is for you to see yourself, as seen by God. To see other people. I think maybe this is the time when we truly come closest to God, and when we become, if ever, most God like, when we have the capacity to see ourselves and others with the eyes that God placed inside us.

November 1975

THE STRUCTURE OF CHANGE

Seasons are changing: you can't miss it if you are aware of color and if you're aware of temperature. I was in my back yard this morning watering some plants, the air was crisp and cool and I watched the leaves falling and this time of year is a very special time, and I was aware that I had to make some changes in my schedule and routine because it's not summertime anymore. I watched people make adjustments in schedule, calendar, different activities. Fall is when your kids go back to school and the adults go to college and we stop a lot of our summertime sports and activities, not much swimming goes on in the wintertime in Abilene or Lubbock or Midland or Odessa, so we find other things to do with our time, simply because our seasons change.

Now I want to ask this morning about change. The person who has the capacity to make changes in his life is happy, healthy, and growing. When a person doesn't make changes, he stagnates outwardly and I think sometimes inwardly and becomes bitter and cynical and sometimes morbid. The difficult thing about change is we have to say goodbye to the familiar and find new ways of filling time and filling activity in order to give a new structure to the new way of life that we've chosen. One of the reasons that I'm talking about this is because after the last week or two, I've heard from a lot of you who have listened to my talk about what to do in the interim period, one person told me that he has swept floors after had heard the telecast. The ability to change and the capacity to change is one of the ways that we copy with grief. When a person can accept the loss of a family member, the loss of a friend, the loss of somebody dearly loved and can go through the experience of change which includes, shock, grief, readjustment, and the rescheduling this person is healthy and he is growing.

I said that we would talk about the structure of change and there are some specific steps that a person can take when he is experiencing change, either out of necessity forced upon him or as a result of choice. Hey, it's a lot nicer when a person experiences a change as a result of choice, rather than going through change because necessity has forced it on him.

The first thing I want to say is that when you look at yourself and your place in the universe, if you see yourself as this person and this is the earth, now the proportion might be off a little bit but that's all right. What I want you to realize is that when you have a relationship with your creator and you have vertical dimension of faith in your life, then you have an anchor and you have relationship with God. How I don't mean that God is up. We all know that,; I'm talking about relationship not direction. When you are related to God and you have an eternal relationship with God, your creator—give Him any name you choose—then you can experience anything, if this is you. Can you see that little dot right there? That's you or me. Then you can experience anything that happens this way or this way, as long as you have this relationship. If you have nothing to tie to outside and beyond yourself, mister, It's going to get rough, or madam. And the longer you live the rougher it gets, because pretty soon when your body starts to wear out and you don't have any place to move, when you have to move out of that body, then it might get crowded in there just before you vacate it.

So, first thing is a relationship with God and when a person has a healthy, active, continuing relationship with God, he can experience any kind of change. He can experience grief; he can experience job change; he can experience reverses in his financial, social, economic position. I don't say that you'll always like it, and that it will not be painful, but it won't kill you. There's a real possibility that after you experience this kind of change, and some of you have written about this in the mail, that after you experience this kind of change you'll find yourself in a situation much happier for you than the previous situation that you were so reluctant to release. Now, I'm going to do some very significant drawings. I think we used this same illustration last week. I want you to imagine a place inside your body and this is your body, and this is a place in your body, relatively speaking, that was filled by a family member—or a friend and this friend dies or this friend moves to another section of the country, or the friendship is broken. Ad there's this much space inside you where, previously, your life had been reserved for this friend. You reserve a certain time to talk with him or think about him or certain value that you placed on him, it may be your husband or wife, son or daughter, mother or father, business associate or just a social relationship. Now, when this person is removed, there's a vacuum and a void in your life and some of you have expressed it this way to me and others: "I feel empty on the inside."

Now change means the capacity to change means you have the capacity to fill this space with a new activity, with a new series of persons, with new commitments, and with new behavior; so, that your life doesn't just crumble in here and die because there's a vacuum in the center. Now, when I say structure change, I mean that one of the ways you fill the space is by establishing new acquaintances and new relationships with people that admittedly are not as significant to you as the old relationship was. When you give up someone that you've had a close intimate and personal relationship with, somebody else won't do, another person just won't do. Now the capacity to change means you will take the unfamiliar relationship with a new person or persons and begin to move it into the space of your life previously occupied by one lived and lost and give yourself time and opportunity for readjustment for a period of trial and error testing and relationships and you'll find that in the years to come new persons will inhabit this area of your life formerly occupied by the friend you lost.

Now I do not say that persons can be replaced, I am only saying that new relationship can be established. If you've lost your mother or father, and you had a good relationship with them,– son or daughter, husband or wife—or even, I know some people who've had dogs for years and years and years and lost their dog and they get another dog, but it was never like the old one. Now, we get attached to these people, and I think—now this is very relative here—the longer we get attached to a person or an activity, I think the stronger the wall grows that outlines the relationship of the person, and that's just a place inside our lives that belongs personally and particularly to the individual place or thing and nobody else can ever take that person's place or the place inside our lives that belongs personally and particularly to the individual place or thing, in some cases, I admit that. I am saying that we are so structured, thank God, that we can find new activities, new places, and new people.

It may mean that eventually the place will have to be changed, and instead of being one large place, you may have several small places in your life, that's where you have put other activities and other persons to take the place of the person or relationship that you've lost. This applies to persons who've lost friends in death or by a break in relationship or by just a geographical change. Now, I mean specifically that when you go through the experience of grief that you can reach out and you can find this other person and begin to establish new relationships with him. I'm saying you will not want to, everything in you will be wishing you could go back to the old places of safety and security. You are running a risk; you will probably be unsure of yourself; it will probably be necessary during the early stages of grief for you to do this when everything in you says, "I don't want to." I don't mean the first week or two or three weeks. And there are always some well-meaning people who say, "What you need to do is..." or "I wish you would...."

When people come on with that, run, and tell them goodbye. Generally, when a person is adapting to grief or loss in its critically stages, you don't need people around to tell you what to do. That could be dangerous because they may be right, but unless and until the decision for change has taken place inside you, you're not going to be happy with what you do.

I do not think that it's an accident that God in His wisdom chose for the earth—this particular planet on which we live—to have seasons; I don't think it is an accident that our life is divided into twenty-four-hour sections on this planet, and at least a third of our time—in order for us to remain healthy—at least one third of our time must be spent unconscious. Sleep is a necessity, work is a necessity, or some kind of creative or productive activity, and also, play is a necessity, and God in His wisdom has designed us so that life to be healthy must have a certain rhythm and routine that involves work play, rest, work, play, rest. In this particular section of the planet, we have season of the year that are relatively cold, some in-between and some seasons that are relatively hot. This give to life a variety which requires change, adaptation, and the establishment of new activities, new routines, and new relationships, and I do not believe that this is an accident. I think God is an intelligent and wise person. He doesn't leave anything to change or happenstance or chance. He also, in His wisdom, has made change the only single constant factor in your life and in mine.

Look around you: I do not care what your life situation is at this present moment, eventually, sir, it's going to change, and you will change, and the change may come slowly, carefully, and gradually, or it may come suddenly like a gunshot in the darkness. It may come like a messenger or missile from outer space, the change comes. I am not sure of this, but it seems to me the more I make the necessary changes in my life, by choice, the fewer changes I find forced upon me. I think that's right. When I take the initiative and make changes that really need to be made and I am the initiator of the change, I find change fewer changes forced upon me. Every house requires some cleaning, regularly, routinely. Every building requires a certain amount of maintenance and cleaning routinely. So does every person's life require cleaning and maintenance regularly and routinely. The body does not adapt itself to neglect. The body—when taken for granted without proper care—has its own way of responding and rebelling. It's also true that your while life does this. Boredom is your way of rebelling against an untended, uncared for life, and when you say, "I'm bored and I'm sick and tired of living," you might look to see how much attention and time you've been giving to your schedule and how much choice you've exercised in the way that you used your time. People who are bored with life are not regularly making choices and selections about what they'll do with their time. When a marriage bogs down and gets to being boring and monotonous, the persons involved—the husband and the wife—have not been exercising choices and initiating change.

The happiest marriages that I know anything about are made up of a man and woman who exercise the freedom and privilege of choice with regularity; who find themselves engaging constantly in new activities; who are excited at the prospect of meeting new people. I do not mean a frantic, frenzied chase of life, but happily married people engaging in activities and relationships that present new fresh attractive stimulating relationships, ideas, and concept; those marriages don't get monotonous and bored.

The same old sevens and sixes—sixes and sevens— whatever the expression is here in West Texas—will choke a marriage to death. Getting up every morning and going through your eight to five process and coming home and doing the same old thing, you'll get tired and you'll get bored or your wife will. And it will eventually play out, just like your body will rebel if you take it for granted and do not give it the proper care and the proper exercise and proper nurture. I believe that a man's relationship with God can become stagnant in very much the same way unless it is fed constantly with new ideas and new concepts and new readings—particularly reading from the Bible—and new fresh relationships with other individuals who are themselves experiencing some excitement and some enthusiasm in terms with their own relationship with God.

This business of worshiping God can also be described—this is a change, Okay? The way I worship God and my relationship with God does not have to do just with what church I choose or the frequency of my attendance at church, it has to do with the way that I see myself in the universe, and it has to do with the way I see myself in the family of Man on this earth. I talked with a friend not long ago. I hadn't seen him in a good while, and I said you know, "How are you doing?"—the usual talk we that we have, and he said, "Well, I've been going through some new stuff."

I said, "What are you doing?"

He said, " My God is growing." How, it shocked me at first, but what he meant was, not that God himself was changing, but that his concept of God was enlarging and expanding in his own mind. When he said his God was growing, he meant that his understanding of God and his relationship with God was a growing thing. He went on, as we talked through t the afternoon, he went on to say that his God had become big enough that he could take care of his health—and he'd recently had some health problems. That his God just kept getting bigger and bigger and bigger all the time, and he added that as his God grew, his own—this person's responsibilities in his life. The more he gave up God's responsibilities in his life, the more time and energy he had to do the things he was supposed to do. A lot of times we kill ourselves trying to do God's work in our lives, when if we would allow God to do His work, we'd have a lot more time and energy to do our own. You will just flat kill yourself trying to be God—and you won't succeed at it—nobody has ever yet succeeded at being God. Now some people have been close to it. Some people have become so perfectionistic in their thinking and have so set their goals on being perfect that they've almost made it, just before the suicide or the nervous breakdown or the total collapse of this person's family and social work. You're not going to ever make it in your effort to be God—you can make it in your effort to be a human being.

Change for you and for me—as far as I know for everybody—change comes when we set ourselves deliberately to the task of experiencing new activities, new persons, new situations, new emotions, and new relationships, which–though they do not have the emotional value of relationships lost—will, in time prove themselves worthy of significant, particular, and special place in our life.

I went through a very significant change in my life three years ago. I found that I was giving up something which was for me one of the most precious things in my life, not one of the most precious persons, but one of the most precious things. I drove to Dallas and I talked this over with a friend. And he said, "I predict that in a year you'll consider this the happiest day of your life when you decided to make this change." I could not see it then but he was right. Within a year, I had decided it was for me the happiest and most significant day of my life. One of the things that makes me comfortable with change is the fact that when Jesus Christ was on earth, he submitted himself with change. The same kind of change that characterizes your life and characterizes mine. He didn't fight against change; He even lost some friends and replaced them with new ones. He gave up His mother and father and experienced the change of moving from the relationship of child to the parents. I encourage you to make your pilgrimage of change.

November 1975

CHANGE

These things I've talked to you about, serenity, courage, and wisdom are prayers that' a described to several people. But it goes like this: The Serenity to accept the things I cannot change, The Courage to change the things I can, and the wisdom to know the difference. Now this is used by a lot of people, it's, I think the most popular prayer by members of Alcoholic Anonymous. It's also used by other people who find it necessary to distinguish between areas of responsibility, their responsibility, and the responsibility of other people. The serenity to accept the things I cannot change is a recognition of one's own humanity, it's a recognition of one's own limitations, it's the willingness on the part of an individual to admit that he's not perfect. It's an acknowledgment that there are areas of human responsibility and areas of divine responsibility, and this is where you really make a decision to accept the limitations and capabilities of your life and you really recognize it. The recognition that there are limits gives you the freedom to establish goals until limits are recognized, and believe me you're very respected. You're not really going to have a happy adjustment and a happy relationship to life.

I'm going to use the blackboard to get some of these things listed. While I make a list here, I'd like for you to make your own list because my list would not coincide exactly with yours and yours would not coincide with mine. Hey, before I do that I wanted to say that I enjoyed the mail, and have renewed some old friendships, recently someone who used to watch the telecast years ago, picked the station up by accident and listened last Sunday morning, and I'm glad you're here. These are the things I cannot change. We had the idea that if we prayed hard enough and long enough that anything was possible for us, and believe me, that's not true. We've gotten the idea in some areas, Christianity particularly, that we could manipulate God and we could control God by praise. We had the idea that we could control the weather and also that we could control other people. Don't you believe it!

God never created man so that another person could control him. I've said this before and said it many times: other people affect us, other people influence us, but other people do not control us. And the more you fix this in your mind, the happier you will be with yourself and your own area of responsibility. Some of the things that I cannot change, recognize and honestly face will give me a new realization of my own capabilities and potential, and I mean some very simple basic things that are a part of your life and mine.

The first thing that I list is: "I cannot change others." The behavior of your wife or the behavior of your husband is not your responsibility. He may never be the man that ·you would like for him to be. She may never be the woman that you would like for her to be. Your children may never be exactly like you would like them to be. And as long as you beat your head against a stone wall trying to make any other person conform to the image you have for them in your mind, the misery and unhappiness and sadness and depression you will experience as a person, I know. You cannot change others. You can influence them, and you can affect them, and you can impress them and you can advise and you can suggest, and you can hope and dream and pray, but ultimately and finally this.is the responsibility of the other person and this applies even to small children. I have heard parents say, I've just done everything I could and he is the most stubborn self-willed child I've ever seen.

There are some like that. I have found that the children who were stubborn and self-willed and headstrong generally had parents like that. That might not help your feelings, but it will help your logic, it's true.. Now,, another thing you cannot change is time. Time passes and time operates in continuum, it moves, you cannot change your age, you cannot change the date, you cannot change the hour, you cannot change the seasons. One of the ways we try to change the seasons is by saying, "I hate summer and I hate hot weather, or I hate winter and I hate cold weather." Or some people hate the wind. I've heard some people say, "I just get so angry when the wind blows." If you don't like the wind in west Texas you might want to consider some other location. The willingness to accept the reality of time as permanent or the continuum as being permanent state in which we live make for a better life. If you dislike growing older, it may be wise maybe if you'd consider the alternative. The alternative to growing older is to die, and it might be that growing old means that you are. still alive, it might be that you're surviving, it might be that you're coping, it might be that God has a place and a purpose for your life on this earth Another thing about people who rebel against time and resist time, is their own appearance. I know some people that get unhappy with their appearance as they begin to age and get older. It might be that this ls one of the ways that we resist the reality of time. One of the things you cannot change is time.

Another thing you cannot change is space. Now, we fight against these things in a lot of little subtle ways. One of the ways that some people resist space and try to change space is by speeding in an automobile or by fretting and always being late. And we say, Oh, look what time it is, I'm late; I need to be there. The fact that you are late and you are here and need to be there does not alter either time or space. And one of the ways that we work ourselves into a frenzy and give ourselves ulcers and cause ourselves to panic is by trying to change the reality of time and space, These two are closely tied in together. When I was thinking about what I'd say today, I was thinking about gravity, you know some people try to change gravity and deny the law of gravity and the other basic laws that give the universe its structure. My freedom to live in this universe is based on my respect for its laws and the basic structure of the universe.

Primarily, in these two things, my freedom to live in society means that I respect the rights and the privileges of others right here.

I want you to take a theoretical situation and suppose I could change you and you could change me, and suppose I'm under your authority and you're under mine: this means that I would never really know where I am, and it means you would never know where you are. It would mean that you would have to check in with me every morning, noon, and night to get your signals, and I would have to do the same thing with you. It would mean, furthermore, that I would lose my identity as a person and you would lose your identity as a person. It would, in effect, mean that I would finally be a robot and so would you. If we could change each other and control each other's lives and feelings and decisions, and if every human being could do this, this earth would be bedlam and there would be no safe place on this earth for you. When we read in these science fiction movies or watch ·science fiction movies or have this kind of talk, we shudder to think about mind-control and thought-control. The people from across the ocean called "communist,"—you notice I said from across the ocean—have come up with an idea called "brain washing;"—I wonder sometimes if brain washing started with communism. I think sometimes in our efforts to love, and I believe it is basically an effort to love, I wonder if we haven't resorted to a form of brain washing which we are tempted as we said to a person, I love you; therefore, you should—I love you, and I wish you would—I love you, and if you love me, you would— and if you love me why don't you— and I know you say you love me, but you did or did not do this. I think this might be a subtle effort on our part to control another person, I think it might be a form of brain washing that we sometimes use on children. When we use love to manipulate, or fear to manipulate or anxiety to manipulate or the uncertainty of a relationship to manipulate and to get a particular kind of behavior in another person.

Recognizing that you cannot change these things will give you a new serenity inside, it will give you a new peace because, when you recognize that you cannot change these things then you are really free for the first time to put your wife into the hands of God or your husband in the hands of God, and you no longer assign to that individual the responsibility for your peace of mind, joy, safety—whatever you are interested in at that particular time.

Hey, now the first part of the prayer is "God grant me the serenity to accept the things I cannot change," and the next part says and "the Courage to change the things I can." Now, this is the "can change" column. Okay, the first thing under the "can change" is: I can change me, with God's help, thank God. One of the exciting and dramatic and beautiful characteristics of a human being is, I am capable of change, I have a flexibility of life, my life is pliable and I can change. This is true of you, it's true of every person who makes the inward decision—and I'm convinced it's an inward decision—who makes an inward decision to choose another pattern of behavior, thought, response, who chooses another attitude, chooses a new lifestyle and a new mind stance. I can change me; I can change the way I use time. I can spend my time working or playing, I can spend my time crying or laughing, I can spend my time worshiping or cursing, I can spend my time building my life, or I can spend my time destroying my life. And *you* do the same thing. When you recognize the things that you can change and you have the courage as a gift of God—and this is a prayer—and you have the courage to change these things, it's a whole new ball game at this. point and you can have a totally new lifestyle. One of the things I can change about myself is the way I use time.

Another thing I can change is the way I use space. I have a certain amount of body space that is mine and this body is a part of me and it's part of my space. I can change the way I feel about my body; I can change the way I use my body; I can change the way I care for my body, assuming I have a different respect for myself.

There are people on this earth, who have since they were five or six years old, been in the process of destroying the body space that preserves their life, You can destroy your body in a lot of ways. Some people destroy with drugs, some people destroy with alcohol; some people destroy the body with food; some with work, some people destroy their bodies I'm convinced with inactivity, there's just a lot of ways you can do it. I've seen a lot of older adults lament the fact that the kids were so deeply involved in the drug scene and I certainly share their concern that the kids destroy their lives with drugs. I also share a concern that an adult destroys his life with food, or work, or inactivity—or more than this—that an adult destroys his life with hatred or anger or resentment, or bitterness or littleness. The beauty of all this: this you can change, it's not one of the things that can't be changed. When you make your decision to change yourself, I change me, you change you. When you make this decision then there's a new destiny that lies ahead for you. When I decide to change the way I use time and the way I use space, then I'm already in the process of changing myself. I can also change the way I relate to others, and I reversed this and put others last, for this simple reason: The way I handle myself through a process of growth which is continuing to change, the way I preserve myself in time and space determines the relationships that I establish with others. What I mean is this, if I'm busy dying and I'm busy killing myself, I'll use time destructively, I'll work too hard, I'll eat too fast, I'll drive too fast, I'll think too slow. And then I'll use space destructively, I'll be one of these persons who has never cared about his own body and does not take care of himself. Then—and this is the important thing—then I will use others destructively the same way I use time and space destructively.

So, when I take courage as a gift from God and set about the task of changing myself, I have everything I need for a happy, scintillating, rich, full, and complete life. It's one thing to sit back and say, "well, my problem is others... the reason that I'm not happy is because of others... the reason that I'm not satisfied is because of others... it's my wife's fault... it's my husband's fault... my mother's... or the reason I'm not happy is because I don't have enough time."

Every person on earth has the same amount of time, or it's the space. It's because I live in Texas or New York or California or Florida. And the reason I'm not happy is because I live here instead of there, and if I just had this other place to live or when I used to live there, then I was happy; that's not true. And it's one of the ways that you cop out on life by dealing continually with things that you cannot change. Now the choice, the alternative here is to live in the area where you're experiencing the courage to change and when you stay with the only person on earth you can change, and that's yourself. You change the way you use time and space and then you change the way you use other people, but the way you relate to other people. This person uses others when he's trying to deal in aeras that he cannot change. This person relates. A miserable, unhappy, sad person is a people user, is a people pleaser, is a people manipulator. The growing, happy, maturing, healthy person relates to people leaving them free and demanding at the same time his own freedom.

Now, after you recognize the things that you cannot change, here's the third part of the prayer, which I think is sheer genius and sheer wisdom whoever the first man was that wrote this prayer, and this is one of those plan-ahead drawings, but his person requires wisdom: "The wisdom to know the difference" between the things I cannot change and the things I can change. I guess maybe this is the single most important part of the whole concept of the whole idea. When I have the wisdom to know where my responsibility begins and where it ends, which is where yours begins. You see, my responsibility begins and ends with myself. Where your responsibility begins, mine ends. To have the wisdom to know where this line is, is the final culminating thought in this particular prayer. If you're miserable and unhappy and you're not doing well on this earth, I can love you and care for you and pray for you. I must also recognize that there's not anything I can do in the area of the responsibility that is yours. I must have the wisdom to know that I cannot change you, and I must have the wisdom to know that I can change me.

Now this is something that I would like you to hear, it does not apply to everyone all the time in every circumstance and in every situation, but it's true some of the time. There's a very real possibility that when I'm working as hard as I can to change you, that I'm doing this because there's something in me that I know that I need to change and I refuse to face it. I may be that you're trying so hard to change your wife so you won't have to face yourself. Or you're trying so hard to change your husband because you know that some things you need to face yourself and then you can change him. Sometimes we do this with children. Sometimes with our parents. Sometimes with others, friend or enemy. So, when you're most disgusted, most displeased, most unhappy with others you might wat to stop...stand in front of the mirror and look at the man who face you in the mirror and say, "What is it in myself that I'm refusing to deal with."

One of the beauties of this man Jesus of Nazareth is right here at this point. I think He came—I know He came—into the world to give us a whole new concept of living and a whole new understanding of ourselves and respect for other people. One of the beauties of His life is the respect that He had for others. He never forced change on anyone. He could have, He didn't. He could have miraculously by summoning the powers that were His by virtue of His being. He could have forced a change, but He leaves men free to be themselves; He leaves men free to make their own choices and to make their own decisions, and He was busy doing His own work.

He respected areas in His life where He needed to make new choices and decision. I think He was a very wise man. This is evidenced in his teachings. When the people listened to him talk , they said, you know, "Where did this man get wisdom like this?" They were talking about the fact that He was acquainted with the wisdom of all ages, that He spoke like one of the prophets who had been schooled and trained for year and years. But the real wisdom and the real beauty of Christ, in my understanding, is that this man recognized the limits and the boundaries of His own human life and these limits and boundaries were voluntarily imposed, but he recognized them and He accepted them. Recognized that there were some things He could not change and some things He could change, and He had the wisdom. Maybe my imitation of Christ—maybe my worship of God—could begin right here.

August 1973

LOVING YOURSELF

(Laity Lodge Retreat)

No statement applies to everyone all of the time under every circumstance and in all situations. So, if you will not take what I say and apply it to extremes, but will keep it In the broad median, it will be easier to accept.

I want to say first that God made you, and that God made you like Himself. He used Himself for a pattern and you reflect the Image of God—not just as a physical appearance, but as a total being, a total entity. God's clearest picture of Himself is you, including the sunrises and sunsets. If you want a clear picture of God—if you want the clearest picture of God you can find anywhere in the universe—look in the mirror. You are made in the image of God: God put His own life in you when you became a living soul. **You** reflect, most clearly, God's image. It is not said of anything, any animal, mineral, or any other entity anywhere that it is created in the image of God—nothing but a human being bears His image. And THAT includes you. With all of the potential and capacity you have–realized and unrealized, dreamed of and not even dreamed of—God's creative work in you, in giving you life, is the basic essence of your personality.

So, guess what! It is all right for you to be yourself. You don't have the right to call yourself a mistake. God does not make mistakes. In a little church in Tennessee, working with a bunch of kids there, I saw signs plastered all over the building: GOD DON'T MAKE JUNK. That's poor grammar, but it's beautiful theology.

You do not have the right to call yourself a mistake. You do not have the right to call yourself a cosmic maverick. You are not a reject. God made you and He made only one you. In all of time and space and eternity, there has not ever been another you. And if the world stands another hundred million years, there will not ever be anywhere, at any time, or in any place, another you. There are about three and a half or four billion people in the world today, and you could line them u four abreast and march them by, in front of you, and look every one of them in the eye, and you would not see you anywhere.

In a very particular, distinctive, beautiful way, there is only one you in all of time and space and eternity. It might be that the unpardonable sin–might be–would be the refusal to be one's own self, and thereby, having rejected God, never knowing the meaning of your life on this earth.

And I need to say, too, that when Jesus Christ died on the Cross, He did not die for people in general or for humanity, He died for you. And if there had been only one person in all the universe who had sinned, and if that one person had been you, Jesus Christ would have died for you alone. In a very real way, He did—just for you. It is just that personal. It's just that intimate, and God's love is just that particular.

I'm glad God doesn't love us in bunches—like bananas. I don't like bunchy love, or lumpy love. And He doesn't love us in tribes or races. He doesn't even love us in political parties, and although this may be hard for some people to accept, He does not just love Texans! He love us as individuals. And if you could take your highest and holiest concepts of a father's love and multiply it by infinity, it would be something like the love that God has for you. (If you have more than one child, you know you don't have to worry about which one you love the most.)

Now, when God made us, He chose—in his wisdom—to make us human, though He could have chosen to make us some sort of angelic beings. (I don't know anything about those, but I assume that maybe they're some sort of creatures that live continually in the presence of God and praise Him night and day; I doubt if they sin a great deal. If they spend all of their time praising God night and day.)

But when God chose your existence on this earth, He gave you and me total freedom. This is what I like about the security of God. He is so secure and so free that when He made Homo sapiens—when he made us—He did not create us with a limited freedom, but so gave us the capacity for determining our own destiny that we can make a decision here about our state even in infinity. How, sometimes I don't like this (and there are other people who don't like it), but I believe that my freedom– and this might be a personal testimony– is so great that I cannot only determine my destiny here but for eternity. If my freedom is limited, then I am allowed to make a few minor decisions here on earth, and finally and ultimately, God is going to wipe out what He doesn't like and say, "Now that you've messed it up, I'm going to straighten it out." thereby, negating the freedom, though I possess it.

That is not true. God gives us the awful freedom to say "yes" to him, and also the frightening capacity to say "no." When you in your humanity are falling, stumbling, falling, learning, and growing, this is part of your own nature. It is not something that happens contrary to God's knowledge and to God's love and to God's plan.

One time, when I was in Del Rio for a weekend, I was out early and saw a father walking in the patio, holding the hand of a small toddler who had on some new tennis shoes and could barely walk. And you know how—when you can barely walk– the toes drag? But this father was very patient, and this unusual—usually (in case you don't know), the mother is taking the child to breakfast—I imagine the mother was sleeping in late or something—The father walked very patiently with him across the patio and took him to the restaurant. Later on—and we didn't get to the restaurant for a good while—he was still trying to feed this kid, who had egg all over him, and the daddy was trying to clean the egg off with a dry napkin. I wanted to say, "Hey, if you wet the napkin in the glass of water, it will do a lot better job." But he nearly scaped the skin off the little kid's face and hands, and he kept looking around to see who was watching. I know he was embarrassed, but finally somehow, a ray of light broke through, and he dipped the napkin in the water. I felt a lot better and felt that the kid breathed a sigh of relief. The daddy had just started on the legs because there was egg all down there, too.

But you know, I got to thinking while watching this man—I got to thinking about God and the way He cares for His children. That father never did spank the child for being a sloppy eater or a poor walker. He knew that, at this stage of the child's growth and development, that spilling food and stumbling as he walked was a very necessary and vital part of his life. The father did not require of this two-year-old the performance of a twenty-one-year-old. And I got the feeling, too, that he wasn't waiting for him to get grown before he loved him.

Sometimes we act as if God will love us when we act mature or when we get full grown or when we stop spilling our food and dragging our toes—when we stop doing all of the immature things and making the same childish mistakes that we make over and over and over. And we think "Boy, when I do, then God's going to love me and everything's going to be great!" I have heard some parents say, "They are the most loveable when they are small."

It might be that, with God, we are most loveable when we're small, when we're new Christians, when we recognize our spiritual poverty and when we need Him so much, rather than when we get to be pastors and prominent members in the church and everybody looks up to us and recognizes our worth and our value—I mean everybody but God—For then, we cannot really come as spiritual beggars to God because we've got to maintain our positions in the church. And we can no longer confess our sins because we have to keep up the pretense of being mature. I think we sometimes cut ourselves off from the love of God and from His gentle, fatherly, parental care when we refuse to allow Him to exercise what I'm sure must be the primary concern in His heart—the freedom to love us.

God made you, and when you're looking at yourself, you're looking at God's handiwork, and, as sure as He made you, He loves you. You are not unlovable to God, and though you might not be able to understand this love and to see how God could love you—well, try to remember that there are a lot of things God is capable of doing that you cannot understand; so just don't sweat it.

I want you to do something for yourself right now. Okay? I want you–mentally–to stand alone. If you have a Hoola Hoop, stand in the center of it, as we do in our group sessions. If not, mentally draw a small circle about yourself. Within your circle, say these three things: (1) God loves me; (2) I love me, too; (3) with the love that God has given me, I love God in return.

This is what it means—it is not all, but this is something of what it means—to be a person. Here is where it starts: it starts with the fact that God made you and loves you, and it is all right for you to be YOU–period—no IFs, ANDs, or BUTs. When this happens to you, there is an internal happing–in the present tense–and you cannot be a worthless individual to yourself.

Now, try it again. Just say, "God loves, and I love me, and, with the love He gives me,I love Him in return." You don't even have to manufacture the love; it's provided. You don't even have to love yourself; it's provided. Just take what He gives you and accept it. That's all. God does not wait for us to be mature persons before He loves us. He loves us as we are, where we are, and as the human beings we are.

You ask, "Well, John, but what about my sins?" We are going to get to that in a minute, but let's stay on this while we've got it started. Most of the time, I think we deal more with sin than we do with God, anyway, so I'm trying to reverse the process.

Now when you're ready to love another person, the only way to love that person healthfully is to love him or her as you love yourself. So, if you can start in this inner world: "God loves me, and I love me—" then you are ready to love another person. But unless I can love me and until I can love me, the best I can give you (or anyone else) in the form of love may possibly be disguised hatred. If I hate myself, yet I profess to love you, You'd better be very careful with me. If I love me, I'm free to love you as myself. If I love you, I can love God. If I love God, I will love you, for I can love you as I love myself.—This forms the circle you are standing within—if I say I love God, yet I hate you, then I lie. In fact, when I start judging you, what I'm really doing is confessing my own sins.

Why is it so hard to love ourselves; Because we expect too much of ourselves—much more than God does. You see, if I say to a gathering, "God loves me and I love me, and I love God in return," some people are repelled and feel that this is ridiculous. Now if I say, "We're going to have a little exercise in honesty: so, will you please list your ten greatest faults?" everyone will be more comfortable because they feel this is more honest. But some feel, "I love myself" is fantasy; it's bragging.

Suppose I cannot forgive myself. Suppose I have to stand alone—under the naked grace of God—and say, "I don't deserve it, and I'm not worth it, but God loves me and God forgives me"? What a miracle of grace! Perhaps one of the reasons we cannot learn to live ourselves is that when we do, we have to get off the throne. If you can her me in theological terms, It is becoming more and more obvious to me that the biggest thing about a human being is his "BUT" —and I do not mean that in terms of anatomy—we are a "Yeah, but" people, and if we do not believe that, let's just listen to our "Yeah, buts":

"God loves me, BUT..."

"God forgives, BUT..."

"Jesus Christ came into the world, BUT..."

"I'm a Christian, BUT..."

Do you know what that does? It gives us an escape at every turn in the road so that we do not have to grow, or experience love, or experience the mercy of God. It always give us a back door.

I've even heard men say, "I'm not going to say 'BUT' anymore, BUT...."

* * *

Would you be interested in making a contract with yourself that you will be Oka?,– Let's say– just for the morning?—Don't reject this before you listen to it! Do you want to go for a morning or do you want to try for the whole day? All right, Let's gamble on a day.—You don't have to tell anybody, so don't feel guilty—Even if you fail, you have done a lot of sins worse than this maybe. Now, you will be Okay for today, and today you will act on the assumption that you are made by God, and you are loved by God, and it is all right for you to be yourself. You do not have to apologize for yourself or compensate for being who you are. You do not have to pretend. You can just relax and be YOU. If, in a conversation, you cannot come up with anything witty or profound, that's all right. It is all right to remain quiet—without being self-conscious. If you fall on your face, and make a social mistake, it is all right.

Just consider the possibilities that this day gives you both license and encouragement to be a person made in the image of God, loved by God, to be one who loves himself, and thereby, makes the others who are around him safe by the quality of love which he extends and by the quality of love which he receives.

You young men who are married might want to take this carefully, because if you start giving your acceptance instead of judgment, and if you start becoming intimate and open with her instead of freezing her out, you might scare the girl to death. This goes for wives, too; you might scare him. When you are all right with you, your spouse will be all right with you, too; for you and I both know that when we most pick each other apart is when we are each most unhappy with our respective selves.

I do not get unhappy with my wife until I have first gotten unhappy with myself. And when I start criticizing and condemning, I'm not saying anything about her; I'm say, "Hey, look what's happened to me." Sometimes I think the Bible is true, particularly when it says, "For with the judgment that you judge others, you condemn yourself, for thou that judges, does the same things."

Now, let's talk about perfectionism—the avoidance mechanism we have that allows us to escape intimacy. Transactional analysis, which is becoming very popular across our country, is dealing a lot with intimacy, and it is being picked up now and is becoming almost a cliché. When I say "intimacy," I don't, of course, mean hopping in bed with someone. I mean the kind of emotional, mental, spiritual nearness that gives affirmation to all parties included in the relationship of intimacy. I'm talking about the kind of intimacy that's communicated in a look; I'm talking about the kind of intimacy and acceptance that is communicated in a "Hi" or the kind of intimacy that can be communicated in a silence or tears or laughter or words, or in the calmness of standing on the balcony and looking at the water or the cliff—this kind of intimacy.

If I am "A PERFECTIONIST," I set such high standards for myself that I guarantee myself failure so that having labeled myself a failure, I can shut myself off from you, living with my decision that I am an inferior human being. Then I don't have to get close to you, because if I get close to you, you will discover me, and if you discover me, you will dislike me. If you should say, "But I really do like you, "then I may say, "But you don't really know me; you wouldn't like me, because y you see, I'm a perfectionist and I've got ten goals here for myself. I made nine of them perfectly, but this tenth one, I missed by about just that much...."

My own distorted sense of accomplishment–my own humanism– blocks out the nine successes and points to the tenth, with "Aha! Look! You've failed again!" Then I can live out my old previously established patterns of failure and worthlessness and I can condemn and ridicule and belittle myself. I can live in a world of silent or verbalized withdrawal and I don't have to get close to you or to anybody else. I don't have to love you because I don't love myself, and I don't have to accept your love because I'm not worth it. I can live my life in a little personally constructed world where all is vacuum and void and emptiness—and I can enjoy my suffering.

This Spanish, crazy man, Una Muno, said—in talking about this same thing—: "Here is where each man hides behind his own mask and feasts on the flesh of his own soul." Now, what that means, interpreted for you and for me, is that we choose loneliness. We construct for ourselves lives and relationships that guarantee and defend our loneliness, so that in the most intimate situations, another person will not ever even remotely approach us. Then we will not stand and say to our wives (or husbands), "I'm lonely and I'm defeated, and I need you," because to do so might bring us into a relationship of intimacy and closeness. We can't say to our sons or our daughters or our mothers or our fathers, because this is the kind of honesty we cannot bear. If we did, we would have to give up our perfectionism, and join the human race. We would have to admit ourselves made by God and loved by God, and therefore free to love ourselves. And then–having been made safe with ourselves–we would have to become safe with others.

I think that God is not a perfectionist when He looks at you and me. That's silly, isn't it? He couldn't be—not if some of us look in the mirror. And God is not threatened by our sins. I had a real vision of God one time—recently–to be truthful— when I did this horrible thing; and I knew that when I looked at God that He would just be devastated. I expected to look at God up in Heaven and see Him, Sprawled on the floor, gasping, "Oh, John, how could you do this?" You know? I knew when I had done it, that I could just hear God–in panic: "John has failed Me." And I looked up there, and do you know what God was doing? He was yawning—full in my face! It came clear to me that God knew me better than I did—that the unreasonable goals that I had set for myself, in my world of fantasy, God had never accepted.

I know pretty well what a two-year-old will do, and a five-year-old will do, and a ten-year-old will do; and when I become a totally unreasonable parent is when I expect them to act other than their respective ages. Now God is as good a father as I am, and He is as good a father as you are (and as good a mother, and if you and I have the capacity to love our children, God has the capacity to love us—one hundred million times more than we could ever love our children.

God is patient. He is not in a hurry with us. However impatient we become with ourselves; God does not get in a hurry. And we cannot shock God—or frighten him. God can stand us even when we cannot stand ourselves, because he made us and He loves us and He works with a timetable that is spelled in terms of eons and eternities and infinities. He does not wear a wristwatch. There is no calendar hanging on his kitchen wall. The sun does not rise and set over a barbed wire fence in Heaven.

So—not for the rest of your life, but just for today of this—you might want to let yourself off the hook and just be YOU. Just relax. Try not to impress anybody. You might be able to do without a tranquilizer or two–or a drink–or your fantasy world.

Now, I'm not unreasonable enough to believe that God could do this for you always. But just for a day? Maybe he could. It is all right for you to be yourself today because God is with you. He has a purpose for your being with him—today. So, enjoy God and enjoy being you right now.

January 1978

THE NEW PAST

(Retreat at Laity Lodge)

There are a lot of you here that I do not know. I would like you to know that one of the things my friends do is interrupt me and then we have a conversation instead of just a lecture. I mean I have some material that I have been excited about. I want your response. Thinking back on other times when I've been here....

If you will, look to see what expectations you have of me. If you do have expectations of me, and tell me about them, I will talk to you about them. If you will not tell me about them, I will not be responsible for them. Is that agreeable? Okay? If I have some expectations of you—and I was asking myself what I expect of you when I was thinking about this—I'll make it verbal and put it out in the open.

I'm going to talk today about the New Past and tomorrow about the New Future and the next day about the New Present.

One of the things I've said here is that you can't change the past. I've changed my mind about changing the past because I've found myself doing just that. The other day, I was reading a book and the author talked about how we constantly change the past. His name is Maslow, and he talked about the capacity for remembering...the capacity for selecting memories. He says, too, that we are products of our past and the part of the past that you have integrated into your person is the degree to which—no, let me say that again—the degree to which you have integrated the past into your person is the degree to which you are allowing the past to control your present. This is one of the sure ways to avoid a meaningful, healthy, happy relationship in the present tense—to bring more from the past into the relationship than you are willing to experience in the present. I think I wrote that man's quote down. Here's what he said, "The past is active and alive only insofar as it has recreated the person and has been digested into the present person."

Will you consider that God is eternal now and look to see if there are areas of your life where you have so integrated your past into the present that you are not open to experience what we are here for now and what I'm about now and what you're about now. This means that if you and I had a disagreement eighteen years ago and it had never been resolved, you would have a great deal of difficulty hearing me now. I would also have a great deal of difficulty hearing you. If you bring some of the problems you've had with me into this present week, everything that could possibly happen between us will be colored, diluted, or diminished to the degree that you bring the past into the present relationship here.

You know what? I've made a tremendous discovery! I've found out why children can forgive so easily and quickly. I am amazed when two children play, and stop and fight and then go back to playing. (I've always wished I could do that with my wife.) We have this little fight and then we go right bac to playing. But I find, that sometimes after a fight, it's necessary to pout for a while...a week...two weeks...or whatever I necessary for her to take not of the fact that I am deeply wounded and deeply injured. I know why children forgive quickly and you can test this out. It's because that child doesn't have the social history that we do.

When you snub me, when you insult me, when you embarrass me, it happens between you and me. I've got a computer and when you run that through my computer, it goes all the way back and brings me out a printed sheet of all the experiences I've had that are similar to that one. I take all of these previous experiences and I use them as an overlay on top of what you've done...and you've lost! Because you see, I've been married 32 years. I've got a lot of memories—so has she. And when she says, "Hello," instead of "Good morning," and I've gotten up with my "I'm not feeling good, please notice" face on and she doesn't notice, then it proves to me once again that we've never been emotionally compatible. "I just wish she could be perceptive like some of my friends are"—who don't have to live with me.

This social or emotional history that you and I have is used as an excuse or as the basis for relating to other people in a particular way. You're doing this to your six-year-old, and when your six-year-old does it, you remember that he's done it in the past and you say, "Oh, my goodness, he never finishes anything he starts, and I'd better begin making him finish things that he starts. He's six years old and he's supposed to be mature"... and then you remember the things in yourself that you don't like and in your husband that you don't like or in your wife that you don't like. Then the six-year-old is standing behind this tremendous wall. All of a sudden, he's lost his identity and you're dealing with the past data that you have not properly assimilated and disposed of. That is a long sentence—did we come out at the right place? Okay—So, children don't have this—Thank God!

When you do me an injury, I hit you and I kick you or you hit me or kick me—it's only one hit and it's over—it does not last for days and weeks. I think this might be something tied in with forgiveness. When I start telling you about my pain, I want you to listen with moist eyes and quivering lips! But if I tell you about my joy, I expect you to lose interest. I am grateful that I have friends who no longer take the pain of my childhood seriously. I used to delight in telling my story—got pretty good at it, too—and got to the place where I embellished on it, and embellished on it, and embellished on it—but people will believe almost anything if they year it often enough.

Will you try a little experiment with me? I haven't done this exact thing before. The purpose is for you to know if it's possible to make changes in your past. If you want to do this—fine. If you don't just sit there with your eyes open and watch me, but don't watch other people.

I want you to close your eyes, please. Go back to your childhood home, preferable in your pre-school years. You go back to your childhood and picture your home. Now, find the place in your house or in the school or community where you were the most uncomfortable, where you experienced the most pain. If it was your mother who didn't love you, or your sister who didn't love you, or your brother...or the time when you spent your loneliest and worst hours. Now, sit down there or stand there and wait just a minute. Now get into the feeling and feel that pain that you have been referring to and depending on—really. Now stay there. Listen to me while you are there. Knowing now what you know—being there and knowing what you know now, find another place with another person that's safe. Do it now and put yourself out of a bad place into a good place. There's no trick to that—that's just one of the beauties of being a human being. Have you done it? Now do this—it's one of the abilities that God has given you as a person—put yourself in a good place, have a fantasy. Have a fantasy with your favorite movie star. Now, when you do that, take what you want and need. Take what you want to take, give what you need to give, share what you need to share, ask, and receive what you needed when you were a child—receive it for yourself, now. Then feel a new feeling about your childhood-self and I promise you it's all right to feel good about your child. You may feel it's sinful— I promise you, it's not a sin. No one will hurt you or punish you for feeing good as a child. I give you permission. Now will you open your eyes?

How many of you could not make the transition from the bad to the good? How many? One? Two? Okay, okay, that's where the verse of scripture is really illuminated— the verse that say, "If it works, don't fix it." So, if you can't find the bad place, Man, don't bother. That God and be grateful. Now what I'm saying to you is that with the exception of two people, every one of you has proved that you can feel any way you want to feel by remembering whatever you choose to remember. You can choose the bad place and you can choose the bad memories, and you can choose the threatening people. Or, you can, in your mind, go to a new place and change your feelings—change your past.

FROM THE AUDIENCE: "Can I go back in my mind and whip that guy that used to beat me up after school?"

JOHN: "Now you've got the point. See? I thought you didn't have one unhappy experience. Sure! Now, that guy who beat you up as a child...you can go back and be just mediocre, or if you want to, you can go back as the blackbelt champion of the city and really chop him up...in a Christian way! "

The beautiful thing about all this is that God has put you in charge of your life and He has not left you at the mercy of your past. I said, nothing has ever happened to you in your past that is so terrible, horrible, or bad that you can't experience the joy, the peace, the love, and the beauty of Christ in the present. If you in your minds think... "But you just don't know...." Yes, I know, because I did that myself. And sometime some of us go to adulthood, remembering childhood abuses and it's almost like we drove a stake down in that place, tied a rope to it—and all of our lives we have been living with our lives tied to that experience back there. That experience back there was someone fondling you when you were six or seven. Or this man exposed himself to you, or this woman exposed herself to you, and you thought "I'll never be the same again." Well, some people have tied themselves to abortions, prison sentence, times when you were publicly embarrassed or disgraced—or the war, or – what did you tie yourself to? "I've never been the same since..." What? Well, don't just sit there, say something if you have to make it up. What are you tied to? You had a heart attack! Yes,... and as long as I live I'll ... and what can you expect of someone who's....

One of my favorite pictures—so vivid to me—is this man, who every time he meets someone, says, "Hello, my name is 'so-n-so. I'm a veteran." He was in World War I, and since World War I, he's been "a veteran." What did you tie yourself to? We're not going any further until you participate.

(RESPONSE FROM AUDIENCE MEMBER who tells of the time she was not invited to a birthday party.)

JOHN: Hey, just do this casually. Have you ever been invited to a birthday party since?

AUDIENCE MEMBER: Yes?

JOHN: See that's the thing.

AUDIENCE MEMBER CONTINUES: "I wasn't invited to this one birthday party when I was 4 and now I'm 54...50 years of invitations have never made up for that one."

JOHN: "So, what you could do is, you know, —while you're here— you could have someone write you out an invitation to that birthday party."

(RESPONSE FROM AUDIENCE MEMBER: " Friday night is my birthday and you're invited."

Beautiful! Hey, that's beautiful! Let me tell you something. My mother never did love me. I've been loved by thousands of people for 50 years since, but because my mother never did...I'm not loveable. And you can stay hitched to that post if you want to, as long as you want to. But when God made you, the only constant that he interposed in your emotional matrix was change—it's a matter of which way. So, you can change. Some of you women are living with husbands and you are still relating to the husband in warmth, touching and intimacy the same way you related to your father when you were a little girl. Now, not anybody who comes to Laity Lodge would hold to something like that, but the people who don't come to areas like this do. Some of you men are still relating to your wives, as far as touch, closeness, caring hearing, warmth is concerned—you are relating to them exactly like you saw your father model the relationship when you were 3 or 4 years old. So, how did you daddy treat your mother? If you want to know, look in the mirror and see the way you treat your wife. It will either be imitation or the exact opposite. And either way, you use your parent for a reference point, when the solution might not be the using the parent for a reference point, but some other place. This is the way you do with your children. You say you have a kid who is untouchable...you don't. That kid has an untouching parent. You say, "Well, when he was born, he was that way." When he was born he didn't know how to feed himself, either—or go to the bathroom. He couldn't even multiply, or dance...but he learned.

Not long ago, I went to the annual meeting of the Sidon Cemetery Association. —I wanted you to know that I've been around. My hometown is Sidon, Mississippi, and when I grew up there, they had about 250 people—more or less—counting the tourists who came through infrequently. But every year the cemetery association has an annual reunion and meeting, and you come back the first Sunday in May. Everybody is expected to go to church and Sunday school—just like when you were a kid. I went with my brother, and he said, "Do you feel like you are being made to do this?" and I said, "Yeah...who's making us? Mother's been dead for years." I don't have permission to go back to the place and not go to Sunday school. I don't know what terrible thing might happen, but we went to Sunday school and we went to church, and I think one of the prerequisites for the ministers of that church is that they be bald-headed and that they shout—and he was and did both—he fulfilled it. I was not disgusted with him when he shouted; he was still my brother...and for that I thank God —Some of you here in this room taught me that.— It rained the whole weekend; we had to have dinner "on the ground" inside the building. Dinner "on the ground" is never quite the same if it has to be held inside a building. Before the meal was over, the place was so full of children, we were slipping on boiled eggs on a tiled floor.

I found out this year that as I looked at my home, the house of my childhood, it had changed. No—I had changed. I think that probably the dimensions of the house are the same but the dimension of the house in my mind are different. The face of the lady who lived in that house (I call her Mother) has changed, too... and I think that is probably because the face of the middle child, the one named John has changed. And that's why I come to you this week to say, "You can change your past." And I'd like to lean on you and push on you and say...You don't have to live with a history of fear or a history of pain or history of trauma—you don't have to.

I talked to this man one time, and he said, "You know, John, I finally made my million dollars—He made lots more than that.—And I went home to my class reunion in my Leer jet, but you know...the airport in that little town wouldn't accommodate my Leer Jet. I had to land about fifty miles away and rent a car, and all they had was a compact model!" It's an empty victory when it's for somebody else.

What I'm talking about now are the decisions that are resident within you, and you alone—the decision that takes the form of something like this: "I will move to a new place" or "I will **not** move to a new place" or "I will experience joy and happiness and acceptance and warmth and openness" or "I'll be the same miserable wet-blanket I have been all my life." Something like, "I'll be depressed all my life. At best, I'll be able to live on tranquilizers."

I want to say that when God made you, He put you in charge of your life and not even God over-rules your authority. The only way God will have charge of your life is by you or surrender. That is a terrible amount of power, isn't it? But the think that makes it safe is that He didn't give you authority over **me**...Thank God! And He didn't give me authority over you. There have been times when persons would like to try to exert this power over other people. But it is not there, and the only way a person has power over your life is when you sell your birthright for a cold bowl of porridge. Then you're probably going to be just fortunate enough to get somebody who will control you. If you are considering giving some control over your life, watch to see what he's doing with his own. And if you 're not sure about this, look at his wife's eyes and see how happy she is—or look into the eyes of her husband and see how happy she has made him. Look at the children—listen to the laughter. If that person is not handling his own—rest assured he will not be able to handle yours, either.

What I'm saying is that no one can make you feel good, bad, sad, happy, mad, or glad...you are responsible for your feelings—you choose them. Other people affect you, influence you—they don't make you feel. The way you experience your past can be changed by you here and now as you selectively release the painful experiences and choose new memories—real or imagined.

One of the other capacities that God has given us is the capacity for fantasizing, which I think is very close to creativity. You might have to be a little creative, but what better fruit of creativity than happiness!

I have a new friend—I'm not sure the other person knows it, but I have a new friend. I have been watching a blind woman for a while. I had a really good feeling of being able to watch this blind woman without her watching me. I noticed that when there was no conversation going on, her hands were usually busy. She was always looking at things. I could tell by the way her head was turned—usually, not all the time—which way she was listening. I never once saw any hint of self-pity. My first thought when I saw this woman was... guess what?: Oh, what a tragedy! I am saying that she chose a lifestyle, has chosen a quality of life that not even physical blindness can limit. In fact, I had the feeling several times in talking to her, that she was seeing more of me than I was seeing of her. I wasn't sure of this until one day, she started talking to me about something—and all of a sudden, I saw myself swallow nervously. Then, I thought: "That's crazy! This woman can't see me." and then I relaxed.

You build for yourself a new parent in your head, a new mother, a new father— (Transactional analyst have called this "re-parenting.")— who will be everything to you that you ever wanted in a mother, or father, brother, sister, grandfather, grandmother...whoever... and if you will not allow yourself any of these, build you a god. I used to preach a sermon on "Homemade gods"... now I think it might not be a bad idea. If you have a God that's you've been afraid of all your life and He's the God who goes around zotting people, and you know that eventually He's going to "get you"—particularly if you are too happy, or too successful, or too relaxed— then try building you another God, one nearer your own choosing. It may be that you'll find out that He's already been born.

The way you see yourself will be the mirrored image of the conception you have of God—will be a mirrored image of the conception you have of yourself, and loving yourself will result from the knowledge that you're loved by God and will result in living yourself.

Then the miracle, the wonder here is that you change. The miracle here is that I change. Then the world doesn't have to. I have spent a great deal of my life waiting for people to change and no little time telling them how they "ought to be" —not finding great throngs who were willing to listen to this for any length of time. I found that the only person whose hearing I could count on only a small percentage of the time was my own—Here you are faced with the choice of deciding what you will do **for** yourself and what you will do **with** yourself.

One of the things that I have worked on with some people is that I try to get people to practice smiling. If you want something new and different, go back to your room, get in front of the mirror and practice smiling. Look at yourself. Then look at the face that greets the people who meet you during the day. Look at the face that your family looks at most of the time. And ask yourself what it would be like to look into that the first thing in the morning and the last thing at night. It may be that you'll want to change this . The external smiling will not, in itself, accomplish anything without the internal change. But I'll tell you that when there has been an internal change, there needs to be an external change, too.

I would like to relieve you of any alibi or excuse you have for not experience what is call in Italian *la dolce vita* —the good life—here and now. I believe that's why God put us here on this earth. Somewhere, in some catechism, is written, "and what is the whole duty of man...to love God and enjoy Him forever." When I was a real fundamental Baptist, I thought that was the most sinful statement I ever heard in my life—because who could be a Christian and be happy. But since I'm not fundamental anymore, but do consider myself to be orthodox, it might be that it's possible for God to wish the same thing for His children that you would wish for yours and I wish for mine—that they would be able to enjoy and experience themselves in their world. I believe that this would move them toward responsibility.

This changing of the past will result in a continually changing response to the present. You will find yourself giving yourself permission more and more to experience life rather than waiting for the time when worse comes to worst and you're going to kill yourself. And you'll find yourself needing less and less to say, "I'd rather be dead than...." And to know an inner peace that is resident and abiding and does not vanish in the face of situation a discomfort. You'll find yourself saying when somebody acts like they like you, "It's all right for them to like me." rather than doing something to make them move back or turning and running.

I the past, all you had to do to get rid of me was to ace like you liked me. Those are not my terms for leaving today...maybe tomorrow, but not today. When you're making these changes in your past, you'll find yourself— simply the way you choose to remember— willing to stand there even when a person is evidencing warmth or intimacy or openness toward you...even when everything in you says, "Flee...run." If you're brave enough and stand there long enough you may find that the love, warmth, or acceptance (however you want to label it) that you receive from this other person, did not originate in him, but merely flowed through. And that even God needed an instrument. I'm not saying that God **can't** love you or me through the ether, but I think that if God has bought at such a terrible price so many lives and has gathered so many of you this weekend her at Laity, that He would be wasting a lot of good human resources if He loved you out of the blue and left me standing idle. I always have a little bit of discomfort when people say, "Well, I just need to get away from you and be with God." And I get to thinking, "What did I do?" Want to be just with God not with His temple. I'm not saying we don't need quiet time—that's not what I'm saying.

Let me tell you something. When you have a different past, and you're feeling differently about yourself, you are going to be different toward me. Because then you will not be quite so occupied in trying to make me start or make me stop, or wishing I would, or wishing I wouldn't, or wonder why I don't, or wondering if I will, or saying "If John had just not..." or "If John had just..." then all of a sudden you will find the same kind of acceptance of me that you are giving yourself. It will be almost like you taking what you give yourself and your mirror it. And do you know something? I will know it! Is that true? —Yes, I'll know it. When you give me this kind of acceptance, I say "acceptance"... I think it is—if I understand the meaning of the term—the nearest to agape love that the human being is capable of experiencing. When you give this to me, I will know it. Although I may never find the courage in your presence to acknowledge it with words, I'll know it. And I will leave you a richer person than I was when I came to you. And if, by God's grace, I can do this with you, you will know it—and nobody will have to tell you.

January 1978

THE NEW FUTURE

(Retreat at Laity Lodge)

I want to say that you can change your past. The decision to change it is yours. Now, if you are unwilling to give u certain kinds of behavior, look to see what you're getting from it. For example, there are a lot of benefits that come from depression. You get a lot of what we call secondary pay-off. What's your pay-off for being depressed?... What do you get out of it that's good?

FROM THE AUDIENCE: ... "Attention, ...sympathy,... aloneness,... don't have to be responsible,... escape,... it's a time-filler."

JOHN: "What do you get out of being sad?"

FROM THE AUDIENCE: "The same thing,"

JOHN: "What do you get out of being angry?"

FROM THE AUDIENCE:... "ulcers, ...control,... self-righteousness... anger from other people... it can cover up a lot of other feelings."

JOHN: "I think that anger is like the big skirt—it covers up a lot of things."

FROM THE AUDIENCE: "Some of these feelings give you your identity, you know. For instance...'I'm a guy who's always depressed.' or 'I'm a guy who's.....,' in other words that gives you security... you don't want to give that up."

JOHN: That's so important—for some people this is the only identity they have ever had. I've seen people who–after they have gotten over a depression–came back and said, 'What do I do with myself?' because it is a fantastic time filler. You have to work to stay depressed–it keeps you busy–just like you have to work to stay mad. You have to register little annoyances and irritants and the way people snub you, or are considerate or thoughtful. Once you do this for a lifetime and make it a primary vocation, then that block of behavior is taken out of your life— you have that much of a gap. Along with the decision to give this up, must come the decision to do other things."

When you change your past, you will find yourself experiencing some new anxieties, and experiencing some new tensions which will be caused simply by the void that's left due to the removal of the previous behavior. For me, my past exists only in my head—it's not recorded anywhere in history. It's written down between my ears. This is my past. If I talk to you about the past, you may say, "I didn't see it that way at all." That means that it is,– in a very particular and peculiar way,– my very own. I am saying that I change my past. I do not change the actual events or experience that I had, but I do change my interpretation of them, and That's the thing that matters most anyway. Because when this person did this thing to me when I was five years old, I doubt if he meant any harm. But if I interpret it with my five-year-old mind, "harm" –then he meant it –or she did. What I'm saying is that my past belongs personally and intimately to me—I make the decision to change.

SOMEONE IN THE AUDIENCE recalls what the other speaker for the week explained...how **God** changes a person's attitude and beliefs, and how John is saying the same thing in a more practical and volitional way.

JOHN'S RESPONSE: "This question comes up every time at Laity Lodge. This is God as I understand Him...My God is not a magician. He does not do magic tricks for me—however much I have pled with him at times to—at times bribed Him to—at times pressured Him. My God does not by-pass the mental and emotional and spiritual factors He has given me in order to get something for me. He gave me a brain, and when He does a miracle for me, He requires me to use my brain. He gave me the capacity to relate to people, at a sociological level, and when I experience healing with a person, I've got to go apologize, or I've got to go make amends, or someone else has to do it.

Now that **could** come out as some kind of a veiled humanism...I am not saying that God **cannot**—I'm saying that God **does** not —walk for me. He shows me how to walk, and I learn how to walk by falling.

Now do you hear this Lloyd? (Lloyd is the other speaker for the week.)

LLOYD: "I would agree with that. What I think I was trying to stress is that our very dealing with the subjective reality of life comes from an objectivity of our God...who He is. In other words, I know that I can love myself with unmerited favor because I have been loved by Him. But until I know that He loves that way, I **can**not love myself that way, nor is that love lasting—apart from the continuing love from Him. I just feel that at this point in history, we need a new vertical thrust in which we understand that the source of all of these basic theories of insights of human nature are rooted in God and the Incarnation and the gospel. There are a lot of distorted ideas about God, salvation, and life which are promulgated by movements and by certain schools of thought that are non-biblical. And that's the reason that I fell that it's time to go back to the scriptures."

JOHN: "Lloyd, when I don't know that God loves me...I don't feel it... and you come and tell me and you say, 'John, God loves you.' Then I have a choice here: I can say, 'All right, I accept that.' Then, even though it's not a feeling decision for me, I can act on that...based on my trust in you, until I trust in God."

LLOYD: "You would have had to feel that from me or you would not have heard the word."

JOHN: "Right."

Now there are people who, when they hear it, there is a light form heaven, their name is called, and they have a mystical, magical, wonderful experience—and then from then on they are forever different—and that's fine. God, bless you, I wish I could be that way. But God requires me to use what He's given me.

I know some people who are particularly involved in healing movements in the churches and various forms of charismatic movements in the churches, and it's very difficult for me to communicate with some of these people, and I would like to. Because I don't have any criticism of the other ways, and if you want to criticize mine, you'll have to catch me to tell me about it, because I'm not particularly interested in hearing that. You don't know anything about me that I don't know better than you do. So don't give me your criticism. Give me your positive affirmation and I'll be stronger and better. But the criticism I don't need.

What I'm saying is ...I don't feed my children... I teach them how to use a knife and fork. I don't think for them and make decisions for them...I let them make mistakes and fall. That's similar to the way I have experienced God.

You can hear this, I think, if you don't make it an "either, or" because I have had some miracles in my life, and I look forward to more. I'm not talking about limiting God at all; I'm mostly talking about how I perceive my own growth. And maybe you are not supposed to grow this way. I doubt if I can see my own growth objectively. But I can, a little bit. Is that okay? (This question is addressed to the person who had commented on what Lloyd had said the previous day.)

THE PERSON FROM THE AUDIENCE: "I don't feel any conflict; I feel that the two tend to support each other. They tend to be very much in harmony."

JOHN: "Yes, I felt this way, too."

I want to talk this morning about the new present. When you change the past, you are different. You have already changed now. I don't know if you know anything about geese. Every morning this goose wakes up in a brand-new world. And you can tell it by the way he moves his neck. When he gets up, he kinda winds his neck around and stretches it, and when it finally get stretched, up he see everything as if for the first time. I think that a person who has changed his past wakes up every morning like a goose—in a brand-new world. So, I'm urging you to be like the goose–in this respect–that you experience this place in time and in reality as being brand-new. You will hear me say this again—'Ladies and gentlemen, this is not a dress rehearsal...this is the final performance.' And you will not come on this stage again for this particular scene or act, and neither will I. And we won't even have a chance to replay it to ourselves after the curtain goes down, because you have not been here before and I have not either.

Now with this in mind—do you know what I told you yesterday about children not remembering things? I learned something else when I learned about the children—I learned why we talk so much about the weather. I promise you that in the last two weeks I have talked about weather, clothes, and food until I could drop! And "What time is it?" This is all I'm going to say about my trip—if you're going to go on a tour, don't go with 500 people. I don't care how much money you save—don't do it!

When you and I have a conversation, there are six people involved, at least. When you talk to me, you talk to John as **you** see me, and the John as **I** see me, and then there's a **real** John. This is the person. When I talk to you, I talk to you as **I** see you, and then there is a you as **you** see you, and there there's the **real** you. So, when you're carrying on a conversation, be aware that you're talking to at least three persons standing there. When I speak to you, I take John as **I** see me, and I talk to you as **I** see you, but when you answer me... you, as **you** see you, and John as **you** see me, and it's just like I was talking to this person, and that person was answering that person, and they didn't even hear the first question.(He's referring to a black board with the six persons drawn there.) It's like a dumb hearer speaking to a deaf speaker...or something like that. (Laughter)

Because I know what you're like and I know the way I have perceived you, I have you pretty well figured out–and on that basis–I address my remarks to you. Not knowing how I have figured you out, you answer from the person **you** think you are, and you address not the John who spoke to you but me as **you** have perceived me. It's a wonder we every get anything said. The only thing to talk about is the weather!

(Someone in the audience tells of a remark one person makes to another and how it was not heard the way it was meant.)

JOHN: "Yes, and you came on trying to help me, and I heard you being critical, so I responded to the critical person after the caring person had spoken. So much of this goes on in a marriage and between parent and child."

The beautiful part of this is that as the friendship matures and as the acquaintance deepens, due to the result of time and experience shared, the conversation reaches a deeper level to where you may come with a person—and this does not happen often, I think rarely—it comes to the point where the real me communicates with the real you, and at this point, we enter what that beautiful old Hebrew introduced us to called the "I and Thou." At this point I am safer with you because I trust your perception of me. And I don't have to impress, justify, camouflage, or conceal, and I don't have to defend. And you can trust my perceptions of you. I think that this is what the man was talking about when he wrote that little verse, "Oh, the comfort...the inexpressible comfort...of feeling safe with a person." This is a relationship that I am convinced would only be experienced by people who had dealt with their past. In fact, if I am in this with you, you would have to have dealt with my past...as far as you were concerned— and I would have to have dealt with your past... as far as I was concerned. At this point, our relationship changes and you are "person" to me, never "thing." And I experience you and I see you for the beauty of who you are, not for any functional value you might have to me.

One of the things that I became aware of when I was working in another job is that when I was talking with a person, I was aware of whether or not he was a potential donor. It was sure a relief not to have to feel that anymore —when I no longer have to parent you, and I don't have to sit in judgment on your statements, and I don't even have to judge your language....

Maslow, whom I've been reading a good bit lately, said that he was sure about one of his colleagues...that if he were up to his neck in —I'll substitute a word here)— salt water—he wouldn't say the word. So, I don't listen to you talk, and I don't judge you by your language, and I don't size you up, and I do not fragment you or segment you by chopping you into little bitty parts to decide whether or not you conform to my specifications and measurements—I take you as a total person and I experience you as a total person, and then I meet you as a total person—and that's enough. When I leave you, I can tell you "goodbye" and walk away. I don't have to take you with me. When I leave you, I don't rehash what I said to you and wish I had said it differently, or I do not rehash the conversation and wonder what you thought about what I said. What I mean is that I can walk away, and I can leave this kind of session so that I will be totally present when I'm with the next person, living in the present. I don't have to gossip and bring into **this** conversation non-existent, or "absent" persons. The degree to which I do this is the degree to which I diminish you. Because, if I am going to experience you, I do not need to be bringing all these imaginary people in and stacking them up on little tiers around me so I can refer to them. I am sure that you all will know what I mean when I say, "I know when I'm being measured."...Do you? And I know when I'm being evaluated. And I have prayed for strength and grace to put it out of my mind and relate to this person anyway, but the most overwhelming feeling I have is that I want to run.

I keep three pieces of glass on my desk—I put them there for my own self, and I did not explain them to anyone for years. One is actually two-lenses—one side is concave and the other is convex. Because I found that I have a habit of looking at every person through this convex lens and magnifying him and walking around as a little pygmy in a world filled with giants. It's like I had a pair of glasses fitted with that. Everybody I saw was bigger than I was. And I lived as an inferior person in the presence of superior individuals—everybody was superior in some way. There is another lens, concave that diminishes and I wish that I had a pair of glasses fitted with that, because you can take that and hold it up in front of a person and you can shrink him down to a very small person—have trouble even seeing him there. I've thought several times—not man, just occasionally—when someone wants to tell me what he thinks of me, I'd like to just take that lens and hold it up to my eye and say, "What did you say?" When working through this in myself, I have been amused to see what kind of glasses other people wear.

I also have a prism. I keep it on the desk in the sunlight and it usually puts a little happy spot on the wall. Without taking this too far...this is a parable—you have to get one point out of it—there are some people who bring color into my life. They do not diminish me, and they do not magnify me...it's almost as if I need no magnification. But I feel that with these people, I have color. And there was nothing but the plain old stuff until my life passed through this person and then there is a brilliant display of color. And I feel sometimes when I've been with a person, like that, I want to go to the mirror, look at myself, and say, "Oh, I did not know that about myself!"

When I am totally present with you, you have color. When I am totally present with my son, and he is not measured by the background of his past failures or my expectations, hopes, and dreams, he has color.

JOHN (In reply to an audience member's remark): "We carry tremendous chronicles in our mind. When you meet a person, you know, you see him against the backdrop of all these memories. If this person has been overboard politically in some area and he starts talking to you about the present administration, you think 'There he goes again.' and you erase his face and think, 'He's a nut.' So, when you're willing to excuse me from my past, and when you're willing to discover me today, as you are continually discovering, revealing, enlarging, and exploring yourself—it may be that love is the continuing exploration of another human being who is in the act of continually revealing himself to you...in a reciprocal relationship."

You see, I love you not because of what I know about you, but because of what I experience with you. I think this is the nature of grace. God's love for us is grace-filled love because of who we are, not what we've done. It's been said here at Laity Lodge may times, "Nothing I can do will make God love me more, and nothing I can do will make God love me less," and the more we experience this kind of grace, the greater is our capacity to love the same way. When you make the decision to be totally in the here and now with your wife, your marriage is going to be different. And when you make the decision to be totally present, in the here and now with your husband, your marriage is going to be different. I think that one of the familiar responses is, "There he goes again— or she goes again." And the same thing applies to our children.

(Someone in the audience questioned what John had said about "leaving" the person you have been with and going to the next one.)

JOHN: "I like to sometimes 'relish,' the experience I just had and re-live it because it was so precious. Don't take everything I say literally...there is no way I can totally leave you and totally meet the next person. Give me a lot of room in language here."

PERSON IN THE AUDIENCE: "It's all right for me to go away relishing the meeting, isn't it?"

JOHN: "Of course, but when you get with me, don't spend too much time relishing the past conversation... unless you want to share it with them, then it becomes something between us."

What I'm talking about is people who have been with you and you know they weren't there. And it's the thing that gave birth to the famous scripture that says, 'You're not listening!' Because you see, the greatest gift I have to give you is my time-presence—I can give you nothing greater. And the greatest gift I can give you is to sit down and focus totally on you and say, "Hello." Then I have given you the most priceless possession I have. But when I meet you and you say, hurriedly, "Hello...I'm so glad to see you....Well, it was nice to see you." (said with much enforced gusto) ...I am disgusted and want to say, "Don't do that to me anymore."

I went one time to a convention. I had a friend who had a high office in the convention, and every time I could stand next to him, I did. He said, "You stay with me, and I'll show you the ropes and you'll get ahead like I did." And I thought, "Boy, that's the way to make it to be President of the Southern Baptist Convention"— he never spoke to **one** person...at least ten. He knew everybody's first name and call ed them by name...and I thought, "I'd never make it — and I don't want to."

That's what I'm talking about. When you give yourself to me, I'll know it. When I give myself to you, you'll know it. And I will know that I have been met by you, and I will know that I have met you, and **you** will know it. This I fully believe...that I will be a richer and more complete person as a result of **any** authentic encounter with **any** human being regardless of social, education, financial—the status has nothing to do with it.

I want to say this again, if you will be patient with me, the clearest picture we have of God in all the universe is the human face.

It is a more accurate picture than a sunrise, sunset, or the mountains, or the sea, or the sky. You are the most God-like entity in the universe. Because, it is said in no other place, of no other thing, that it was made in the image of God. Only **you** are made in the image of God. So, when I stand before you I see you in His image and I see myself in His image. Now, listen to me...and then the third Person make His presence known and we have meeting. He is there... He is here...I believe He will even come if you meet no one but your wife. I believe He will even come if you meet no one but your husband. He has promised.

(John draws on the board.) If you let this line be "time" and this line be "place"...here's where we are right now where this "x" is. If I am with you, and I'm with you here, and I'm with you now, we have an authentic meeting. If I meet you here, physically, but my mind is back with my conversation with Bill this morning, there is no authentic meeting. I'm not sure of this, but I believe Christ **will** not come—I did not say he **could** not— he will not come to any meeting that I half-heartedly attend myself. This is what eternity is. Eternity is this minute...right now... in this place. And eternal life is my being here, right here and now in this place with you. And my willingness to experience life eternal may possibly be measured by the degree to which I am willing to be here, now...with you...knowing that as I am here, now with you, so is He. As you are here, not with me, so is He. Otherwise, we cannot claim His presence. So, when we have a cup of coffee together, I drink the wine and you drink the wine—even though it may not be the same color. In this kind of meeting with you, my soul is sustained. My spirit is fed. And I do not go away hungry, or empty, or lonely. Because I know I have been touched. And I know that as you have touched me in His presence, I can rise and take up my bed and walk. I know that my sins are forgiven, because all the drama of the meeting of this Nazareth Jew with all the needy people of His time is re-enacted as He in His spirit through you meets me again today. It is re-enacted as He, in His spirit, through me, meets you today.

That's the reason that your past is not important. Don't tell me about your past...**meet me...** because sometimes I think we avoid the meeting when I see you and say, "Well, hello! Let me tell you about what happened to me ten years ago." It's like the Christians who get together and brag about their spiritual birth and part of the Christian testimony is tell you about the time when they were born as Christians. This is good for some people...but I have had a vision of meeting someone sometime and say, "Hey, let me tell you that I was born. Here, I can prove it with my driver's license. And I've got a copy of my birth certificate...Would you like to see it?" If I did that, you would think I was some sort of nut, wouldn't you? That's the way some of us do as Christians. "Let me tell you about my conversion experience." I believe that, for some, this is a cop-out to keep from being real and genuine and authentic in the present tense. The business at hand might not be the rehashing of the details of your birth...or mine.

Because I live in a different present, this meeting with you is different from any other meeting we've had before, because I am a product of a different past and I am in the process of "becoming," and I've been enriched and changed or disciplined and challenged and tempered by the experiences I've had since the last time you saw me, and you have, too. So, when I meet you, I am a new person meeting you, and when you meet me, you are a new person meeting me, and the knowledge of the change will not be necessarily communicated by the rehashing of events, but by result in the meeting between two qualitatively different human beings.

This is one of the great criticisms that the church must bear today. It is the absence of authenticity in inter-personal relationships. And sometimes we work so hard at being joyous, joyful, triumphant Christians, when I think it would be wise for some of us to just try being average human beings. It would be infinitely easier. I get so tired with "triumphant Christians"— and so bored. And if you don't ...that's all right.

Is there anything that needs clearing up before I stop?

FROM THE AUDIENCE someone asks if she has grown and changed and meet someone else who has grown and changed, is it not okay to tell the other person about what has been happening with her since they last met?

JOHN: "It's okay. This may be my need. I may need to say, 'Let me tell you what's happened.' Because not having any knowledge of that, you would really not understand what you're getting from me. But if I insist on rehashing the details of the past, in order to avoid the meeting of hearts...I believe that I am enriched when I meet you, though...I know it. You have helped me to learn this."

(AUDIENCE MEMBER asked a question inaudible on the tape.)

JOHN: "I think that's a very good point. I'm glad you brought it up. My scars are a part of my person. But do not let us get together and worship my scars. Please don't forget that they are there, but don't let me make them into idols. And if I am in the act of destroying myself, do not be my friend. If I continue to stay depressed or continue to stay in a self-defeating pattern like abuse of alcohol of drugs, do not befriend me beyond getting me to a source of help. I am of the firm opinion that more people have been helped into their graves by would-be-helper than have been allowed to live—if that's not introducing a new subject. I was saying that in conjunction with the scars."

FROM THE AUDIENCE: "What **do** you do with somebody who's depressed?"

JOHN: "Send them to a psychiatrist, or a psychologist, or to a counselor. But don't **you** help them...I mean real **depression,** not someone who is down in the dumps.'"

FROM THE AUDIENCE: "What does one do when a friend or business associate repeats the same story or problems every time you see him?"

JOHN: "It depends a lot on the relationship between the two persons. If you're working with him, one way to get away from his is to say, 'Excuse me...

I have to go to the restroom.' Another way is to say, 'Here come the supervisor.' Or, if this is friend and you care for this friend, one way to handle it is to say to him, 'Are you aware that you've told me this already ten times? Is there something you want me to hear that I'm not hearing? I care enough about you not to continue to tense up every time you go into this rehash. Let me tell it back to you once and see if I heard it properly.' It may come out what' he's trying to say. This is a whole different subject, but one of the things we do not often do is say what we mean."

January 1978

THE NEW PRESENT

(Retreat at Laity Lodge)

You 'll not have a different future, regardless of how many resolutions you make in your mind until you make decisions. The decision is the important thing, and one of the capacities that human beings have is the capacity to make a decision. You can make a decision about feelings as well as about behavior. You can make a decision about your awareness. One of the ways to make a valid decision is to make it in the presence of another person, and let that person be your witness. This is part of the value of small groups. It's one thing to sit in the office with a counselor—just the two of you — and do your work. You make a lot of decisions and reach a lot of conclusions, but the decision is socialized when I say what I have decided in the presence of ten people. It's a different thing saying, "I have decided that I will stop depressing myself. And instead of depressing myself, I will speak with people, I will listen to what they are saying. I will share my feelings when I feel that I should not share my feelings." When I say this in the presence of nine or ten people, and sometimes someone asks for clarification, and sometimes I give it, and in the clarification I understand it better myself.

Specifically, if you are from the kind of background—if the past you are considering changing takes you back to a family where no one ever expressed their feelings, where you never washed the family's dirty linen and put it out on the line for all the neighbors to see—if you lived with a mother or father who never expressed feelings, you grew up with the idea that that was right. In your child's mind, expressing feelings would be wrong. You probably even carried that into your faith and made it a part of your relationship with God—so much so because the childhood decisions we made are sacred. They are sacred because they were made in the presence of the only God you knew until you were 5 years old—that was your mother or father. What your mother and father said was right. You had no basis of comparison—you could not compare what they said with anything else because you did not have any social history. So, you come up with a certain behavior pattern that to you is right, and that behavior (and this is the crucial and import thing)—that behavior feels right. What I'm talking to you about is a decision that will initially feel wrong—I am talking to you about in the areas of life where you are in trouble—so what I'm asking you to do is to do something wrong. When you are in trouble, that is the time to make a new decision. Or, if you're not in trouble but are just uncomfortable, sometimes this first hint of trouble may be discomfort. When you're uncomfortable or in trouble, make the decision, regardless of the feeling. Generally, it's best to make the decision in the presence of another person or persons who can witness it and to whom you can report with some degree of regularity. This is just to sort of keep you honest. You may need the permission of the people in the group to give you the strength to make the decision.

It may be appropriate for some people in this room to make the decision, "I'll stop criticizing myself in my head. And when I say things, I will not say to myself in my head, 'You stupid thing! Why did you say that?'" Then you say in the group, or you say to a few friends, "I'll stop doing that to myself. I won't do it to you and I won't do it to myself." Then, when you make this decision, the awareness will be heightened and your perception will be sharpened. Then you will begin, when you initiate the new action, to experience a new feeling. You will begin to feel differently about yourself. And that's true—You'll feel differently about yourself. And, Boy! That's a great day!

You'll find, then, that you don't feel inferior, or you don't feel inadequate, or you don't feel lonely like you have in the past. The way you change your behavior is with the decision, preferably one that is expressed verbally to one, two, or three trusted friends who stand witness to this work that God is going to do in your life.

I think that this is one dimension of the nature of the early church. It was one of the things that was behind the Holy Spirit's inspiration for the writing of a particular verse of scripture that we read very rapidly. It says, "Confess your faults one to another, forgiving one another even as God, for Christ's sake has forgiven you."

It was Gibran, I think, who said, "If we all confessed our sins, each of us would be amazed at our own lack of originality." So, we say, "Why take up anybody's time?" You don't get up and pour out your insides to the church. Because, you see, I haven't really trusted you when I don't tell you about my sins. I'll tell you about my sins and watch you walk away. But I'll tell you about my dreams—quickly. And neither will I tell you about my strengths. I have not shared at depth with you when I criticize myself. But if you hear me tell you the things that are good and positive and admirable and beautiful about me—know well, my brother—that you are trusted. I think sometimes we use this confession bit like some people use sex—as a means of getting rid of people. The decision not to put myself down, in my head, first, would be followed by your witnessing this decision. And then here is the beautiful part of the whole thing, and here's the part of the whole dynamic of church. When I stop doing it to myself, I will no longer do it to you. When I stop mistreating myself, rest assured, I will stop mistreating you. When I am being unkind to you, be gently with me, because you can know for sure that I'm being unkind to myself. When I'm criticizing you deal with me gently because inside I am literally beating myself to death. I think that if our God had seen fit to enlarge on these words, "And thou shalt love thy neighbor as thyself," then we would not have needed

Martin Buber. But maybe He saw that the Martin Bubers would be born, and that's the reason He didn't enlarge on the verse.

I have a book in my library that I have read a couple of times. It's entitled *If God Does Not Die.* The content of the book I know just sketchily—the title is indelibly imprinted on my mind. What author says is that if God does not die, I've got to live differently now. I have to live in the context of eternity, and I have to think of infinity as an unending continuum, and my life is moving along this line of infinity. So, if I have a new future, the future that is mine will be the unfolding of the life that is based on decisions made in the present. It's going to be open-ended.

I think during the first 35 years of my life, when I was having such a miserable time, I always held out the option of suicide. And I always knew that if things got too rough, I could—one way or the other—end this thing. I received a little decoration in the war—I didn't tell anyone this for a long time. It wasn't much—It's what they call the Bronze Star. At that time what I wanted to do more than anything in the world was to die. I can remember some of the experiences I had, looking back, and I know some of the other men who had the same inner motivation I did. You see, when the future would be nothing but more of the past, I needed an escape hatch.

Now a new future, lived by a new person in a new present, with a new past, the future is open-ended, so I don't plan any trips down dead-end streets. Most dead-end streets are well marked, and when you turn down one, there are even signs at intervals saying, "Dead-End." Even one-way streets are marked. And I make a decision—a decision that I will not kill myself accidentally or intentionally. And I won't say, "If worse comes to worst, I can always...." And I erase from my vocabulary, "I'd rather be dead than...." I do not carefully mark back door exists labeled, "Alcoholic Abuse," "Drug Abuse," Automobile Abuse," or "Work Abuse." I will not work myself to death, or drive myself to death, or starve myself to death, or eat myself to death. Once I have decided that the future is new, I won't kill myself, and I won't kill anyone else. I will do no murder. I will not murder people by attacking their reputation with my words or my silences. I attack and murder people neither by direct accusation or by insinuation. I will not murder a relationship by threatening harm. And I will not hold people in a state of continuing anxiety, promising approval but never giving it—if the future is new for me. This will leave me free to assign to you the same respect and the same gift of dignity that I claim for myself and expect from you in the relationship that we establish.

One of the real corners in my life was when I decided to respect myself—this is where I turned a corner. Then I found that I felt differently and I treated other people differently. Then I had a new capacity to say "goodbye." My "goodbyes" have not been easy. I usually conclude the meetings I have with the Lord's Prayer, so I can leave while everybody's head is bowed and eyes are closed, and I don't have to say "goodbye." I know a lot of reasons for it, but I just don't like to say, "goodbye." Probably someday I will get in therapy and grow up in this area, but it's one of the areas where I don't want to grow up. I don't even **want to** want to know how, so I probably just won't learn. But if you are interested, and if you want to learn how to say "goodbye," you can work on it in this area. I think this problem has something to do with the sense of abandonment.

If God does not die, I have eternal life and it is a possession. You have eternal life—it's a possession. I must deal with you as I'm dealing with myself, as you're dealing with yourself, as you're dealing with me in context of eternity, because I'm not going to go away—and neither are you. You're going to have to deal with me sooner or later, so why not now? This thing is open-ended, see? I have to be reconciled to you. The pouting, the holding a grudge, the silent treatment–kind of like an ailment, but sicker. These behaviors are no longer appropriate for me. I had written most of this before I left recently and when I met that man I told you about, I remember these lines...I must be reconciled to you...this behavior is not appropriate. That thing will always be open-ended.

You see, my being-ness—now I'm not talking about my profession, and I not talking about behavior. The reconciliation I'm talking about right now is within me. I don't mean that I've got to be a friend to everybody—do you know that? I will have some disagreements that will never be reconciled between two people. If you can do otherwise, you'll be beating the track record of Jesus Christ—and that would be embarrassing to God; so, don't do that. There are some people that He never did become reconciled to. And this is where, I think, we get the childhood Sunday school concept that some of us were reared with—that a Christian loves everybody. I don't know about you, but this Christian doesn't. And I don't even need to or want to anymore. That's unrealistic for me—I don't have that much love. If a relationship is harmful to you, then it's your responsibility to mend it or break it off. Sometimes this is the only way you can survive. You do not do God a service if you stay in a relationship until you finally lose your mind or kill yourself, and then they mark on your tombstone: "Well, he really hung in there." I knew a marriage counselor who felt very strongly about divorce, and he got this couple back together —after they has sworn they wanted a divorce and he worked long and hard with them—the counselor got them back together. Three weeks later, the husband of the re-united couple killed his wife—That's a true story.

There are some differences that won't be reconciled, that are harmful and destructive to one or both parties. You break that relationship. Don't tell me it's hard—I know it is! But since you are an eternal being, you do not take into your being anything that destroys you.

Since my being is eternal and my future is open-ended, I will not waste my life in resentment, anger, or fear. I recognize that when I am busy resenting you, or busy telling myself scary stories so that I can stay frightened about what might happen tomorrow (and I can think of up ten thousand "what ifs" for everyone I hope) . Then I realize I am destroying the capacity I have for happiness, for contentment, for joy and for peace in the present with the people in this room. You see, you are my present—for the time being— and I am—for the time being—a part of yours. And this moment is eternity—the only segment of eternity we can touch. So, what happens here and now is eternal. It's happening between beings that are eternal who have infinite worth and value in the eyes of God, and therefore, you in your eyes and me in mine.

QUESTION FROM THE AUDIENCE: "Can another person destroy me?"

JOHN: "We've bandied this around a whole lot... you have to have permission."

SAME QUESTIONER: "I'm really troubled with that."

JOHN: "Man, I have been, too."

You have to have my permission...in most cases. We said this yesterday...Nothing I say applies to everybody all the time—you understand that. If I stay with you knowing that the relationship id draining and is punitive, exacting, demanding, and the more I see myself diminished by you—YES, you are destroying me and I'm permitting it. I want to talk about the exception to that. There are some people who, because of time, circumstances, and events, do not have the ego-strength, the will power to say to this person, "Leave me alone." I've seen some people murdered by degrees. And I think it's a very ungodly form of torture. There are some people who do not have the strength to say "no"—do you know what I mean? When you talk to them about saying "no," they say, "I don't know what you are talking about." You know, that's not an option.

QUESTION FROM THE AUDIENCE: "For a person to destroy me, I've got to believe what he says about me and buy into the relationship and accept the causation for the problem, and a whole bunch of things in addition to—I've got to participate actively in my own self-destruction, do I not?"

JOHN: "Yes, and I've got to keep coming back for more, too."

QUESTION FROM ANOTHER IN THE AUDIENCE: "What do you do with somebody who can't say 'no'?"

JOHN: "I think this is why we have families and societies that make laws. Ideally, our society would take care of that person through an institution or an agency–as on the part of a child.

"We have laws that govern mental incompetence, but what I'm talking about, and I assume that you are, is emotional incompetence. And this is a nebulous thing –a gray area– and it's hard to identify."

COMMENT FROM THE AUDIENCE: "But, there are some people who have the strength to say 'no,' but live in a situation because they think it is the Christian thing to do. And they come to the point of almost being destroyed before they will finally say, 'no.'"

JOHN: This is where I keep coming back to a statement that Wayne Oates made when I was a seminary student sitting in one of his classes, and it really set me free. He said, "What some people call 'religion' Jesus Christ calls 'sin.'"

Nearly everything I've learned about God I've learned from other people—even had other people teach me the Bible and tell me how to interpret it. And when I want the interpretation of a passage, I go to three or four favorite people that I have on my bookshelf.

So, I said that I am going to talk Friday about the new God. If my concept of God does not change as my self-concept changes, then I'll always be a prisoner. Do you hear that? So, what I'm saying is that your concept of God must be a growing, changing concept. The God that I knew as a child is not the God that I have grown to know through Jesus Christ. He was a God that was in a brick building and He was a tough hombre. He zapped people, you know, and sent them to hell and had a great big book —and that kind of stuff. I'm saying that God in Himself has not changed, but my own growth and awareness has changed and this is a part of the "new me" because the God that I know now is the God and Father of our Lord Jesus Christ, and the characteristic and attributes of Jesus Christ are the revelations of being and the person of God. I ask is—is the God you know today the same as the God you learned about as a little girl?—or as a little boy? —or has He changed with your growth and new awareness?

QUESTION FROM RALPH IN THE AUDIENCE:"I guess it's a matter of time, maybe, and a world that's in a hurry or something—it's still troubling me. I notice that we pray for and we work with our medical skills, for instance to heal somebody who has emphysema, or has hyper-glycemia, diabetes, or heart disease, or something like that, and we turn all the resources of science and the church over to the healing of that person. And we're willing to wait a year, two, three, four or five years working towards the healing of the person. We get a fractured relationship in marriage however and we tend to look at that and say, 'Well, this is destroying one of the people—maybe they ought to get a divorce.' In a month, six months, a year, two years, ten years, fifteen years—because so often, healing **can** occur, healing **does** occur, emotional maturity **does** come around, and that party who was in such a terrible place...."

JOHN (INTERRUPTING): "Do you mean what you are saying?"

RALPH: "I not only believe it, but I've witnessed it so many times that I regard it as one of those things that has been tested in time and history, and I've lived through it vicariously and directly."

JOHN: "Do you think God can heal an injury that a man has inflicted on his wife?"

RALPH: "He certainly can heal the memories...there's no question about that."

JOHN: "Can He hear an injury that a woman has inflicted on her husband?"

RALPH: "No question about it."

JOHN: "That a parent has inflicted on a child?"

RALPH: "I would say that all those things have happened in my own marriage."

JOHN: "Are you healed?"

RALPH: "I really am."

JOHN: "Thank you."

RALPH: "I really love my wife."

JOHN: "I believe you."

RALPH: "And thank God, I didn't make the decision that I ought to leave her because of the injury we were doing to each other. I just don't know the answer to that."

JOHN: "Yes, you do—you just spoke it.—Yes, you know the answer."

(after a pause) RALPH: I don't know whether that applies to everybody, but I know that it has to me."

JOHN: "Don't dilute it...it's great! Leave it just like it is. Don't overkill it."

If this is not true, then we Christians have no hope. If there's no forgiveness, then , "God, have mercy on us all." And if forgiveness does not exist between persons, then where in the universe does it exist? We certainly can't afford to pray and say, "...and forgive us our trespasses..." if forgiveness does not exist.

Because of the new future, I don't waste you and I don't waste me. And I'm aware that in the future, when we meet, He will join us there as He joins us when we meet in the present. Always the company will consist of more persons than one plus one. It is almost like we become like Melchizedek—no past, no future, but a fantastic present! And because I have a new future, I have time—I have all the time I will ever need, and I don't have to hurry anymore. Now, I don't believe that, but I **want** to believe it. My prayer is, "Lord, make me **want** to want to." I don't live in a state of frenzy or turmoil. The only thing that matters in the face of this new past and new future is the new present, so I live this moment here and now with you. When I am here now with you, I'm neither back there in the past or out here in the future. I'm not at another place in my mind, and I'm not with another person in my mind—I'm here, now, totally with you. And I open the inner chambers of my heart to admit you, so that to me you are here now, totally with me, else I cannot entertain God. I believe that.

I wrote down here a long time ago, "I don't even have to get through on time." so when we have lived this moment, it's all right for us to leave and to arrive—to break friendships and to make friendships. We can go on to something else because what we have dealt with is completed. Then, at this moment, at this time, in this place, the past and the future merge, and we live here and now as we bring the future into the present. Since this present is eternal, I will treat myself and you in a different way, because I am going to last, and you are going to last, and I see myself in the present as acceptable to God.

I learn something of late and I no longer allow myself the luxury of saying, "I wish I had known this earlier." I have learned of late that my children are perfect. At their present stage of growth with the knowledge they have, with the training they have, with the resources that are available to them, they are doing the best that they can possibly do at the present time. And I believe that. And right now, at this moment, I don't want any of them to do any better than they are doing. I believe that of my wife, of my friends—and in my better moment—I believe it of myself. Because, you see, if God sees in a dimension of timeless-ness which we call "eternity," He is aware that you are His growing child and that you have not learned to walk yet, and that it's going to be necessary for you to fall and get bruised, but you will eventually learn to walk . He sees that you have not learned to use your spoon, and that's why you get oatmeal on the ceiling. But he does not take the spoon or food away because the "messiness" is simply a necessary prerequisite to dining in an acceptable manner at the banquet.

I am in growth process, and God—as I understand Him—allows me to grow, which means simply: He give me a future. Because if there is a future, there is no growth. And I see you as acceptable in the present, acceptable to me, and acceptable to God, and I give you the gift some call love of accepting you where you are and allowing you time to learn to stand erect and take your first faltering step, or to take the spoon and move the food laboriously and tediously from the bowl to your mouth. I wait on you, and I allow you to wait on me without embarrassment and without apology—"I'm so sorry to keep you waiting"— and I don't beat myself for not growing fast enough. "Well, it looks like as long as I've been a Christian, I should..." Neither do I push or shove you, because the place you are is yours and the place I am is mine and this is my place and my time in eternity, and that is your place and your time in eternity. I don't need to alter either your time or your place. The endless quest for the right place is over. I've got news for you—I've just found out where your place is— it's where you are sitting right now, and I've looked for a place all my life. I have never had a "home" until recently, but I've discovered of late that my home is within. It is real and it is mine in the light of the fact that I'm a new person.

My new past, my new present, and my new future give me a new place. Now, I have permission to enjoy and experience you in your place while I'm in my place since I no longer have to move you to another place before I can enjoy you or move myself to another place before I can be enjoyed. I know that some of you know what I mean when I say that I have lived a great deal of my life waiting until, you know, — and until..., and until..., and until. I don't do that anymore. That "until" is "now." The place that you've always waited for is the place where you are now and you experience yourself, God, existence, beauty, and meaning, now or never. Don't change—meet me as you are. Then when I'm gone from you, I will not suddenly become aware that I never did let myself be here with you, and I wish I had—I wish I had. I've been to meetings and I've been with people and then when I was leaving the meeting and going to the next one, I was aware that "so-n-so" was there and this person was there and I never really experienced them. Driving down a lonely road late at night trying to get to somewhere in a hurry, I'd think, "Was that person really there? I never did experience him."

Now in this new relationship, I don't need to do **to**...or be done **by**...I am just going to be, and I'll experience you, and I will let you experience me. I have a great temptation to take one of the ways that I've protected myself from happiness is that I've taken my grief and I've set it between myself and a person and said, "I cannot come close to you because of my grief," or I've taken my guilt and used this as protection and said, "You could not really like me or really know me because, look here...." Then, when I'm going from the place I can leave you and experience the next moment with the next person, because I have finished with this time and place with you. I experience the new time and place that comes to me from the future. I always know because of the new being, the new creation and the transformation of the past, the present, and he future—I always know that the best is yet to come. That means that I can release this moment because what God has ahead for me is surely better, and I can release you because what you have and I have in the future is better than what we have with each other here, now. That's true. This means that nothing could happen here and nothing could have happened in the past that would prevent me from experiencing a higher and holier place in the future.

Because of some experiences, I have said—and I think I have said them here—that I consider myself an emotional cripple. I am not—not anymore. Because God did not bring me into this world crippled and limit my ability and my capacity to enjoy the moments of present—like the one I have with you here, and like the one I had with you here yesterday, and like the one I will have with you here, now tomorrow.

Through the mystery of His working, He takes the experience of the past, transforms by His blessing into capacities for perception, particularly, I think intuitive perception, understanding, sensitivity, openness, awareness, receptivity, and the thing that yesterday was my pain is in the moment of the present "my blessing." And it may be that what happens to you today that I interpret as pain may be tomorrow's blessing.

Also by John N DeFoore Sr.

A Few Stories For God's Children
Anyone You Know?
To The Latter Years
Narratives Musings and Memories
A Place To Talk